ANCIENT TRADITIONS

SHAMANISM IN CENTRAL ASIA AND THE AMERICAS

ANCIENT TRADITIONS

SHAMANISM IN CENTRAL ASIA AND THE AMERICAS

GARY SEAMAN
AND
JANE S. DAY

Editors

A joint publication of

University Press of Colorado
and
Denver Museum of
Natural History

in cooperation with

Ethnographics Press
Center for
Visual Anthropology
University of
Southern California

Published by the University Press of Colorado
P.O. Box 849
Niwot, Colorado 80544

Ancient Traditions: Shamanism in Central Asia and the Americas is based on the proceedings from "Nomads: Masters of the Eurasian Steppe," volume 4 of the Soviet-American academic symposia in conjunction with the museum exhibitions.

The University Press is a cooperative enterprise supported, in part, by Adams State College, Colorado State University, Fort Lewis College, Mesa State College, Metropolitan State College of Denver, University of Colorado, University of Northern Colorado, University of Southern Colorado, and Western State College of Colorado.

Library of Congress Cataloging-in-Publication Data
Ancient traditions : shamanism in central Asia and the Americas / Gary Seaman and Jane S. Day, editors.
   p.   cm.
   "In cooperation with Ethnographic Press, Center for Visual Anthropology, University of Southern California."
   Papers from a symposium held at the Denver Museum of Natural History, June 1989.
   Includes bibliographical references and index.
   ISBN 0-87081-342-0
   1. Shamanism—Congresses. I. Seaman, Gary, 1942– . Day, Jane Stevenson. III. Denver Museum of Natural History.
BL2370.S5A48   1994
291.1'4—dc20   93-47593
                                                              CIP

Cover illustration © 1994 Martin Prechtel
Book design and composition by Cathy Holtz

The paper used in this document meets the minimum requirements of the American National Standard for Information Sciences—Permanence of Paper for Printed Library Materials.
ANSI Z39.48—1984

CONTENTS

CONTENTS

CONTRIBUTORS

Vladimir N. Basilov
Institute of Ethnography, Academy of Sciences of the USSR, Moscow.

Robert S. Carlsen
Research associate in the Department of Anthropology, University of Colorado at Boulder, Campus Box 233, Boulder, CO 80309–0233.

James A. Clifton
Scholar in residence in the Department of Anthropology, Western Michigan University, Kalamazoo, MI 49008.

Vladimir Diachenko
Institute of Ethnography, Academy of Sciences of the USSR, Leningrad.

Vera P. Diakonova
Institute of Ethnography, Academy of Sciences of the USSR, Leningrad.

Peter T. Furst
Professor of anthropology at the State University of New York in Albany, and research associate at the University Museum, University of Pennsylvania, 206 Hyland Avenue, Devon, PA 19333.

Larisa R. Pavlinskaya
Institute of Ethnography, Academy of Sciences of the USSR, Leningrad.

Martin Prechtel
3650 Cottonwood Lane, Berthoud, CO 80513.

Gary Seaman
Associate professor and chair, Department of Anthropology, University of Southern California, Los Angeles, CA 90089–0661.

Omer C. Stewart (deceased)
Professor emeritus in the Department of Anthropology, University of Colorado, Boulder.

Lawrence E. Sullivan
Director of the Center for the Study of World Religions at Harvard University, 42 Francis Avenue, Cambridge, MA 02138.

Robert J. Theodoratus
Professor of anthropology at Colorado State University, Fort Collins, CO 80523.

Johannes Wilbert
Emeritus professor of anthropology at the University of California, Los Angeles, CA 90024–1553.

PREFACE

This volume is the result of a symposium held at the Denver Museum of Natural History in summer 1989, in association with the exhibition "Nomads: Masters of the Eurasian Steppe," which drew thousands of visitors to the museum. This brilliant, colorful exhibition from the great museums of the former Soviet Union focused on the cultures of nomadic tribes that once dominated the open steppe lands of Central Asia. From the Scythians to the Huns to the Mongols, they swept through history on horseback from their homelands in Central Asia, reaching into the heart of Eastern Europe. In spite of their warlike nature, these cultures were rich and diverse, and underlying them all was the common practice of shamanism.

Shamanism, which may be humankind's earliest belief system, relates humans to their environment through the strong, dominating figure of the shaman, whose rituals are concerned primarily with hunting, fertility, healing, and death. Shamanism has deep continuities from past into present, and many of its manifestations appear to have migrated with hunting bands from northern Europe across the cold steppes of Russia and Siberia into the New World.

During the exhibition in Denver, as we talked with our Soviet colleagues, it became ever more apparent that the ethnographic record demonstrates that many traditions from Central Asian shamanism also exist in shamanistic practices of native peoples of the Americas. The Soviet team of scholars-curators became fascinated with the intriguing relationships they recognized between Asian and New World shamanistic rituals. This interest triggered the idea of a symposium at which Soviet and U.S. scholars could gather and share ideas and information through papers and conversation. This was the period just before the great upheavals in the Soviet Union, and little opportunity had existed in the past for this type of open intellectual exchange.

Our Soviet colleagues were anxious to meet not only other scholars but actual shamans as well. As a result, in June 1989, a stimulating two-day gathering was held at the Denver Museum of Natural History, with twenty Soviet and U.S. scholars and two practicing shamans participating. A rapt audience of two hundred and fifty people listened eagerly as scholars, who had long worked in the same field but had never met, discussed the perceived similarities and differences in Old World and New World shamanism. It was a memorable weekend for us all, and it is to these colleagues who now face new problems in the emerging chaotic freedom of Russia that we dedicate this book.

JANE STEVENSON DAY
CHIEF CURATOR
DENVER MUSEUM OF NATURAL HISTORY

ANCIENT TRADITIONS

SHAMANISM
IN CENTRAL ASIA
AND THE AMERICAS

INTRODUCTION: AN OVERVIEW OF SHAMANISM

PETER T. FURST

This collection of essays on shamanism in Soviet Central Asia and the Indian Americas appears at a time when the shamans of the traditional world are increasingly the focus of two contradictory trends. On one side we have, as the by-product of headlong destruction of tropical environments, an unprecedented assault on their very survival. And if shamans and shamanism disappear, with them would go irreplaceable stores of empirical knowledge and experience—the special expertise of shamans in the natural environment, which could ultimately benefit all of humanity.

Against this potential disaster, the dimensions of which are becoming apparent only now that it is almost too late, we see an upsurge of interest in, and a new respect for, shamanism as a phenomenon of religion. The symposium that brought Soviet and U.S. students of shamanism to the Denver Museum of Natural History in the summer of 1989 was one expression of that growing interest.

The symposium was held in conjunction with the opening of a remarkable traveling exhibition of objects from Russian and Siberian collections of arts and crafts created by the native peoples of Central Asia. As the considerable audience attending the symposium demonstrated, there is great interest in shamanism, not only among ethnologists and historians of religion but also within the general public. True, this popular fascination with shamanism may in part be a function of what Vladimir N. Basilov (1990:46)—a well-known Russian ethnographer of shamanism who was also chief curator of "Nomads of Central Asia"—once referred to as "the motley mystical teachings" that have proliferated in the West, especially in the United States, to which one might add that mysticism is hardly a stranger to Russians either.

These so-called teachings may be all wrong, or they may be deplorably superficial, but that is not to say that something is inherently invalid about interest in shamanism outside of scholarship. Many of the central tenets of shamanism seem to respond to some very basic human needs, even to plug into our biological being at a fundamental level. It is a very ancient phenomenon, and the shaman's vocation, as Basilov has suggested, is probably the first real profession in the history of humanity. Some scholars see it as the universal *Ur* religion, and there are good reasons to think they are right—even if, strictly speaking, we take the different forms of shamanism to be phenomena of religion rather than religions in and of themselves.

THE SHAMANIC WORLDVIEW

Perhaps it would be better to conceive less of a universal shamanism than of a *shamanic worldview* as originally the common property of humankind. Its great antiquity finds support in striking correspondences in some of the basic assumptions of shamanic beliefs and similar paraphernalia and techniques in many places in the traditional world. No doubt, there have been exceptions to or violations of the rules, but in general shamanism expresses a philosophy of life that holds all beings—human, animal, or plant—to be qualitatively equivalent: all phenomena of nature, including human beings, plants, animals, rocks, rain, thunder, lightning, stars and planets, and even tools, are animate, imbued with a life essence or soul or, in the case of human beings, more than one soul. Generally speaking, the origin of life is held to lie in transformation rather than, as in Biblical tradition, creation ex nihilo. It conceives of a long-ago time of origin in which animals and people were indistinguishable from one another and were able to change their outer form at will, a talent that eventually came to be the shaman's alone. It is a worldview in which, typically, the earth is Mother and the sky is Father. Relations between the human realm and that of gods and spirits are governed by the principle of reciprocity: for whatever you take, you must give back something of equal value. Plant and animal species have spirit "owners," or masters and mistresses, who might exact retribution if those in their charge are killed without regard for their spiritual sensibilities and welfare—if, for example, more are taken than are needed to sustain life: the offended species might be withdrawn from the environment by its spirit owner, or the angered spirit of an individual animal or plant might visit sickness on the one who neglected or abused it. Propitiation and respect are required because the shamanic worldview assumes no human superiority over the rest of nature: people, like other life forms, exist within and depend upon nature and the goodwill of the spirits that animate and rule over the environment.

Shamanism, then, is in a very real sense an ecological belief system. And it is surely the foundation on which the many local religions of Native Americans evolved, as it is also that of the peoples of Central Asia; indeed, it must be self-evident that everything enumerated here is part and parcel of the traditional religions of Native Americans. It is not too much to say that shamanism is the substratum beneath all of the world's religions, not just those of American Indians, except that among the latter it shines through more powerfully than it has been allowed to do elsewhere. It is little wonder, then, that Western people also feel themselves drawn to it— even if what is presented to them as shamanism may be greatly truncated and the putative Indian "spirituality" is lacking in both context and history.

Scholars sometimes make the mistake of seeing the real world as a classroom in which passive listeners are expected to absorb the proffered wisdom and regurgitate it faithfully at exam time. But in the real world, people want to participate, especially when they perceive a yawning spiritual emptiness in their lives. Purists may deplore the self-help books that profess to teach us how to become our own "shamans" and the self-described spiritual guides who advertise their services to put us in touch with Indian "teachings" and "the divine universal consciousness." Surely, there are arguments to be made against kits with rattles and tapes of drumming and chanting being shortcuts to spirituality and "journeys of the soul." Shamans use rock crystals, so "crystal power" will cure whatever ails you. There are even tours to see shamans in their native habitats. But even if a few grains of experiential truth do not make a loaf, are they not better than nothing?

Those who insist upon purity also bemoan the fact that some Indian people willingly cooperate in some of these dubious enterprises. But can we blame them for cashing in on prepaid adventures in shamanism? If white people want to spend hard cash for a version of shamanism that sounds more genuine because it is in a language they cannot understand, why not derive some modest benefit? And is it not ironic that after centuries of trying to force Indian people into a Judeo-Christian mold, white people now feel compelled to come to Indians in hopes of recovering the vital spiritual center they have mislaid in their race for material satisfaction? So, much as we may despair at times over what we feel to be misrepresentation and commercialization of a misunderstood Native American spirituality, and much as anthropologists like to think of themselves as the only legitimate interpreters of native cultures, the fact is that no one has granted the members of the academy an exclusive option. At any rate, it should come as no surprise that, as people in Western cultures increasingly find themselves drifting toward the end of the millennium without a spiritual anchor, romantic notions of what shamanism is and what shamans are able to do should abound or that, as Basilov (1990:46) also said in "Chosen by the Spirits," shamanism may spring up "in new forms—based not on a common tradition, but on infatuation with mysticism."

But if we decry vulgar distortions of the ideology, techniques, histories, and functions of shamanism, we also need to be clear about what shamanism is and is not. How else can we expect the converted to know what they may be missing?

A volume of essays that for the first time collects diverse manifestations of American and Central Asian shamanism, "pure" or attenuated, under one roof seems to be as good a place to do this as any. Fortunately, Mircea Eliade has already done it for us, and the following summary is based largely, with some added observations, on his overview—written from the point of view of comparative religion—in the thirteenth of the sixteen volumes of the new *Encyclopedia of Religion*, of which he was general editor. It appeared in 1987, the year of his death.

UNIVERSAL THEMES IN SHAMANISM

Traditionally, shamanism has been regarded as primarily a phenomenon of the tribal religions of Siberia, Central Asia, and the Arctic, Eliade noted in what was to be his final contribution to a subject that had held his attention for so many years. In a sense, that perception is an accident of history: more learned and open-minded travelers, especially the natural historians, came upon and studied the phenomenon earlier in Siberia than elsewhere. In recent years, scholars have come to realize that the old geographical and cultural limits were too narrowly drawn, because the same cultural conditions and religious ideologies that made the Siberian or Inuit (Eskimo) shaman the center of tribal magico-religious life also existed, and to a degree still persist, in the Indian Americas and in other places as well. (The old definition of *shaman* has likewise been recognized as being too restrictive, but the term is now used so indiscriminately, for so many different kinds of specialists in the sacred, the occult, and the healing arts—authentic and not so authentic—that a return to greater semantic precision would not be amiss.)

Still, Siberia and Central Asia bequeathed us the terminology and the basic definitions (shaman came into English and other languages by way of Russian, from the Tungus *saman*). And these definitions do apply across the board: he or she is technician of the sacred, master or mistress of ecstasy and of spirits. Further, shamans function primarily in those societies that not only value the ecstatic trance but regard it as the primary religious experience. (Perhaps that is also too restrictive, but it certainly applies to the indigenous shaman in traditional religious contexts.) In any event, it is applicable no less to American Indian peoples than to those of Siberia and Central Asia, where shamanism was first recognized and studied (for summaries of shamanism in Siberia and Central Asia, North America, and South America, respectively, see Siikala 1987:208–215; Gill 1987:216–219; Furst 1987:219–223).

What we have heard thus far alone would surely justify studying shamanism not only in its culture-specific manifestations but also cross-culturally, comparatively, as a near-universal phenomenon—so long as we recognize that, universals aside, much in shamanism is culture-specific, that shamans are not necessarily the only religious specialists in a given society, that shamanism may coexist with other forms of religious belief and ritual and shamans may coexist with professional priests. There is also this: shamans are indeed specialists, but only rarely do they follow their vocation full-time.

In so-called tribal societies, shamans usually function side by side with chiefs, although occasionally the two offices may be merged in a single individual. (A classic study of the interacting roles of chiefs and shamans is that of Anna Gayton [1930:361–420] of the Yokuts and Mono of Northern California. Yokut/Mono chiefs are primarily political leaders, and shamans are specialists in the sacred and healers of illness. Nevertheless, Gayton was told, the shamans also "were political factors of tremendous importance." The ethnographic literature from Siberia and South America contains many similar examples.)

Although every shaman has a command of magic, Eliade continues, obviously not every magician is a shaman. And although every medicine man is a curer, not every healer is a shaman. Shamans employ techniques of curing that are exclusive to them, because they alone have access to those spirit forces that divination and dreams have identified as the ultimate source of an illness. However, many shamans are also expert herbalists, a point to which I return later.

As for the trance, notwithstanding the shaman's mastery of ecstatic techniques, there are varieties of religious ecstasy that do not properly belong with shamanism; hence, not every ecstatic is or was a shaman. As Eliade (1987:202) puts it, what sets the shaman apart from other mystics or ecstatics is that he or she specializes in an ecstatic trance "during which his soul is believed to leave his body and ascend to the sky or descend to the underworld."

Another distinction concerns the special relationships the shaman has with spirits. Many people claim to have such an intimate connection, whether in the form of controlling spirits or being possessed by them. But the shaman's affinity with spirits is of a different order: the shaman recruits helpers from among the spirits of animals, plants, and other phenomena to assist him or her in encounters with the extra-human sphere, with the supernatural masters or mistresses of game and plants, the rulers of sky or underworld, and the ghosts or shades of the dead. The helping spirits accompany shamans on celestial or chthonic out-of-body journeys, assist in overcoming obstacles and dangers, do battle at their side or in their place against demons and sorcerers, help locate and retrieve lost or stolen souls of clients, and so on. And although there is an occasional report of a shaman having been possessed, these are exceptions rather than the rule. Typically, shamans are the masters of spirits, not their instruments.

Shamans are recruited by various means: they may inherit their vocation or receive a supernatural call, most commonly through a serious illness that responds to no treatment until the candidate agrees to obey the summons to shamanism. Others may decide to take up shamanizing of their own free will, or they may be designated for the purpose by family, lineage, or clan (as among the Tungus). However, almost always the individual "chosen by the spirits" (the title of an essay by Basilov, which appeared in English translation in a highly recommended collection of recent Russian writings on shamanism edited by Marjorie Mandelstam Balzer [1990]), or who has inherited the office, is thought to have greater power than one who was self-made.

Future shamans are often recognized by their fellows by their strange behavior—moodiness; preference for solitude; long and solitary walks in the forest, desert, or mountains; visionary experiences; singing while asleep; attacks of unconsciousness; and similar actions. The Siberian Buriat, for example, believe that during bouts of unconsciousness, the future shaman's soul has been carried off by spirits for instruction; it is also widely thought that only with the first initiation does the soul return to regain complete control over the shaman's body (cf. also Eliade 1964:13–23). Shamans may also believe themselves to have been selected by virtue of having survived some dramatic event or accident: "for example, among the Buriats, the Soyot, and the Inuit (Eskimo), after being struck by lightning, or falling from a high tree, or successfully undergoing an ordeal that can be homologized with an initiatory ordeal, as in the case of the Inuit who spent five days in icy water without his clothes becoming wet" (Eliade 1987:203).

Whatever the route by which the shaman may have come by the office—and shamanic training, more often than not, requires years of perseverance and self-sacrifice—to be recognized he or she must have undergone two different kinds of instruction. Eliade gives these as (1) the ecstatic route, in which the novice is taught by the spirits and ancestors through dreams and trances, and (2) instruction by a master in the shamanic techniques, the different rituals, the identity and function of the multitude of spirits, the sacred geography and the mythic histories and genealogy of the shaman's society, special songs, magical invocations and words—indeed, an entire special language to which only shamans are privy—and so on.

Whatever has been said about the relationship of the future shaman's aberrant behavior to psychopathology—and there is a considerable literature making that (false) analogy—Eliade (1987:203) believes the question has been wrongly put: "On the one hand, it is not true that shamans always are, or always have to be, neuropathics; on the other hand, those among them who had been ill became shamans precisely because they had succeeded in healing themselves" (Eliade 1987:203). In fact, the shaman's initiation is frequently "equivalent to a cure. To obtain the gift of shamanizing presupposes precisely the solution of the psychic crisis brought on by the first symptoms of election or call" (Eliade 1987:203).

What is clear from the cross-cultural evidence is that the shamanic vocation often implies a crisis that simulates the symptoms of madness. But one cannot become a shaman until one has resolved this crisis, usually by overcoming sufferings that are exactly like the ordeals of passage from youth into adulthood or into a new status in the society: "Just as in puberty rites or rites of entrance into a secret society the novice is 'killed' by semi-divine or demonic beings, so the future shaman sees in dreams his own body dismembered by demons" (Eliade 1987:203).

This element of dismemberment by an initiatory demon is found in many places, from Siberia and Central Asia to the Canadian Arctic and southward through the tropical forests of Amazonia to the Tierra del Fuego. An example from tropical South America is the ecstatic experience of the future *héwiawan* shaman of the Sanemá, a subgroup of the Venezuelan Yanomami. In his initiatory trance, triggered by a hefty dose of intoxicating *Virola* snuff (discussed later in this chapter), the novice penetrates deep into the forest. Here he encounters Omáokóhe, a giant bipedal supernatural jaguar, who is Master of all Felines. Omáokóhe strips the flesh from his bones and replaces it with that of a bat—hence the designation of this class of shaman as héwiawan, literally "Bat Person" (Wilbert 1963:222). He also rips out the candidate's internal organs and replaces them with magical ones. The cultural, geographical, and chronological distance between the Sanemá, who until recently were hunters and food collectors, and the Classic Maya of southern Mexico is substantial, but a class of burial figurines dating to A.D. 600–700 from the Late Classic Maya cemetery on the island of Jaina, Campeche, appears to represent precisely the same initiatory trauma: a giant, semianthropomorphized jaguar is shown in the act of disemboweling a young man seated on his lap. There is no sign of terror or resistance; on the contrary, the youth's hand is raised in a gentle touch to the jaguar's face.

With respect to the erroneous but persistent equation between shamans and the mentally ill and epileptics in some of the older literature, Eliade also points out that shamans have an astonishing capacity to control even ecstatic movement, and they usually not only have more mental and physical energy and endurance than other members of their social group but—as guardians of the rich traditions and esoteric knowledge, and as performers of a vast corpus of sacred and magical songs and invocations—often also command a vastly larger vocabulary than their compatriots. Thus, "the poetic vocabulary of a Yakut shaman contains twelve thousand words, whereas the ordinary language—the only language known to the rest of the community—has only four thousand. The same observation applies to the shamans of other regions, such as North and South America, Oceania, and Australia" (Eliade 1964:29–30; 1987:203). Anthropologist Johannes Wilbert, who for more than three decades has worked with shamans of the Warao of the Orinoco Delta in Venezuela, and whose essay on South American tobacco shamanism appears as Chapter 3, has found the same differential between the vocabulary of the Warao specialist in the sacred and that of ordinary Warao.

◣◥

SHAMANISM AND MENTAL ILLNESS

In his classic work, *Shamanism: Archaic Techniques of Ecstasy* (1964), Eliade effectively demolished the oft-repeated notion that the Arctic shaman's spontaneous ecstatic trance could be explained as a form of "arctic hysteria," that is, as a psychopathological condition brought on by an environment of extreme cold, desert solitude, long nights, and vitamin deprivation. Even as recently as 1939, wrote Eliade, Åke Ohlmarks proposed a differentiation of a supposedly "pure" shamanism in the polar regions, where the nervous constitution of the people—especially of shamans—was influenced by "cosmic oppression," giving rise, on the one hand, to such forms of mental illness as arctic hysteria and, on the other, to the shaman's ecstatic trance. In Ohlmark's view, only in the Arctic could one properly speak of a "great shamanism," that is, of the ceremony whose culmination is a real cataleptic trance "during which the soul is supposed to have left the body and to be journeying in the sky or the underworld." According to this interpretation, in the sub-Arctic, in contrast, the shaman—no longer subject to the stresses of the polar environment—can also no longer spontaneously put himself or herself into a "real" ecstatic state and hence has to be content with a semitrance with the help of narcotics or else to "mime the journey of the soul in dramatic form" (Eliade 1964:24).

In refutation, Eliade (1964:27) points out that the alleged psychological maladies and nervous predisposition of candidate shamans to their mystical vocation are not exclusively Arctic phenomena but can be found among shamans all over the world. From this alone it follows that this and all attempts to explain the shamanic phenomenon as "mental illness" must be rejected. "The mentally ill patient," he writes, "proves to be an unsuccessful mystic, or, better, the caricature of a mystic. His experience is without religious content, even if it appears to resemble a religious experience." The shaman, in contrast, is *homo religiosus* par excellence, the true specialist in the sacred.

This is also the view of Basilov (1990:5), who notes that the conception of the shaman as mentally ill, which reigned in the literature for over half a century, was effectively refuted early on by such experienced Russian field workers as S. M. Shirokogorov (1919:1) and by some other scholars in the West, even though in their day their views on the subject were largely ignored. In any event, Basilov writes, the entire mental illness hypothesis is untenable on the cumulative evidence of a century of

◥

study: "The shaman is not a haphazard figure in the history of humanity. He is a person who has taken on the functions dictated by the norms of his culture" (1990:5). In short, then, the shaman is eminently sane, and more than sane, he or she is reflective, the true intellectual, the philosopher of his or her society.

THE ECSTATIC EXPERIENCE

Later in this chapter I say more about shamanic techniques of ecstasy, but for the present the definition in Eliade's overview (1964) is helpful. In the most basic sense, he writes, a shaman is one whose mystical experience expresses itself in the ecstatic trance. "Shamanistic ecstasy signifies the soul's flight to Heaven, its wanderings about the earth, or its descent to the subterranean world, among the dead" (Eliade 1987:205). The shaman never undergoes these profound experiences lightly or for frivolous reasons but always on behalf of an individual client or the community as a whole. Eliade lists four principal reasons: first, to encounter the spirits and the gods face-to-face and bring them offerings from the community to gain a favor or to give thanks for favors bestowed; second, to find and recover the soul of a patient that is thought to have strayed from its body or been abducted by demons; third, to guide the soul of a dead person to its new abode; and fourth, to gain new knowledge through encounters with the higher, nonhuman realm.

Of course, shamans already know the sacred geography, the road to the center of the world, the opening in the sky through which they can climb or fly to the highest heaven, and the terrestrial aperture through which they can descend to the land of the dead. They know the signposts for dangers and how to overcome them, having apprehended all of this essential expertise through long and demanding training by master shamans and through the ordeals of their initiatory experience. They have learned how to become spirit: "Because of his ability to leave his body with impunity, the shaman can . . . act in the manner of a spirit: he flies through the air, he becomes invisible, he perceives things at great distances . . . sees the souls of the dead and can capture them, and is impervious to fire" (Eliade 1987:203). Indeed, shamans typically are "masters of fire."

According to Eliade, what the shaman does in ecstasy is to re-establish the communicability that existed *in illo tempore* between this and Otherworlds; the difference is that the ancestral beings could pass freely between them without need for trance, whereas now this is possible only in a state of ecstasy (or what has been called, less elegantly, an altered state of consciousness): "temporarily and for a limited number of persons—the shamans—ecstasy re-establishes the primordial condition of all mankind" (Eliade 1964:486). At the same time, by mastering the dangerous passage between the two realms—the "mouth of heaven" that opens and closes in an instant, clashing icebergs, scissor-sharp dancing reeds, the snapping jaws of a monster, and the like—the shaman proves that he or she is no longer a human being but has become spirit; in other words, "has transcended the human condition . . . indeed, this 'paradoxical' passage can be accomplished only by one who is 'spirit' " (Eliade 1964:486).

Here I should add that the shaman, like the hero of Classic mythology, is spirit only temporarily, for were that state to become permanent, he or she would be dead and could not return. And that perhaps explains why in many of the shamanic myths of the dangerous passage, the shaman or his or her conveyance is given a blow or made to suffer some other nonfatal injury precisely at the moment of passing from this world to the other. Thus, in one shamanic tale from the Arctic, clashing icebergs from which there is no escape seek to bar the way for an Eskimo shaman as he paddles his kayak in search of the hole in the sea leading to the home of the Mother of Sea Animals. In that split second when the dangerous gateway to the Otherworld opens, he paddles with all his strength to push his skin boat through, but the monstrous icebergs close on the kayak's stern and crush it. The shaman continues on in his damaged craft, finds the hole, visits the sea goddess in her submarine abode, and successfully pleads with her to release the seals to feed his hungry people. Inevitably, such culture-specific stories call to mind the classic tale of the Symplegades, the clashing rocks through which Jason, with the aid of the goddess Athena, steered the Argo in his quest for the Golden Fleece. The Argonauts make it, but not before the rocks close in on their ship and crush its stern. Similar traditions of what Eliade calls the "paradoxical passage" are found worldwide in shamanic, funerary, and heroic mythology.

SOUL LOSS AND SICKNESS INTRUSION

There is, further, the power of transformation: shamans can at will transform themselves into animals; they can kill at a distance, foretell the future, and perform all manner of magical tricks and thus proclaim to one and all that they share in the condition of the spirits. Because of the current fascination with out-of-body journeys, I cannot emphasize enough

11

that the shamans' travels to the underworld always have a purpose—to gain knowledge of death and the dead and to bring that knowledge back to comfort the living—that they are not searching for the unknown but through their training are familiar with the pathways between the human and the spirit worlds. Indeed, in traditional contexts one of the most important tasks of the shaman is to act as a psychopomp, a guide of the soul, either to return it to its owner or escort it after death into the community of the ancestors.

Soul loss is widely perceived in Asia and the Americas to be one of the two principal causes of illness, the other being sickness intrusion—that is, the shooting of a sickness projectile into the victim from a distance by supernatural means, by an offended spirit or deity, perhaps, or a human enemy who has engaged the services of a sorcerer or prevailed upon a god or a spirit to act on his or her behalf. There are also instances in which the shooting of a magical projectile can have different purposes, a common one being the "killing" of the novice and that novice's subsequent revival in his or her newly acquired quality. Thus A. L. Kroeber (1929:274) tells of master shamans of the Southern Maidu in California shooting novices with magical objects called *ci'la* as part of their training; the novices would fall to the ground as though dead and be revived by the shaman who, against payment of a fee, would suck the magical projectile from their bodies and continue to treat them for several days, until the initiates had regained their full strength. Shamans also shot each other in contests or demonstrations of their magical power: "the shaman would smoke," Kroeber writes, "then take his arrow-like ci'la and, looking between his legs, shoot it from a miniature bow of quill with a woman's hair, at a man perhaps 'a mile off,' who dropped. Then the shaman . . . revived him, and he was new, stronger than before" (1929:274). Brushing the intrusive pathogen to some central place and sucking it out, in the form of a concrete object—a thorn, perhaps, or a seed or pebble (for an example from a Mexican Indian culture, see Chapter 5)—is a part of shamanic curing all over the world.

It used to be assumed that soul loss and sickness intrusion were mutually exclusive, but the literature shows that although the one may predominate over the other in some instances as the primary cause of illness, more commonly the two coexist. According to Eliade, in Siberia and Central Asia, "rape of the soul" is by far the most widespread among the several conceptions of the cause of illness; hence its recovery is one of the principal aspects of the shaman as healer. In fact, curing sickness, which requires the discovery and neutralization of its supernatural cause and not just the removal of symptoms—sometimes through great expenditure of psychic and physical energy on the part of the curer—is surely one of the primary and most immediately apparent functions of shamans in traditional societies, whatever other roles they fulfill.

SHAMANISM AND "ECOLOGICAL WISDOM"

Lest it be assumed that because much illness is laid at the door of the supernatural all curing must also follow supernatural lines, the religious specialist of traditional societies, and even ordinary people, often have command of many practical remedies, with herbal pharmacopoeias containing three hundred to five hundred different medicinal plants by no means unusual, at least in the tropics. And it is this empirical area of the shaman's practice, often overlooked in our fascination with the mystical, that is increasingly facing extinction, an impending tragedy to which the *New York Times* drew attention in its science section of June 11, 1991 (pp. C1, C6).

"Shamans and Their Lore May Vanish With Forests," read the headline. "Botanists fear a loss of valuable knowledge about healing plants." They do indeed. Shamans, according to science reporter Daniel Coleman,

are a dying breed. Like a bellwether species whose decline signals that an entire ecosystem is in peril, the dwindling number of shamans is a sign of the demise of their cultures.

Today most shamans are elderly, members of the last generation to have fully learned the native lore. Ethnobotanists report that, around the world, younger generations are rapidly losing interest in learning what the local shaman knows, lured away by the pull of the modern world (p. C1).

The article quotes ethnobotanist Mark J. Plotkin of Conservation International, a foundation based in Washington that seeks to save endangered ecosystems and the myriad plant species that have served Indian shamans as herbal remedies for hundreds and thousands of years and of which some might contain that elusive substance to combat the scourges for which Western science has found no cures (cf. also Plotkin 1993). That, indeed, is what has happened in some of those instances— and they are far too few—in which the pharmaceutical industry chose not to put aside, as it has done far too often in the past for reasons of economics, the testimony and experiences of Indian shamans. No one would assert that all herbal remedies prove to be as effective as they are claimed to be, but—as Bernard Ortiz de Montellano, in his excellent book, *Aztec Medicine, Health, and Nutrition* (1990), has shown to be the case with herbal pharmacopoeias of the ancient Aztecs—many are. And, as ethnobotanists remind us, many thousands of plants remain, especially in tropical environments, whose beneficial effects may have been known to the indigenous inhabitants but that have never even been classified, much less tested, by scientists. In fact, as Michael Balick, director of the Institute for Economic Botany at the New York Botanical Garden, points out in the same *New York Times* report, "of the more than 265,000 known plant species, less than 1 percent have been tested for medical applications, or even for the chemical compounds they contain. Yet out of this tiny portion have come 25 percent of medicines."

There may even be answers to that terrible and elusive modern plague, the AIDS virus, in plants some South American shamans use to cure a variety of illnesses. Balick, who received his Ph.D. at Harvard under Richard Evans Schultes—long-time director of the Harvard Botanical Museum and the pre-eminent authority on the ritual hallucinogens of the New World—has been engaged for some time in a research project in Belize to which the herbal expertise of the local shamans has proved essential. Balick used two approaches—one in which plants are collected at random, the other concentrating only on those plants for which the local shamans made therapeutic claims. The two collections were turned over to a cancer research center in Maryland, where extracts made from them were placed in test tubes containing human blood T cells infected with the AIDS virus.

"Of the 20 plants collected on the shaman's advice, five killed the AIDS virus but spared the T cells," reports the *Times*. "But of 18 plant species gathered randomly, just one did so. The findings do not mean that the plants necessarily are a cure for AIDS; many substances that kill the virus in the test tube are ineffective or unusable in the body. But all the plants that showed promise in this test will go through further testing" (June 11, 1991, C1, C6).

There are apt to be "great medications to be discovered in the other plant species," Balick told the *Times*. "But because the species—and the people who know their uses—are disappearing so quickly, we have just ten to 15 years to do this work" (June 11, 1991, C1, C6).

The urgency of conservation, not only of the rain forests but of the knowledge their indigenous inhabitants have amassed over thousands of years—not to mention of the peoples themselves—was brought home with special poignancy recently in the public debate over the fate of the Pacific yew tree (*Taxus brevifolia*). From the bark of this tree, a tradition-al source of medicines for Indian peoples, scientists recently isolated a chemical that proved to be effective against ovarian and other types of cancer, which they named taxol. The tragedy is that in decades of clear-cutting, tens of thousands of these trees were customarily discarded as useless weeds. It had, in fact, long been known—but evidently not regarded as important—that North American Indians made the bark, leaves, branches, and twigs of the Pacific yew and its sister species, *Taxus canadensis*, into decoctions, infusions, and poultices to treat, among other ills, problems of the lungs, coughs, colds, rheumatism, external and internal wounds, and stomach aches (Moerman 1986:477).

Taxol was approved at the end of 1992 for the treatment of ovarian cancer, amid fears that the enormous amount of bark required for just one patient—four hundred trees—would soon doom the Pacific yew to extinction. However, taxol was also discovered in European species, and, most recently, it has been successfully synthesized.

Yet, the story of taxol is a warning of what we stand to lose if envi-ronmental degradation continues at the present pace and indigenous cul-tures disappear, together with their forests. As Balick has warned, "The 1990s may be the last chance to preserve what native healers know about the rain forest. We're in danger of losing this knowledge in the next gen-eration. There's already been tremendous loss" (June 11, 1991, *New York Times*, C1, C6). Indeed there has. Many shamans are old, and they die without having passed their knowledge on to their disciples.

There are a few bright spots, however. Conservation International is sponsoring a shaman's apprentice program under which the Indian peo-ple select individuals to be trained by experienced shamans. The pro-gram is well underway among the Tirió of Surinam, Plotkin reports in his recent book, *Tales of a Shaman's Apprentice* (1993), as well as among the Bribri of southern Costa Rica, where four shamans have selected four apprentices for a four-year training program (Plotkin 1993:287). That is a drop in the bucket, but it is a start.

There is, finally, the long-overdue question of compensating the native specialists for sharing their precious knowledge. "It's a question of intellectual property," anthropologist Jason Gray of Survival International told the *New York Times* (June 11, 1991). "People whose medical lore leads to a useful product should have a stake in the profits. Unless we return some profits to them, it's a kind of theft."

Here, too, the future looks brighter than the past. Pharmaceutical companies have new interest in the potential of tropical forest plants. Several are negotiating with environmental groups such as Conservation International and Amazonian Indians for collaborative work on medicinal plants. Eli Lilly is engaged in a venture with a West Coast company called, appropriately, Shaman Pharmaceuticals to search for antifungal compounds from rain forest plants, with an agreement that a percentage of profits will go to the native peoples. A nonprofit organization called the Healing Forest Conservancy has also been established expressly for that purpose (Plotkin 1993:287). Clearly, the potential is enormous: in their recent book, *The Healing Forest* (1990), Richard Evans Schultes, the foremost ethnobotanist of our time, and phytochemist Robert F. Raffauf identify nearly 1,500 medicinal and toxic plant species native just to northwestern Amazonia of which the shamans have knowledge; for half of these, little or no scientific investigation of their chemical and pharmacological properties has been undertaken. The task ahead, then, is to salvage as much as possible of the knowledge of the surviving specialists in the sacred *and* the healing powers of plants before more of the forest is gone and with it its peoples and cultures. Perhaps better than anyone else, anthropologists included, the ethnobotanists engaged in this desperate race against time, need, and greed know the world of difference that exists between "the motley mystical teachings," to quote Basilov's apt characterization, which are so often mistaken for the real thing, and the practical ecological wisdom that lies every bit as much at the core of authentic Native American shamanism as do out-of-body travels.

SHAMANISM AND THE PSYCHOTROPIC FLORA

Except for the shamanic uses of tobacco, there was unfortunately little discussion during the Denver symposium of the specialist in the sacred as empirical, practical healer—that is, as specialist also in the therapeutic properties of plants. In part this can be explained by the absence of ethnobotanists from the list of speakers. Ethnobotany, rather than anthropology, pioneered the study of that remarkable class of plants—the botanical hallucinogens—employed by the shamans of some Native American peoples to facilitate the ecstatic trance that is an indispensable component of shamanism. These plants, too, are classified by shamans as therapeutic—as "medicine"—but in a somewhat different sense from the medicinal species discussed earlier. As noted, all plants are regarded as having souls or spirits, but the so-called hallucinogens are of a different order. Their users credit their extraordinary effects, which science knows to be due to certain alkaloids, by themselves or in combination, to supernatural power. The plants are sacred, and at least some are personified as deities that must be treated with care and propitiated with offerings, lest they turn their powers against those who use them. Because of these special qualities, some students of the phenomenon have proposed to do away with *hallucinogen* and replace it with *entheogen*, a compound term that means "containing deity" or "the god within," thus conveying more accurately what is meant in the indigenous universe.

The psychotropic flora has a cultural history in the Americas that goes back millennia. The fact that these plants occupied an important place in ecstatic shamanism, divination, and curing has been known for nearly five centuries, since Columbus and his men saw "Indians" intoxicate themselves with a mysterious snuff on the Caribbean island they named Hispaniola. This was followed by descriptions, by Fray Bernadino Sahagún and other sixteenth-century chroniclers, of Aztec use of peyote, morning glory seeds, mushrooms, and other ritual intoxicants. The literature on these remarkable plants is considerable, much of it published since the 1960s on their botany, chemistry, history, and functions in different cultures. I will say here simply that traditional peoples do not use their sacred plants for recreation or entertainment or to search for "nonordinary realities" or to escape unbearable conditions of daily life but to confirm, in direct contact with the superior beings and ancestors, the validity of their culture. Typically, youths return from their first out-of-body excursion in the initiatory ecstatic trance reporting that "it is exactly as our shamans told us, as our fathers and mothers said it came to be," or words to that effect. What they see for themselves is what they have heard described on countless evenings around the fire, what they have seen being enacted in the rituals, and what has been pounded into their heads during their initiatory instruction. As the Colombian anthropologist Gerardo Reichel-Dolmatoff, who has published important studies in English on hallucinogens and shamanic practice and imagery among the Tukano of the Upper Amazon, once told me, "In a certain sense, yajé and the other ritual plants provide the candidate with a blank screen upon which, in his ecstasy, he projects his cultural experience."

In this connection it is useful to summarize some insights and concrete data to which both anthropology and ethnobotany have made crucial contributions and that, in my view, have greatly advanced our understanding of the shamanic complex in Native American religions. I begin
with what I have long regarded as a real milestone in the investigation of
ecstatic shamanism in the Indian Americas. In 1970 Schultes posed a statistical question that had to do with the then known number of hallucinogenic plants employed in the two hemispheres and to which Weston La
Barre, in a path-breaking essay in *Economic Botany* (1970:368–373), sup-
plied an ethnological answer that pushed the study of American Indian
religions in new directions.

At first sight, a journal published by the New York Botanical Garden
would appear to be an unlikely vehicle for speculations about religion.
Actually, the choice was eminently logical. La Barre was attempting to for-
mulate a reasonable explanation for a statistical problem that emerged
from Schultes's long-time study of the hallucinogenic flora, going back to
his early field work in Oklahoma that led to his 1937 doctoral dissertation
on peyote and its role as the sacrament of the pan-Indian Native American
church and to a number of pioneering studies on Mexican ritual hallucinogens (on the peyote religion and its relationship to traditional Indian beliefs
and practices, see Omer C. Stewart [1987] and Chapter 6 in this volume).

While compiling a list of the botany and chemistry of hallucinogenic
plants then known to have been employed in shamanistic ritual in both
the New World and the Old World (Schultes 1969:3–16,15–27;
1970:25–53), Schultes was struck by a curious statistical imbalance:
whereas the indigenous populations of the New World had discovered
and utilized somewhere between eighty and one hundred "hallucinogenic" species (a number more recent research, by Schultes and others,
has nearly doubled), all he could find for the Old World were eight to
ten plants that were used for similar purposes. Prominent among these
were the fly-agaric mushroom, *Amanita muscaria*, and hemp, *Cannabis*
spp. The discrepancy was all the more puzzling, Schultes wrote, because
the Old World floras were presumably as rich as those of the New World
in potential hallucinogenic species; further, the Old World comprised a far
greater land mass, in which human populations had been present for a
much longer time span than in the Americas and thus had had far longer
to explore their environments for, and experiment with, the psychotropic
flora and to incorporate its effects on body and mind into their belief systems, pharmacopoeias, and rituals. Given these facts, Schultes suggested,

the reasons for the puzzling difference in the number of intoxicating plants employed anciently or recently in the two hemispheres could not be found in nature. And if not in nature, the answer had to lie in culture.

Quite right, replied La Barre, who, as author of *The Peyote Cult* (1938, 1969, 1974, 1975), also had a long-standing interest in the uses to which people have put the hallucinogens that are naturally occurring in their environments (cf. also La Barre 1972). In this path-breaking essay, La Barre explained the demonstrably greater interest in such plants among the aboriginal inhabitants of the New World, as compared to the Old World, as a function of the greater survival in the former of an archaic, Late Paleolithic and Mesolithic Asiatic shamanism, which he said is the "base religion" of the Indian Americas. One of the hallmarks of shamanism is the ecstatic trance. And such plants have found their place in culture to facilitate this highly valued mystical state, in which people—especially the technicians of the sacred—travel or project their souls into the realms of spirits and gods.

The pre-Columbian New World, he pointed out, did not undergo the profound socioeconomic, demographic, and, especially, religious transformations that in the Old World displaced and suppressed the old shamanism and the shamanistic nature religions, which valued personal encounters with the spirit world in ecstatic trance. In the Americas, in contrast, shamanism was never suppressed or displaced by the spread of new religions whose practitioners tolerated no rival faiths or gods. (Typically, Native Americans respected the validity of anyone's pathway to the supernatural; even the militaristic and expansionist Aztecs did not force people incorporated into their tribute empire to abandon their religions and embrace that of the victors. More commonly, indeed, it was the conquering Aztecs who assimilated some of the gods and rituals of the defeated.)

And there was always the undercurrent of the old shamanism. Shamanism, La Barre pointed out, not only survived as socioeconomic conditions and lifeways changed but continued to inform the religious beliefs and practices of the indigenous populations, from hunters and food collectors all the way to the complex civilizations of Mesoamerica and the Andes (La Barre 1970:368–373).

La Barre contended that the centrality of the ecstatic trance in Paleo-Asiatic shamanism may actually have predisposed, not to say culturally programmed, the small hunting bands that wandered out of northeastern Asia across Beringia into what is now Alaska and beyond, to explore their new environments for plants capable of facilitating the mystical experience. Just when these first small, incremental migrations occurred is still a matter of controversy, with estimates ranging from fifteen thousand to forty thousand years ago; what is certain is that they began sufficiently early to allow for the amazing diversity of Indian languages to develop and for the presence of human beings in Chile eleven thousand or more years ago.

La Barre assumed that the linear ancestor of hallucinogenic plant use in the Americas was an archaic Eurasiatic form of the shamanistic fly-agaric cults that survived in Siberia until well into the present century. This idea was inspired by the work of R. Gordon Wasson, the leading student of the cults of sacred, intoxicating mushrooms in the Old World and the New World (e.g., Wasson and Wasson 1957; Wasson 1968, 1980; Wasson et al. 1974; Furst 1976).

Granted that a generalized shamanistic worldview and techniques are clearly discernible in the religions of hunter-gatherers and even of peoples practicing horticulture, was La Barre correct? Can this really be claimed for, say, the Aztecs? Had not the professional and hierarchical urban Aztec priesthood come much too far from the shamans of their seminomadic past to allow for the survival of any but the most distant echoes of an archaic type of shamanism? Far from it. The ethnohistorical sources from the sixteenth and seventeenth centuries make it clear that Aztec religion and iconography, and also the ritual manipulation of the sacred, contained a powerful shamanistic core—major elements of a common archaic shamanistic substratum, concepts, and techniques that are, sometimes to a surprising degree of correspondence, shared with both North and South American and Asiatic shamanism and that continue to this day to underlie the religions of the indigenous inhabitants of the New World.

Aztec priests as much as the rural shamans, about whose stubborn "idolatries" and "superstitions" the parish priest H. Ruíz de Alarcon complained in 1629 (Ruíz de Alarcon 1953; Coe and Whitaker 1982; Andrews and Hassig 1984), valued the ecstatic trance. We gather from the writings of the Spanish clergy that Aztec state religion, and its counterpart on the "folk" or village level, featured such typically shamanic concepts as transformation and qualitative equivalence between humans and animals, initiatory illness or sickness vocation, journeys of the soul, sentience and soul matters inherent in all phenomena—even those we would regard as inanimate—sacred mountains, a stratified universe around an *axis mundi,* spirit helpers and animal allies, the bones as seat of life and the head as locus of the soul, soul loss or sickness projectiles as magical causes of illnesses and their corresponding cures, and so on. Like the Siberian shaman, the Mexican counterpart— or, rather, his or her spirit—traveled to dangerous places to recover a client's soul or sucked the pathogen from the patient's body.

And, as noted previously, the early sources describe an entire series of intoxicating, or hallucinogenic, plants by means of which priests, diviners, and curers, or "doctors," sought contact with the spirit world and which they invested with sacred and magical powers or to which they even ascribed divinity. Ruíz de Alarcon complained bitterly that his Aztec-speaking charges in Guerrero revered *ololiuhqui*, the psychotropic seeds of the morning glory, as a deity and had a greater fear of offending it than of the punishment of the clergy.

In a 1972 essay on hallucinogens and shamanism, La Barre wrote that on the basic shamanistic level, it may strike us as strange that throughout the entire distribution area of hallucinogenic plant use in the Indian Americas—which included the Aztecs—it is the "doctor," that is, the curing shaman, who takes the "medicine" rather than the patient. But that is foisting our own pharmacodynamic category of secular medicine on the first Americans. In fact, the shaman's taking the supernatural "medicine" is eminently logical, because the shaman requires the super-natural power in order to diagnose the cause of the illness and effect its cure (La Barre 1972:274–275).

This was the case with Aztec shaman-curers and priests, who ingested for these purposes such psychotropic plants as peyote (*Lophophora williamsii*) (traded to them by Teochichimec hunters from the northcentral desert, to which little cactus is native), morning glory seeds (*ololiuhqui, Turbina corymbosa, Ipomoea violacea*), *Datura inoxia* and related species, mushrooms (*teonanácatl, Psilocybe* spp.), hallucinogenic members of the mint family, tobacco (*Nicotiana rustica*), and so on. All but tobacco grow wild and so would have been available without modification or activation of admixtures for thousands of years before the first tentative beginnings of agriculture, around six thousand or seven thousand years ago. Tobacco, however, as Wilbert writes in Chapter 3, and in a path-breaking 1987 book, was one of the earliest plants to be domesticated by South American Indians, presumably from the first as a special kind of shamanis-tic intoxicant; in any event, the demonstrable interrelationship between important elements of shamanic ideology and the effects of nicotine intox-ication are seen by Wilbert to be largely responsible for tobacco having become over time the most widely distributed sacred plant of Native American ecstatic shamanism and religious ritual.

By now, as noted, the ethnobotanists have compiled a list of nearly two hundred hallucinogenic plants (some as yet known only by their native names) that were, or still are, utilized by Native American peoples as triggers for the mystical experience. Of these the one with the longest cultural record is *Sophora secundiflora*, whose potent seeds were utilized in the southwestern United States for thousands of years, beginning in those distant times when Paleo-American hunters were still pursuing mastodons and other large Pleistocene game. Their use as intoxicants in the initiation rites of ecstatic shamanistic medicine societies in the Southern Plains died out only in the latter half of the nineteenth century. The oldest cache of *Sophora* seeds was even older than the beginnings of the Desert Culture phase, c. 7000 B.C., because archaeologists found them in association with the bones of giant bison of the long-extinct species *Bison antiquus* and Folsom and Plainview projectile points. This bone bed has been dated at 8440 B.C. and 8120 B.C., respectively, providing the use of *Sophora* with an uninterrupted genealogy of over ten millennia. Thereafter, the potent red seeds occur in every cultural level in rock shelters occupied by Desert Culture people in the trans-Pecos region from about 7000 B.C. to A.D. 1000, often together with another psychoactive species, *Ungnadia speciosa* (Furst 1976:8). Two peyotes also found in one of these rock shelters were recently dated at c. 5000 B.C. by the UCLA radiocarbon laboratory (Furst 1989:386–387). Such impressively early dates for plant hallucinogens clearly support La Barre's explanation.

Those familiar with Eliade's (1964) *Shamanism* may recall that this distinguished historian of religion once had a very different notion about the historical place of hallucinogens in shamanism from that proposed by La Barre. Whereas the latter derived the widespread New World hallucinogenic complex from a heritage of ecstatic shamanism in Siberia, specifically the use of the fly-agaric mushroom, Eliade viewed the use of plants, including the fly-agaric, as well as alcohol to trigger the shaman's ecstatic trance as degeneration from a supposedly purer, spontaneous, or organic trance that was thought to be the standard for Siberian and Central Asian shamanism before it came under the influence of foreign religions. "Narcotics," he wrote, "are only a vulgar substitute for 'pure' trance." When Siberian shamans do use the fly-agaric mushroom, *Amanita muscaria*, and other chemical means of attaining the ecstatic state, it is "a recent innovation and points to a decadence of shamanic technique."

Noting that in a number of Ugrian and other Siberian languages the Iranian word for hemp, *bangha*, and its derivatives had come to designate both the pre-eminently shamanic mushroom *and* intoxication, and that the ancient Iranian hymns to the divinities "refer to ecstasy induced by intoxication by mushrooms," Eliade proposed that the magico-religious resort to intoxication for achieving ecstasy was of Iranian origin (1964:400–401).

But here we must remember that this work of Eliade's was a translation into English of a French edition published years earlier (1951). At that time, the vast panorama of ritual hallucinogens in the New World was, except for a very few species, virtually unknown. Few people were aware of the *Sophora* seeds found in Texan archaeological sites, and their great antiquity was unsuspected. The Wassons' research into the prehistory of the fly-agaric in Eurasia was barely in its infancy (their first book, *Mushrooms Russia and History*, was not published until 1957), and Gordon Wasson's personal foray into the survival of ancient Mesoamerican shamanistic-divinatory mushroom use among the Mazatec Indians of Oaxaca was still three years in the future. Although the basic chemistry of peyote, and of the South American *yajé* (*ayahuasca*) (*Banisteriopsis* spp.), had been known for decades, it was not until the 1960s that Albert Hofmann, the Swiss chemist who discovered LSD in 1938, identified the LSD-like lysergic derivatives in the seeds of morning glories or the tryptamine alkaloids that accounted for the extraordinary effects of sacred mushrooms of the genus *Psilocybe* and related genera.

If we can now see clearly that La Barre, and not Eliade, was right, in justice to the latter I should note that in the last years of his productive life, although unable to amend his views in a new, revised edition of *Shamanism*, he had discarded his view of the use of hallucinogenic plants as "degeneration" of the shamanic techniques of ecstasy. The work done by ethnobotanists and ethnographers on the vast complex of shamanic uses of sacred plants in the Americas, the emerging philological evidence for widespread and very ancient use of the fly-agaric mushroom in Europe, and, finally, the new radiocarbon dates from the American Southwest, he told me not long before his death, had convinced him that we were indeed dealing with an archaic phenomenon and that there was no phenomenological difference between the techniques of ecstasy, whether "spontaneous" or triggered by the chemistry of sacred plants. Another element that entered into his reconsideration, he said, was the recognition that the Arctic was settled relatively late in Siberian prehistory.

Arctic forms of shamanism could thus no longer be held to be ancestral to shamanism in the more temperate regions of northeastern Asia.

None of this is meant to suggest that the ecstatic trance experience is dependent upon ingestion of a particular ritual intoxicant. There are large areas in which visions and the ecstatic trance are highly valued and even considered essential but in which no psychoactive substances are employed for this purpose. The Plains in particular come to mind, for here many people—mostly men but also some women—sought visions to acquire guardian spirits, a phenomenon not unrelated to the shaman's recruitment of spirit helpers. But they did so through lonely vigil, exposure to the elements, sensory deprivation, even self-torture, and never by means of the psychoactive flora. Tobacco was smoked but as prayer, not, as among some South American peoples, for ritual intoxication and ecstatic communication with the spirit world.

As a final observation, it is not too much to say that neither the "Nomads" exhibition and the symposium on shamanism nor the joint Soviet and U.S. "Crossroads of Continents" exhibition of Alaskan Indian and Siberian art and artifacts that preceded "Nomads" in touring U.S. museums could have become reality had it not been for the fresh winds that, beginning with Mikhail Gorbachev, began to blow outmoded and increasingly discredited ideological cobwebs off Soviet social science even before the dissolution of the Soviet empire. It is not that Soviet scholars had been prevented in the past from studying or writing about shamanism, sometimes even with objectivity. Several volumes in English translation of essays on Siberian shamanism by Russians, Hungarians, and others attest to that. But in contrast to studies of shamanism among indigenous peoples in North and South America, Siberian shamanism was largely treated as a historical, rather than a living, phenomenon—as interesting but not very relevant. Worse, whether for reasons of conviction or political pressure, such studies were often viewed through the distorting prism of dialectical materialism. If such a philosophy still existed at the time of the Denver exhibition, its hold was clearly increasingly precarious. More and more, scholars in the former Soviet Union, including members of some of the nationalities of the Soviet Far East (where shamanism was already enjoying something of a rebirth), have been writing of it without the taint of ideology, with respect and even excitement. Some of this is evident in the Russian contributions to this volume, especially that of Basilov; in the spirited informal exchanges of observations and theories we had in Denver; and in such recent collections as that edited by Marjorie Balzer (1990). Indeed, Balzer's ongoing ethnographic field research in Siberia, which began when Siberia was still under Soviet domination, would have been unthinkable only a few short years ago. In all, the future of studies of shamanism—whether in the particular or as a universal phenomenon of religion, in Central Asia and Siberia or in the Indian Americas—seems assured. If the future of shamanism itself seems less certain, past reports and predictions of its demise have all proved to be greatly exaggerated. Experience suggests they will be so again.

REFERENCES

Andrews, J. R. and R. Hassig.
   1984.   *Treatise on Heathen Superstitions.* Norman: University of Oklahoma Press.

Balzer, Marjorie Mandelstam, ed.
   1990.   *Shamanism: Soviet Studies of Traditional Religion in Siberia and Central Asia.* Armonk, N.Y.: M. E. Sharpe.

Basilov, Vladimir N.
   1990.   "Chosen by the Spirits." In *Shamanism: Soviet Studies of Traditional Religion in Siberia and Central Asia,* Marjorie Mandelstam Balzer, ed., pp. 3–48. Armonk, N.Y.: M. E. Sharpe.

Coe, Michael D. and Gordon Whitaker, eds.
   1982.   *Aztec Sorcerer in Seventeenth Century Mexico. The Treatise on Superstitions by Hernando Ruíz de Alarcón.* Albany: Institute for Mesoamerican Studies, State University of New York at Albany.

Eliade, Mircea.
   1964.   *Shamanism: Archaic Techniques of Ecstasy,* Translated from French by Willard R. Trask. New York: Bollingen Series 76. Distr. by Pantheon Books.

———.
   1987.   "Shamanism: An Overview." *Encyclopedia of Religion,* Mircea Eliade, gen. ed., Vol. 13:201–208. New York: Macmillan.

Furst, Peter T.
   1976.   *Hallucinogens and Culture.* San Francisco: Chandler and Sharp.

———.
   1987. "South American Indian Shamanism." *Encyclopedia of Religion,* Mircea Eliade,
          gen. ed., Vol. 13:219–223. New York: Macmillan.

———.
   1989. Review of *Peyote Religion: A History,* by Omer C. Stewart. *American
          Ethnologist,* Vol. 16, No. 2, pp. 386–387.

Gayton, Anna H.
   1930. "Mono/Yokuts Chiefs and Shamans." *University of California Publications in
          American Archaeology and Ethnology,* Vol. 24, No. 8, pp. 362–420.

Gill, Sam D.
   1987. "North American Indian Shamanism." *Encyclopedia of Religion,* Mircea Eliade,
          gen. ed., Vol. 13:216–219. New York: Macmillan.

Kroeber, A. L.
   1929. "The Valley Nisenan." *University of California Publications in American
          Archaeology and Ethnology,* Vol. 24, No. 4, pp. 253–290.

La Barre, Weston.
   1938. *The Peyote Cult.* New Haven, Conn.: Yale University Publications in
          Anthropology, No. 19. Fourth revised and augmented edition, 1975, Schocken
          Books, N.Y.

———.
   1970. "Old and New World Narcotics: A Statistical Question and an Ethnological
          Reply." *Economic Botany,* Vol. 24, pp. 73–80.

———.
   1972. "Hallucinogens and the Shamanic Origins of Religion." In *Flesh of the Gods:
          The Ritual Use of Hallucinogens,* Peter T. Furst, ed., pp. 261–278. New York:
          Praeger. Revised and reprinted, 1990, Waveland Press, Prospect Heights, Ill.

Moerman, Daniel E.
   1986. *Medicinal Plants of Native America,* Vol. 1, p. 477. Ann Arbor: University of
          Michigan Museum of Anthropology, Research Reports in Ethnobotany,
          Contribution 2.

Ortiz de Montellano, Bernard R.
   1990. *Aztec Medicine, Health, and Nutrition.* Salt Lake City: University of Utah Press.

Plotkin, Mark J.
   1993.   *Tales of a Shaman's Apprentice.* New York: Viking.

Ruíz de Alarcon, H.
   1953.   *Tratado de las Idolatrías, Supersticiones, Dioses, Ritos. Hechizerías y Otras Costumbres Gentílicas de las Razas Aborígines.* México: Ediciones Fuente Cultural (new edition of the 1629 manuscript).

Sahagún, Fray Bernadino de.
   1969.   *Florentine Codex. General History of the Things of New Spain.* Translated from Aztec by Charles E. Dibble and Arthur O. Anderson. Santa Fe and Salt Lake City: School for American Research and the University of Utah.

Schultes, Richard Evans.
   1937.   "Peyote (*Lophophora williamsii* [Lemaire] Coulter) and Its Uses." Unpublished Ph.D. Dissertation, Harvard University.

————.
   1969.   "The Plant Kingdom and Hallucinogens." *Bulletin on Narcotics,* Vol. 21, No. 3, pp. 3–16; Vol. 22, No. 4, pp. 25–53 (1970).

————.
   1972.   "An Overview of Hallucinogens in the Western Hemisphere." In *Flesh of the Gods: The Ritual Use of Hallucinogens,* Peter T. Furst, ed., pp. 3–54. New York: Praeger. Enlarged and revised edition, 1990, Waveland Press, Prospect Heights, Ill.

Schultes, Richard Evans and Robert F. Raffauf.
   1990.   *The Healing Forest: Medicinal and Toxic Plants of the Northwest Amazonia.* Foreword by H.R.H. Phillip, Duke of Edinburgh. Portland, Ore: Dioscorides Press.

Shirokogorov, S. M.
   1919.   "Opyt issledovaniia osnov shamanstva u tungusov." *Uchenye zapiski istoriko-filologicheskogo facul'teta v g.,* Vol. 1. Vladivostok.

Siikala, Anna-Leena.
   1987.   "Siberian and Inner Asian Shamanism." *Encyclopedia of Religion,* Mircea Eliade, gen. ed., Vol.13:208–215. New York: Macmillan.

Stewart, Omer C.
   1987.   *Peyote Religion: A History.* Norman: University of Oklahoma Press.

Wasson, R. Gordon.
1968.   *SOMA: Divine Mushroom of Immortality.* Ethnomycological Studies, No. 1.
New York: Harcourt, Brace and World.

———.

1980.   *The Wondrous Mushroom: Mycology in Mesoamerica.* New York: McGraw-
Hill.

Wasson, R. Gordon and Valentina P. Wasson.
1957.   *Mushrooms Russia and History.* New York: Pantheon Books.

Wasson, R. Gordon, George and Florence Cowan, and Willard Rhodes.
1974.   *María Sabina and Her Mazatec Mushroom Velada.* New York: Harcourt Brace
Jovanovich.

Wilbert, Johannes.
1963.   *Indios de la Región Orinoco-Ventuari.* Caracas: Fundación La Salle de Ciencias
Naturales.

———.

1987.   *Tobacco and Shamanism in South America.* New Haven, Conn.: Yale
University Press.

THE ATTRIBUTES AND POWER OF THE SHAMAN: A GENERAL DESCRIPTION OF THE ECSTATIC CARE OF THE SOUL

LAWRENCE E. SULLIVAN

During *ecstasy,* the human soul leaves the body. Ecstatic specialists control the deliberate passage of the soul out of the body. On behalf of their clients, they also regain the controlled self-possession of an ungoverned soul if it has spontaneously exited the body during dream, fright, anger, sneezing, coughing, or sickness.

The shaman is arguably the most important—and certainly the most famous—ecstatic specialist in Central Asia and the Americas. But the term *shaman,* originally borrowed from Central Asian communities, has often been applied so generally that it risks conveying no particular meaning. The specific character of the shaman risks dissolving with the definition of a word frequently used to designate any kind of religious leader or mystic.

The extraordinary meeting of Soviet and U.S. scholars in Denver in June 1989 called for some broad definitions of the subject matter of our discussion. Within the context of these broad remarks, which Jane Day invited me to offer, lively discussion of more specific cases and issues could follow.

This general description, or phenomenology, of shamanism is based on reports filed about shamanic practices and beliefs over the past two hundred years, especially among Native American communities. It is possible to sketch a profile of the features frequently associated with the ecstatic power on which shamanic authority rests. This outline stresses the intrinsic relationship that exists between the nature of ecstasy and the cluster of attributes characteristic of the shaman. A general description must serve only as a starting point for exploring finer, important distinctions made in individual communities and for attending to variations in ecstatic experiences and techniques that

This text, with slight modification, was originally published in Lawrence E. Sullivan, *Icanchu's Drum: An Orientation to Meaning in South American Religions,* New York: Macmillan, 1988, pp. 651–660. It is reprinted here with permission from Macmillan Publishing, 866 Third Ave., New York, NY 10022.

exist from one community to another. This general description, then, should not be taken as a norm or as a strict definition against which one measures local practices, as if against some standard. On the contrary, this general outline serves only as a first orientation—a way of looking at practices and beliefs carried out most authentically in specific locales.

Shamans are experts in the movements of the human soul, because they not only control the ecstasy of their own souls but specialize in the knowledge and care of others' souls as well. Shamanism arose during the period described in myth, and its mythical origins link human life to the destiny of supernatural beings who were model protoshamans, such as gods, cultural heroes, and primordial ancestors. The apparel, techniques, and responsibilities of the shaman first appeared during these mythic times. Knowledge of the sacred and successful origins of shamanism is communicated through myth, and such knowledge gives courage to the community. Shamanic specialists who follow in the way of the mythic shamans face with confidence those dangers that confront the community, whether such perils come from manifest or unmanifest realities. Primordial shamanism no longer exists, except as a model for imitation, repetition, or approximation. If a power exists to communicate directly with supernatural beings today, it belongs to other species of beings, such as supernatural birds of the upper air or mysterious animals of the forest, sea, or underworld.

The training of apprentice shamans dramatizes a world filled with supernatural adventure, power, and danger. In their dreams, hallucinations, heightened senses of hearing, or extrasensory perceptions, apprentice shamans manifest a special sensitivity to the world of spirits. They enter the supernatural realm of images that are increasingly under their own control, and the novices learn to embody wishes and conflicts at will so they give clear conceptual form to the desires or fears of the soul (whether their own or those of their clients). Such adventures of the shamanic soul accompany dramatic manipulations of the body. The shamans' extraordinary physique has been transformed by their knowledge of the spiritual world. Shamans emerge from their training equipped with special techniques for contacting supernatural realities (to cure patients or destroy enemies) and with a fund of practical knowledge (regarding music, hunting, cycles of game, astronomic lore, and meteorology).

Shamanic apprenticeship cannot be equated with general education. School for shamans has a mythical structure derived from the accounts of the first shamans' accomplishments. Knowledge is acquired in a manner that befits the shamanic vocation and ecstatic temperament. In many cases, separation from one's natal group is essential to contemplative spiritual experiences. The isolation of initiatory illness and the psychic isolation brought on by the strange circumstances of the shaman's vocational call contribute to the disintegration of the individual's social and psychic being. For example, strange supernatural forms may appear before the eyes of the initiate as he or she enters other realms of the spatial universe. Magical items and objects of power are inserted into his or her body space. In addition, substances are extracted from the human being in the form of vomit, blood, sweat, fat, or mystical objects. The apprenticeship of a shaman essentially takes place on the spiritual plane. Fasting, vigil, and physical trial are symbolic expressions of activities that conform to the ideal patterns of myth. This guarantees that the shaman's experience in ecstasy is neither insuperably individualistic nor uncontrolled.

The presence of a master is essential to shamanic apprenticeship, because novices "die" to their former life, and there is danger that this ecstatic death might become permanent. Candidates must prove themselves capable of dealing with the spiritual world and of finding the path that opens to the experiences of resurrection. Acting as both executioner and coroner, the master ensures that an authentic ritual death occurs and, at the same time, prevents the loss or disorientation of the novice's ecstatic soul during that fatal experience. The master not only advises on practical matters—such as when to sleep, wake, and wash, what to eat, and how to prepare ritual paraphernalia—but also offers spiritual direction that guides initiates through strange supernatural terrain. The novice's master is an example of the kind of ritual partner frequently assigned to those undergoing a rite of passage. Through the presence of a master, novices grasp the meaning of their own experience of the sacred and, through comparison and contrast, examine the nature of their own consciences. The ultimate master is the first mythical shaman.

During apprenticeship, novices survive a series of ordeals, from simple quizzes on matters of fact to demanding physical feats or harrowing psychological episodes. These trials deconstruct fixed patterns of thought and behavior in order to rearrange the novice's sense of things. Reality is questioned and reconfigured, and the candidate's perceptions are placed on trial. The goal of ordeals is to obtain a new spiritual state, and the tests establish that worthiness they signify. They function sacramentally, which is why the path to other worlds is marked off into stages by these ordeals. The accomplishment of each test moves the candidates further along the trail of ecstasy and toward knowledge of other conditions of being. The dismemberment of the candidates' body (which the novices see in gory detail during delirium, dream, hallucination, vision, or in the special effects of some staged magical illusion) is the paradigmatic ordeal of shamanic apprenticeship. The candidates' experience of radically different modes of time—the time of the first primordial world or of the underworld of the dead—renders the experience of their own bodily space disjointed. When this sense of time is reconditioned, their bodies are likewise reordered and refashioned in extraordinary ways; they can never be the same.

Many shamanic technologies deliberately push shamans to the brink of disorientation in space and time: tight-rope walking, enormous swings that send the shamans hurtling through space, twirling ropes that make the shamans dizzy or subject them to vertigo, hypnotic songs, extreme fasting, seclusion and social alienation, as well as sexual abstinence. Shamans leave their accustomed senses of space and time and travel to other supernatural realms by manipulating the powers of magical plants, music, motion, dress, behavior, or mood. Hallucinogens stimulate the desired visions and color sacred realities. The ecstatic's systematic science of the soul not only rearranges the sense of the physical body but reconfigures the social network within which experience takes shape and has meaning. Apprenticeship is a time when the shaman learns to live within the new social network created by these new experiences and techniques. The apprentice's relations with other novices, fellow shamans, the master of initiation, the guardian spirit, other helper-spirits, his or her spouse, clients, relatives, neighbors, and enemies determine the success or even the life-or-death outcome of ecstasy.

Shamans move into the company of spirits. Their individual personalities, styles of behavior, physical appearance, and ultimate destiny change, depending upon the spirits with whom they develop rapport. In addition, the spiritual and physical life of the community hinges upon the supernaturals with whom the shaman keeps ties. Spirits reveal their sacred name, symbolic form, or character to the novice. Such systematic knowledge of the sacred, divulged by supernatural helpers, is itself an extraordinary power. On the one side, spirits often reveal sacred realities to shamans because they have to. Many helper-spirits find themselves stalled in the midst of a cycle of transformations that began during the mythic period. These helper-spirits seek aid from the shamans, who are masters in the subtle movements of spirits, in order to continue their transmigration. Some helper-spirits, however, are motivated by the will to save humankind or maintain cosmic order in the form of game protection, weather control, or crop growth. In either case, self-revelation on the part of the spirits discloses not only their power but their desires, needs, and vulnerabilities. Helper-spirits are frequently ravenous for spiritual food or for the essence of material food in the form of smoke, alcoholic ether, vapor, or odor in order to nourish their spiritual bodies.

Especially in the Americas, tobacco smoke is a prime craving of helper-spirits, because they no longer possess fire as human beings do. Fire has the capacity to "spiritualize" tobacco and other material substances through consumption by flame, and the nicotine from the plant helps spiritualize the shaman by consuming his or her body and inducing an experience of ecstatic death. To gain the help of spirits, the shaman must become familiar with the meaning of such spiritual cravings and the consumptive processes that typify the spiritual life.

In addition to mastering fire, serving food offerings to spirits rests upon knowledge of spiritual appetites. Such knowledge is a goal of shamanic training that discloses how the desire to consume is innate to the spiritual dynamism governing the cosmos. Spiritual helpers not only need food but are like food, often entering and residing in the body of the shaman just as nutrients are ingested and stored in the human body. Meditation on the meaning and nature of their spirit-helpers draws novices into reflection on the meaning of their own appetites and on the ways in which those cravings draw them into relationships with all of creation. Novices come to view themselves as consumers of visible and invisible realities and as the outcomes of relations that are predicated on interpenetrating consumptive processes. Their knowledge of these processes and their physical experience of them make shamans ideal candidates for the role of curer.

The transmission of knowledge and spirit-helpers is often a visceral and material process. Shamanic power may be transmitted from master to novice or from mythical shaman to the living one by the ingestion of magical substances or by the insertion of darts, thorns, arrows, or other penetrating images of primordial power into the novice's body. The master of ecstatic passage from one realm of being to another must master the passages of his or her own body through controlled diet, regurgitation, exits of breath during song, or exits of the soul during dream or ecstasy. The shaman's body, its desires, and its appetites become identified with helpful or harmful spiritual powers at work in the cosmos.

As a caretaker of souls, the shaman must master the consumptive processes that produce transformations of spirit. In many mythic reports concerning the origins of the world and of society, fire (supernatural heat or primordial cooking) produced a number of transformative orders over which the shaman, as master of fire, presides. These transformative orders emerge from a primal, cosmic fire and include reproductive physiology as it is seen in warm blood, in menstruation, birth, growth, and death. Another transformative order emerging from the devastation of the cosmic fire is the speech or sounds related to the separate species of animals and human-language groups. As master of fire, the shaman also controls feverish sickness, seething poison, and venom, as well as their remedies. And mastery of fire also often includes control over symbolic actions, especially initiation rites that "cook" candidates or subject them to the heat of incubation. The shamanic master of fire is responsible for transformative processes burning at the core of spiritual life: the symbolism at the center or hearth of social units, community groups, all civilized human life, and the cosmos itself. Ecstatic specialists also prevent recurrence of the total cosmic fire by summoning their helper-spirits and doing battle on the marginal frontiers with the causes of the cosmic fire that once reduced the earth to cinders.

Endurance of the heat and light shed by heavenly beings demonstrates the shaman's mastery over fire. Quartz crystals that embody celestial light and heat glow and simmer inside the shaman's rattle, medicine pouch, or body organs and become emblems of the shaman's relationship to heavenly powers. The shamanic experience of consumption correlates directly with ecstasy. Consumption by fire signifies the death inflicted by supernatural powers during ecstatic trance. Ecstatic death consumes the spiritually awakened or inflamed human being, who is transported to an illumined state of consciousness. This is why dazzling displays of pyrotechnics during shamanic demonstrations of power are important cultural spectacles. Fire walking, fire eating, glowing in the dark, and flashing across the sky like shooting stars are shamanic stunts that fasten the spectators' reflection on the nature of fiery heat and light and on the power of the human specialist who "knows" them intimately in his or her inner being and substance.

Through ecstasy, shamans experience the supernatural life-conditions of the many strange spaces composing the universe. The shaman's soul assumes the physical form of a bird, beam of light, lightning bolt, cloud, breeze, or meteor. The metamorphosis invests shamans with the power of magical flight by means of which they visit diverse cosmic realms. Shamans need not await death to take on the form of free souls who ascend to heaven, but they may rise to other planes of existence at will and do so concretely and sensually. The reachievement of the free-moving and weightless state of the first age is a reminder of the shortcomings of the present human condition and a critique of the status quo. Ordinary mortals become free of their present state and fly to celestial existence only after they die, whereas living shamans pass in and out of all realms. Shamans descend into the underworld or travel to realms on the horizons of the world. In some cases, the entire mythic universe is open to the shaman; in others, types of shaman are distinguished by the type of cosmic realm they visit or by the worlds from which their spirit-helpers come.

Shamans are completely transformed by such travel. Even physical appearances change so that, for example, the shamans' skin radiates with celestial light or their body organs become immortal stone or crystals of light. The ability of shamans to pick their way through the perils of postmortem existence guarantees their own ultimate destiny and empowers them to serve as psychopomps who guide souls to their appointed supernatural destinations after death.

Because shamans can make human existence (their own) adjust itself to the inaccessible reaches of the universe, they serve as mediators between incompatible modes of being. The ecstatic helps individuals and communities adjust to new circumstances. Thus, shamans guide the souls of the dead through the afterlife and return lost souls to their ailing bodies. As political leaders, shamans interpret the encounters with colonizers and foreigners whose reality is shaped by other conditions of time and space.

Shamans possess extraordinary vision, because they see spaces and times that are no longer fully manifest. Their ecstatic passage enlightens their sight. Shamanic "seeing" is a total experience and not just an exercise of the eyes as independent organs. Immersed in pure light, shamans are imbued with the unimaginable colors of sacred realities that concentrate themselves within them as crystals, visions, or dreams. Supernatural light remakes the shaman's eye so that it can see the heart of invisible realities and penetrate the darkness that obscures distinctions between forms. Shamans see reality in its immediate state. The shaman's clairvoyance overcomes distance. Solid matter presents no obstacle to the penetrating vision of shamans. Concealed objects, such as pathogens hiding in the primordial darkness within a patient's body, appear clearly, as do souls that were lost, stolen, or hidden at enormous distances in the forest or underworld.

The reciprocity between supernatural light and the shaman's vision explains the shaman's invisibility. Clairvoyance and invisibility are part of the same process of transformation. As the shaman gains acuity of vision to see the spiritual world, so the shaman's presence, at first invisible and insignificant, becomes more visible and tangible in the world of spirits until the spirits recognize the shaman among their company.

Visions of supernatural realities are induced by sacred plants. Through sound and lighting, shamans orchestrate hallucinogenic seances in which luminous images are sparked by ingesting, snuffing, or drinking plant powders and potions. Because sight of this sort is a total existential condition, the shaman's vision effects his or her intimacy with sacred beings and with unmanifest dimensions of existence.

Shamans are also masters of sound. The noises of the primordial world—the significant groans, roars, squeaks, and tinkles described in myths—become the bass line for magical music. In replicating those sounds, the shaman creates variations on primordial themes and evokes new ways of existing. In the Americas, the gourd rattle is often the epitome of the link between sacred sound and shamanic power. Elsewhere, especially in Central Asia, it may be a drum or some other percussion instrument.

Like the shaman's soul, emitted sound has an ecstatic quality. In mythical times, the sound of primordials assumed a fully autonomous life outside and beyond them and opened up the existence of a new realm of the cosmos. Those sounds are represented in the shaman's rattle or drum and its noises. They become images of the shaman's own soul. The sound is expressed or extruded from some body (a mythic figure, a rattle, a drum, or a shaman) and stands as a well-defined presence of its own with a concrete structure, like the shaman's soul in ecstasy. The shaman fills the rattle or constructs the drum with elements he or she collects in voyages to other cosmic realms (from which the rattle or elementary structures of the drum may have come). The instrument contains powers fully present in worlds that normal mortals enter only at death, and the rattle or drum may cause dangerous mystical death if touched by the wrong hand. The rattle or drum is frequently a microcosm of active powers, because its construction, the designs painted or etched on it, and its component elements amount to a creation of the far-flung reaches of the cosmos. The instrument may be viewed as the womblike space that contains primordial, fecund forces, or its physical construction may bring together male and female elements (such as the haft and gourd or the rattle, or the round frame and crosspiece or mallet of the drum). The union of female and male elements in producing sound re-creates life in the cosmos. Cutting mouths or symbols of teeth into the gourd reinstigates the cosmic hunger for being and stimulates the appetites of spirits, who are fed with tobacco smoke, fire, sound, or the bodies of sick patients consumed by fever or disease.

A similar logic of sound explains the shaman's mastery of song and other forms of music. The acquisition of melodies and rhythms and the uses toward which they are put remain consonant with the ecstatic vocation.

All extant beings have a sonic structure that, given certain levels of perceptive awareness, becomes audible. Silence is a sonic form that many potent entities assume, just as invisibility can be their parallel visual form. In ritual blowing and breathing, shamans perform powerful demonstrations of silent sound. Magical blowing stretches the limits of perceived, meaningful sound and can only be heard by spirits and shamans with extremely subtle senses. The relationship of blowing to spirit-sound allows for interchangeability and creativity along the entire acoustical spectrum, on which lie also the unintelligible lyrics of shamanic songs and esoteric languages comprehensible only to the initiated. The language that orients one in this life must transcend speech in order to situate one in the presence of creative powers apparent only in other realms. Esoteric speech and arcane liturgical cant make sense in other conditions of existence. Thus, secret language bespeaks the shaman's acculturation to the spirit world.

Shamanic mastery of sound and song sets ecstatics apart, just as other forms of their knowledge do. Secrecy and esotericism are not simply functions of hiding information from others. Because mastery of sound requires a fundamental rearrangement of the senses, the experience of ecstasy underlying shamanic vocations isolates shamans from the general public, which does not share that experience. In the sound of its shaman, the human community learns that the cosmos makes sense—a sense that is not merely common sense. In the sounds of the shaman's rattle, drum, feathers, leaf bundles, breath, ventriloquism, bird calls, and esoteric languages, the community hears snatches of meaning from the paradisal life that existed before the mythic world's catastrophic division into separate species, babbling and senseless. The shaman demonstrates how humankind can live and communicate more freely with all kinds of beings.

Several of these explanations converge to explain the shaman's association with animal forms. Shamans possess intimate knowledge of other kinds of space (that is, they know the secrets of nature) and are expert in the consumptive processes underlying the food chain that includes animals. Their transformed physiology sometimes takes on the forms of primordial animals—the experience of life-forms conditioned by other kinds of space. In South America, for instance, shamans frequently become jaguars. Total transformation of the human condition and reappearance in the form of a jaguar is an immense spiritual achievement. Everything ordinary about the human condition of the shaman is devoured, digested, and left as waste. Consumption by the jaguar, the consummate consumer, parallels consumption by fire and by ecstatic death. All three forms of consumption produce spirit, and mastery over them assures control of the changes that compose spiritual life.

The shaman's bodily transformation is connected to cyclic transition through time. By transforming themselves into primordial jaguars, birds, snakes, or other animal forms, shamans recover some of the knowledge lost in past times. The continuity of life and society depends upon this recovery procedure through animal transformation. Each animal with which the shaman identifies has a power and meaning revealed in myth. The power of shamans to assume the bodily shape of mythic animals relates directly to their power to penetrate and endure the conditions of other forms of cosmic space. Familiarity with changes of form may make the shaman expert in costumery and disguise, transvestism, or homosexual experience. Shamanic management of space through this manipulation of bodily experience, especially through the animal imagery of mythical beasts, situates the entire community in proper relationship to the powers that define its territory and its place in the world.

As a specialist in space, the shaman cares for the health of the human body, the spatial home of the soul. Shamans restore well-being by reinstating lost souls to the body or by extracting from the body's inner space the sickening elements that may have lodged in the body and that only the shaman can see. The curing shaman directs cosmic traffic, safeguards the good order of cosmic spaces, and polices the qualitatively different areas of the universe. The knowledge of physics possessed by the shaman-physician thus guarantees the significance and integrity of human physical space in the universe when it is threatened by the disorder of disease.

Sucking is a technique of cure that attends the emphasis on the body as a spatial microcosm. The shaman sucks a toxic element out of the patient's body and often transforms the pathogen into a beneficial power.

The efficacy of the sucking cure relates directly to the shaman's mystical physiology, especially the ability of the shaman's mouth and stomach to engulf, transform, and extrude spirits who appear in the form of physical objects such as tobacco, hallucinogenic beverages, stones, splinters, snakes, insects, and songs. Swallowing and vomiting are moments of the sucking operation. They highlight a spirituality of cosmic matter centered on the transformative locus of the shaman's mouth or the mystical channel inside the shaman's chest, legs, arms, hands, or rattle. The opening serves as a mystical canal of passage from one state to another.

Shamanic cure is theatrical. Public display of the sick and dramatic triumphs over the forces of disease are themselves spectacles that promote good health. The ill become a public and effective sign of well-being. This explains why shamanic cure is so often miraculous, in the literal sense of the word: a deliberate exhibition of normally invisible powers. Shamanic cure astonishes spectators and compels them to admire what is real and life-giving. Miracles publicize realities that are ordinarily unseen or stashed beneath the threshold of awareness. Truth telling in shamanic medical practice requires that the performance amaze the audience with a startling demonstration of that truth. To communicate truths of this kind, shamans must make available to the naked eye what they see with their clairvoyant penetration of the spirit domain. By means of such miraculous performances and shamanic miracle plays, the audience is able to see reality reflexively, the way shamans see it. The miraculous apparition of those sacred powers who had hidden behind the symptoms of sickness moves the audience into a healthier state; the appearance of an extracted pathogen, sucked out of the body of the suffering patient and held up for all to see, gives the audience a broader vision of reality and thereby re-establishes the world order that is fundamental to wellness. Dramatic performances of cure that re-enact the gestures of mythical shamans give the public what ecstasy offers the shaman: a visible encounter with the forces that are at work on other planes of existence. Curing rites frequently stage for the public audience the journey of the shaman's soul into faraway, invisible realms. This knowledge of other realms, obtained by the shaman during ecstasy and publicized in curing rituals, sustains public health and well-being.

The shaman has many attributes, but the profile of features is surprisingly coherent, because it is consistent with the shaman's special expertise in the movements of the soul. Through control of the ecstatic outpouring of their own souls, shamans specialize in the knowledge and care of others' souls as well. The more we learn about shamanic techniques that control the ecstatic soul, the more we discover about the religious basis of human culture. Shamanism points us to the underlying aims of theater, spectacular entertainment, visual art, poetry, music, medical therapy, and all cultural strategies that counter the terrors of social existence or individual dreams that might alienate self-possession. How we probe the history of ecstasy and how we interpret the variety of experiences of the soul determine how we face the mysterious sources of human creativity.

REFERENCES

Baer, Gerhard, and Wayne W. Snell.
"An Ayahuasca Ceremony Among the Matsigenka (Eastern Peru)." *Zeitschrift fur Ethnologie* 99, Nos. 1 and 2 (1974):63–80.

Barandiaran, Daniel de.
"Mundo Espiritual y Shamanismo Sanema." *Antropologica* (Caracas) 15 (December 1965):1–28.

Bartolome, Miguel A.
"Shamanism Among the Ava-Chiripa." In *Spirits, Shamans, and Stars: Perspectives from South America,* ed. David L. Browman and Ronald A. Schwarz. The Hague: Mouton, 1979.

Basso, Ellen B.
A Musical View of the Universe: Kalapalo Myth and Ritual Performances. Philadelphia: University of Pennsylvania Press, 1985.

Bastide, Roger.
The African Religions of Brazil: Toward a Sociology of the Interpretation of Civilizations, trans. Helen Sebba. Baltimore: Johns Hopkins University Press, 1978.

Bastien, Joseph W.
"Qollahuaya-Andean Body Concepts: A Topographical-Hydraulic Model of Physiology." *American Anthropology* 87 (1985):595–611.

Browman, David L., and Ronald A. Schwarz, eds.
Spirits, Shamans, and Stars: Perspectives from South America. The Hague: Mouton, 1979.

Butt, Audrey J.
"The Birth of a Religion." *Journal of the Royal Anthropological Institute of Great Britain and Ireland* 90 (1960):66–106.

———.
"Realite et ideal dans la pratique chamanique." *L'Homme* 2, No. 3 (1962):5–52.

Califano, Mario.
"El Chamanismo mataco." *Scripta Ethnologica* 3, No. 3 (1976):7–60.

Chagnon, Napoleon A.
Yanamamo: The Fierce People. New York: Holt, Rinehart & Winston, 1968.

Chesser, Barbara.
"The Anthropomorphic Personal Guardian Spirit in Aboriginal South America." *Journal of Latin American Lore* 1, No. 2 (1975):107–126.

Civrieux, Marc de.
Religion y Magia Kari'na. Caracas: Universidad Catolica "Andres Bello," Instituto de Investigaciones Historicas, 1974.

Clastres, Pierre.
Chronique des Indiens Guayaki. Paris: Plon, 1972.

Cortez, Roberto.
"Dialogo Ceremonial e Dialogo Mitologico entre Os Tiriyo," *Boletim do Museu Goeldi-Antropologia* (Belem-Para) 61 (November 1975):1–25.

Cossard-Binon, Giselle.
"La Fille de Saint." *Journal de la Societe des Americanistes de Paris France* 58 (1969):57–78.

Fock, Niels.
Waiwai: Religion and Society of an Amazonian Tribe. Nationalmuseets Skrifter, Etnografisk Raekke, Vol. 8. Copenhagen: National Museum, 1963.

Fulop, Marcos.
"Aspectos de la Cultura Tukana: Cosmogonia." *Revista Colombiano de Antropologia* 3 (1954):99–137.

Furst, Peter T.
"The Roots and Continuities of Shamanism." *Artscanada 30,* Nos. 5–6 (December 1973/January 1974):22–60.

Gillin, James.
The Barama River Caribs of British Guiana. Papers of the Peabody Museum, Vol. 14, No. 2. Cambridge, Mass.: Peabody Museum of Harvard University, 1936.

Girault, Louis.
Kallawaya: Guerisseurs itinerants des Andes. Memoires de l'Institut Francais de Recherche Scientifique pour le Developpement en Cooperation, Vol. 107. Paris: ORSTOM, 1984.

Gow, Rosalind, and Bernabe Condori.
Kay Pacha. Cuzco: Centro de Estudios Rurales Andinos "Bartolome de las Casas," 1976.

Gusinde, Martin.
"Der Medizinmann bei den Indianern Sudamerikas." *Ciba Zeitschrift* (Basel) 4, No. 38 (1936):1,302–1,306.

Harner, Michael J.
"The Sound of Rushing Water." In *Native South Americans: Ethnology of the Least Known Continent,* ed. Patricia J. Lyon. Boston: Little, Brown, 1974; reprinted from *Natural History Magazine* (June-July 1968):28–33, 60–61.

Hartmann, Gunther.
"Zigarrenhalter Nordwest-Brasiliens." *Ethnologische Zeitschrift Zurich.* Festschrift Otto Zerries, Special Supplement no. 1 (1974):177–189.

Henry, Jules.
Jungle People: A Kaingang Tribe of the Highlands of Brazil. New York: Vintage Books, 1964 (1941).

Izikowitz, Karl Gustav.
"Calabashes With Star-Shaped Lids in South America and China." *Comparative Ethnographical Studies* 9 (1931):130–133.

Jacopin, Pierre-Yves.
La Parole generative de la mythologie des Indiens Yukuna. Ph.D. dissertation, Universite de Neuchatel, Faculte des Lettres, 1981.

Kensinger, Kenneth M.
"Cashinahua Medicine and Medicine Men." In *Native South Americans: Ethnology of the Least Known Continent,* ed. Patricia J. Lyon. Boston: Little, Brown, 1974.

Krugh, Janice.
"The Mythology of the Pemon Indians of Venezuela: A Survey of the Work of Father Cesareo de Armellada." *Latin American Indian Literatures 4,* No. 1 (Spring 1980):29–35.

Lathrap, Donald W.
"Our Father the Cayman, Our Mother the Gourd: Spinden Revisited, or a Unitary Model for Emergence of Agriculture in the New World." In *Origins of Agriculture,* ed. C. A. Reed. The Hague: Mouton, 1977.

Lyon, Patricia J., ed.
Native South Americans: Ethnology of the Least Known Continent. Boston: Little, Brown, 1974.

Mariani Ramirez, Carlos.
"Personalidad del Hechicero Indigena. El Machi o Hechicero Mapuche." In *Anales del Tercer Congreso Latinomericano de Psiquiatria,* October 25–31, 1964, ed. Carlos Alberto Sequin and Ruben Rios Carrasco. Lima: Asociacion Psiquiatrica de America Latina, 1966.

Mariscotti de Gorlitz, Ana Maria.
Pachamama Santa Tierra: Contribucion al Estudio de la Religion Autoctona en los Andes Centro-Merdionales. Beitrage zue Volke-und Anthropolgie des Indianishcen Amerika, Vol. 8. Berlin: Gabriel Mann Verlag, 1978.

Maybury-Lewis, David.
Akwe-Shavante Society. Oxford: Clarendon Press, 1967.

Melatti, Julio Cezar.
"Myth and Shaman." In *Native South Americans: Ethnology of the Least Known Continent,* ed. Patricia J. Lyon. Boston: Little, Brown, 1974.

Metraux, Alfred.
"Religion and Shamanism." In *Handbook of South American Indians* 5, pp. 559–599. Washington, D.C.: Smithsonian Institution, 1949.

Moesbach, E.
Vida y Costumbres de los Indigenas Araucanos en la Segunda Mitad del Siglo XIX. Santiago de Chile: Imp. Universitaria, 1936.

Nimuendaju, Curt.
The Apinaye. Catholic University of America, Anthropological Series, No. 8. Washington, D.C.: Catholic University, 1939.

Olsen, Dale A.
"Music-Induced Altered States of Consciousness Among Warao Shamans." *Journal of Latin American Lore* 1, No. 1 (1975):19–34.

Palavecino, Enrique.
"The Magic World of the Mataco," trans. and ed. J. A. Vazuez. *Latin American Indian Literature* 3, No. 2 (1979):61–75.

Reichel-Dolmatoff, Gerardo.
"Funerary Customs and Religious Symbolism Among the Kogi." In *Native South Americans: Ethnology of the Least Known Continent,* ed. Patricia J. Lyon. Boston: Little, Brown, 1974.

———.
"Training for the Priesthood Among the Kogi of Columbia." In *Enculturation in Latin America: An Anthropology,* ed. Johannes Wilbert. UCLA Latin American Studies, Vol. 37. Los Angeles: UCLA Latin American Center Publications, 1976.

Riester, Jurgen.
"Medizinmanner und Zauberer der Chiquitano Indianer." *Zeitschrift fur Ethnologie* (Braunschweig) 96, No. 2 (1971):250–270.

Roe, Peter G.
The Cosmic Zygote: Cosmology in the Amazon Basin. New Brunswick, N.J.: Rutgers University Press, 1982.

Sauer, Carl O.
"Cultivated Plants of South and Central America." *Handbook of South American Indians* 6, pp. 487–543. Washington, D.C.: Smithsonian Institution, 1950.

Schaden, Egon.
"A Origem e a Posse do Fogo na Mitologia Guarani." *International Conference of Americanists,* 31st Session, pp. 217–227. Sao Paulo, 1955.

Seitz, Georg J.
"Die Waikas und ihre Drogen." *Zeitschrift fur Ethnologie* 94, No. 2 (1969):266–283.

Wagley, Charles.
Welcome of Tears: The Tapirape Indians of Central Brazil. New York: Oxford University Press, 1977.

Weiss, Gerald.
   The World of a Forest Tribe in South America. Anthropological Papers of the American
   Museum of Natural History, Vol. 52, Part 5. New York: American Museum of Natural
   History, 1975.

Whitten, Norman E., Jr.
   Sacha Runa: Ethnicity and Adaptation of Ecuadorian Jungle Quichua. Urbana:
   University of Illinois Press, 1976.

Wilbert, Johannes.
   Yupa Folktales. Los Angeles: UCLA Latin American Center, 1974.

———.
   "Eschatology in a Participatory Universe: Destinies of the Soul Among the Warao
   Indians of Venezuela." In *Death and the After-life in Pre-Colombian America,* ed.
   Elizabeth P. Benson. Washington, D.C.: Dumbarton Oaks Research Library and
   Collections, 1975.

Wright, Robin M.
   History and Religion of the Baniwa Peoples of the Upper Rio Negro Valley, 2 vols. Ph.D.
   dissertation, Stanford University, 1981.

Yacovleff, Eugenio, and Fortunato L. Herrera.
   "El Mundo Vegetal de los Antiguos Peruanos." *Revista de Museo Nacional* (Lima) 3,
   No. 3 (1934):241–322; 4, No. 1 (1935):29–102.

THE CULTURAL SIGNIFICANCE OF TOBACCO USE
IN SOUTH AMERICA

JOHANNES WILBERT

Any consideration of traditional Native American tobacco practices inevitably leads back to the shaman as principal actor, because from prehistoric times to around A.D. 1700, tobacco served Indian peoples primarily for religious purposes and related practices of healing (Cooper 1949:526). In both of these areas the shaman is the specialist.

The principal species of tobacco utilized in the Indian Americas, *Nicotiana rustica* and *N. tabacum*, are cultivated hybrids and thus represent the end products of long processes of experimentation. There is reason to believe that tobacco cultivation for religious and healing purposes, including for use in the shamanic trance, occurred at about the same time as the beginnings of tropical forest agriculture in South America, approximately six thousand to eight thousand years ago; it may, in fact, have been the first true cultigen on the South American subcontinent.

Whether shamans of South American hunting and food-collecting societies discovered and utilized one or more of the many other psychotropic species available to them in their diverse environments at the same time as, or even earlier than, tobacco is impossible to say. It may be that before the advent of horticulture, most relied not on psychotropic plants but on such endogenous, nonchemical techniques as rattling, drumming, dancing, or sensory deprivation to trigger the ecstatic trance states that are principal hallmarks of shamanism everywhere. An equally good argument can be made that the discovery of the hallucinogenic potential of different species, including various Solanaceae other than the nicotianas, owes nothing to agriculture, and that the shamans of archaic hunter-gatherer peoples—who, as we know, relied as heavily,

For a broader discussion of the general topic, and for detailed documentation, see J. Wilbert, *Tobacco and Shamanism in South America*, New Haven, Conn.: Yale University Press, 1987, on which this chapter is largely based (courtesy Yale University Press). My thanks to Peter T. Furst for editing the original paper.

if not more heavily, on the vegetable kingdom for sustenance as they did on game—could have consciously searched the environment for the plant allies used to this day in many parts of South America (Furst 1976, 1989). Be that as it may, around eight thousand years ago, the large Pleistocene mammals, which for thousands of years had served the hunters as a staple food source, became extinct. Some hunters turned to the coast and the rivers and became dependent upon seafood and riverine resources, a fairly subtle shift. Others turned inland and subsisted increasingly on wild vegetable foods and eventually on cultivated crops. Because the open savannas of southern South America are largely unsuited for agriculture, the changeover from hunter to planter entailed leaving the open lowlands and entering the tropical forest of Amazonia and beyond. Among the crops planted by early agriculturalists was tobacco.

WILD AND CULTIVATED NICOTIANAS

Tobacco-producing plants belong to the genus *Nicotiana*, a branch of the nightshade family, or Solanaceae. Of the sixty-four recognized species that make up the genus, thirty-seven, or 58 percent, are aboriginal to South America. The rest are found in the Australo-Pacific region (27 percent); North America, including Mexico (14 percent); and Africa (1 percent). Wild nicotianas pertain to three morphologically and cytogenetically determined subgenera. Two of these, *N. rustica* and *N. tabacum*, are peculiar to South America. The third subgenus, *Petunioides* (with the exception of section *Undulatae*), occurs in all three major regions of the world in which nicotianas are found—South America, North America, and Australo-Pacifica. (Recently, a single species has also been found in Africa, but its taxonomic position remains uncertain.)

To determine the geographic origin of *Nicotiana,* it is significant that a direct relationship exists between the *Petunioides* of South America and those of the Australo-Pacific region. But although the North American species of the subgenus are also directly related to South American species, they are related only indirectly by way of South America to those of the Pacific and Australia. This distribution "points to South America as the center of current distribution of *Nicotiana* and, together with other pertinent data, argues for the origin of the genus in that continent with subsequent dispersal to North America and to Australia and the South Pacific" (Goodspeed 1954:8) and, we must now add, to Africa (Merxmüller and Buttler 1975). Lest this raise the specter of pre-Columbian contacts across the Pacific and Atlantic, I hasten to add that we are speaking of dispersals that occurred not thousands but millions of years ago.

The homeland of most South American nicotianas appears to have been in the Andean region. Their distribution area includes the Andean highlands of southern Ecuador, Peru, northcentral Bolivia, and northern Chile. Subsequently, *wild* nicotianas invaded practically the entire southern continental cone south of Matto Grosso. Again, human beings could not possibly have been instrumental—voluntarily or involuntarily—in the dispersal of the genus in its wild state, because this occurred in remote geological eras, the Mid-Cretaceous to the Upper Cretaceous and the Pliocene, somewhere between 10 million and 100 million years ago.

The initial settling of the Americas by small hunting bands may date back to 40,000 years ago, when the first of successful small waves of nomadic bands of hunters and food collectors migrated out of northeastern Asia across Beringia into what is now Alaska in pursuit of large Pleistocene game. From Alaska they traveled slowly southward through ice-free corridors of western and coastal North America, reaching the South American subcontinent perhaps 20,000 years ago. Recent radiocarbon dating of a well-preserved settlement site in southcentral Chile places people in southern South America as early as 13,500 years ago (Dillehay 1984). Certainly, by 11,000 years ago the descendants of the early hunters and gatherers had penetrated the southern lowlands of Patagonia, the Pampas, the Gran Chaco, and possibly southeastern Brazil—regions that appear to have been more suitable to their Paleo-Indian lifeways than the "closed" landscapes of Amazonia.

Ethnographic evidence from historic preagricultural societies suggests that their archaic forebears roamed about in small bands, each headed by an experienced elder, who served as the political guide, and a shaman who catered to spiritual needs. Eurasian and American shamans were and continue to be religious specialists who mediate between their communities and the spirit world. Through ecstatic trance they communicate with the supernatural powers and solicit protection and well-being for their people. Shamans of the Upper Paleolithic, ca. 17,000 B.P., are depicted on the cave walls of such sites as Trois Frères, France, and in their well-documented capacity as mystical specialists and technicians of the sacred were probably present in most prehistoric and historic bands of hunters and seminomadic horticulturists.

It is significant in the present context that the ancient homeland of Paleo-Indian hunters in the southern cone of South America coincided largely with the original world distribution center of that wild representative of the genus *Nicotiana* from which all tobacco-producing plants are ultimately derived. However, it is equally remarkable that although surrounded by a large number of *Nicotiana* species, the early hunters of the southern lowlands, like their descendants in historical times, appear to have ignored tobacco altogether.

Instead, tobacco use by indigenous South Americans is largely confined to horticulturists, who cultivated a dozen or so species, led by *N. rustica* and *N. tabacum*, and dispersed these cultigens throughout the Americas. Accordingly, in considering the geography of South American nicotianas, we must distinguish between the culturally insignificant natural distribution of wild species throughout the southern lowlands of the subcontinent and the culturally very significant distribution by human agency of cultivated species throughout the northern part of South America and the Caribbean.

And here we must underscore that the interest of people in *Nicotiana*, historically as well as prehistorically, has been exclusively motivated by nicotine, its principal alkaloid. Because not all nicotianas are producers of nicotine or tobacco, only a dozen or so came to be particularly favored as tobacco cultigens. *N. rustica* and *N. tabacum* were among these high-yielding species, a circumstance that almost certainly accounts for their unrivaled dissemination—the former even more than the latter—throughout the Indian Americas. Indeed, not one of the wild species growing in Australia, Oceania, or Africa is known to have been cultivated for tobacco in pre-Contact times.

As is well-known, certain species of *Nicotiana*, including *N. rustica*, and of several other members of the solanaceous family, including *Datura* (spp.), tend to grow spontaneously in disturbed soil—that is, at the edges of paths, trails, and roadways, on fields, and especially on the turned-over and enriched soil of burial sites. It is likely because of this latter characteristic that tobacco became widely identified with the ancestors, whom many Indian peoples, in South America as well as North America, credit with causing it to sprout from their graves as a special gift from the spirit world to their surviving kin. In this way too, tobacco became a sacred plant, although the principal reason for the phenomenal diffusion of tobacco throughout native America was likely its utility as a vehicle of ecstasy and altered states of consciousness in which those specialists who used it could communicate with the ancestors and with the spirit world at large.

Thus, as indicated earlier, from first discovery until roughly the beginning of the eighteenth century, tobacco use was restricted to the shamanic practices of conjuring and curing. It was considered the prerogative of a minority of practitioners but was generally taboo for ordinary people. However, although in many places it has continued to play this sacred role as vehicle of ecstasy and food for the spirits, from about 1700 onward ethnographic reports increasingly reflect a gradual shift in the purpose of tobacco practice from the exclusively or predominantly religious to the profane. By this time, Western society, which before the end of the fifteenth century had been completely ignorant of even the existence of tobacco, much less its effects, had thoroughly adopted it as a hedonistic drug. And as Europeans entered increasingly into contact with the Indians, they also introduced tobacco use (especially smoking) as a purely secular custom to be imitated by ordinary members of the community—initially men and then, more gradually, also women. In the ensuing process of acculturation, shamans and their religious tenets suffered a serious loss of face and credibility, making the general adoption of tobacco as a secular drug even more acceptable.

Currently, shamans in many Indian societies continue to practice in the traditional way, using tobacco as a significant psychotropic drug essential to their arts. But tobacco is no longer restricted to a few practitioners of the sacred in every local group. Instead, it has become available to all—men, women, and often children—with the same ill effects on health of which Western consumers have become increasingly aware in recent years.

THE HISTORICAL RECORD

Following their first landfall in the West Indies on October 12, 1492, Columbus and his men were soon introduced to tobacco and its uses. Columbus was presented, inexplicably to him, with the ungainly leaves as a token of friendship between the natives and his men. Then, upon meeting a solitary traveler in a canoe near Fernandia Island, he again saw a supply of these shriveled vegetables among the boatman's meager provisions but remained in complete ignorance of their purpose. Only several weeks later, upon their return from an exploratory excursion through coastal Cuba, did two of Columbus's crew finally report on how they had become the first Europeans to have witnessed the custom of smoking tobacco in the form of cigars. Soon the Spaniards began to experiment with the inhalation of tobacco smoke, eager to experience the purported intoxi-cating qualities of tobacco and the analgesic properties ascribed to it.

In 1535, the chronicler Gonzalo Fernández de Oviedo y Valdés pub-lished the first volume of his monumental account of the first encounter and the early decades of the Conquest. In it he furnishes the earliest printed reference to tobacco smoking and the first mention of "tabaco."

With reference to the Caquetio of northern Venezuela, Oviedo (1851–1855, 2:298–299) commented on the practice of divinatory tobacco smoking by shamans and the methods of tobacco cultivation. Oviedo (1851–1855, 4:96 [1549]) also reported the use of ceremonial cigars by the Nicoya of Nicaragua and knew that Captain Grijalva's men had been offered reed cigarettes by Maya Indians off the coast of Yucatan (Robicsek 1978:11). Benzoni (1967 [1565]), on his travels in 1541–1555, reported on the shamans of Hispaniola and certain Central American provinces, relat-ing how they "poisoned" themselves with tobacco smoke during a curing seance. In the process, some men fell to the ground as though dead and remained "stupefied for the greater part of the day or night." Upon com-ing back to their senses, they would tell of their visions and their encounter with the gods.

As these early reports on tobacco smoking in the West Indies and along the Latin American–Caribbean rim were being filed by the chroni-clers of that part of the newly discovered world, others witnessed cigar smoking on the coast of Brazil. Here, at some point during 1555, the Franciscan friar André Thevet (1928 [1557]) made contact with the Tupinamba Indians and found them using cigars to suppress hunger and thirst and to deliberate in council.

His report, and similar information by the German Hans von Staden (1557), was essentially confirmed several years later by Jean de Léry (1951 [1578]) who, in addition to smoking, witnessed a second mode of tobacco use among the Tupinamba—ritual tobacco blowing. Employing a four-foot to five-foot-long cane, chiefs blew tobacco smoke repeatedly on the heads and faces of circumambulating participants in a war dance, purporting to impart to them the "spirit and fortitude" required to over-come their enemies. Canes may also have served the Tupinamba as tubu-lar pipes. But elbow pipes are definitely an American invention, because sometime in 1535 or 1536, Jacques Cartier (1545) found them in early use among the Iroquois Indians of Hochelaga (Montreal).

Another method of tobacco consumption may have been reported very early by Oviedo (1851–1855 [1549]) by the Taino of the Greater

Antilles, who supposedly used a forked tube, "about a span long and less than the thickness of the smallest finger," through which they inhaled tobacco smoke. I say may have because a bifurcated tube of this type was mentioned first by Columbus as an inhaler of psychotropic snuff. Also, the Catalonian friar Ramon Pané, in the first ethnography ever written (1497) and published (1511) on any native American population, refers to a similar tube in use by these same Indians, not for smoking but for inhalation of a psychotropic snuff called *chohobba* or *chohuba (cohoba)* (Anghiera 1912). Cohoba is believed by some scholars to have been *Anadenanthera peregrina* (L.) Speg. (Safford 1916), although the Winikina-Warao of the Orinoco Delta still employ cohoba as a term for ritual tobacco.

Thus, the bifurcated tube Columbus and Pané mentioned as an insufflator for cohoba snuff, and that Oviedo documented as an inhalator for tobacco smoke, may have been used by the Taino for both purposes. It might also have served to snuff tobacco powder, but this remains uncertain. In any case, both powders, pure or blended, are, as suggested by S. A. Dickson and P. H. O'Neil (1958–1969, 1:19), capable of producing the acute states of intoxication mentioned by Oviedo. This would also be true if the tube had been employed for the inhalation of tobacco smoke, especially, as is likely, if the tobacco used had been the stronger *Nicotiana rustica,* which was grown in Indian plantings from Chile to Quebec long before Cuba became famous for its milder *N. tabacum* (Sauer 1966:56).

Finally, among the earliest reports of tobacco use in the New World is one by Amerigo Vespucci (in Waldseemüller 1907:126–127), who mentions what seems to have been tobacco chewing with lime, which he observed on some coastal island off northern South America; this island has been variously identified as Margarita Island, the Guajira Peninsula, the Paria Peninsula, and even Marajó Island in the mouth of the Amazon. Vespucci also failed to identify the plant material he saw being chewed by the Indians; hence it is possible that something other than tobacco— specifically coca—was involved. For, as T. Plowman (1979:198) has noted, "the custom of chewing whole coca leaves with powdered lime . . . was widespread along the Caribbean coast of South America at the arrival of the Europeans and still persists there today."

Yet, the chewing of tobacco powder with ashes or pulverized shell was common among the Carib of the Lesser Antilles and the northeastern mainland at the time of the first encounter. Hence, as in the case of early tobacco snuffing, the evidence for pre-Contact tobacco chewing remains ambiguous. The available documentation may refer to the chewing of either coca or tobacco, but it may also indicate the practice of chewing a blend of the two substances.

In short, in the course of the first decades following the initial encounter, the Europeans had learned about several different ways of ingesting tobacco: cigar smoking, pipe smoking, rhinal smoke inhalation, smoke blowing, and possibly snuffing and chewing. Many explorers had learned that tobacco was addictive and multipurpose, although the Europeans largely failed to appreciate why the Indians considered it to be sacred. But the plant was already known to be of variable (biphasic) effect: in small doses tobacco served as a stimulant, as a depressant of hunger and thirst, and as an analgesic; large doses produced altered states of consciousness. For social purposes tobacco products were ingested to seal friendships, to conduct tobacco palavers, war councils, and dances, and to strengthen warriors. It was taken to forecast propitious weather and to predict successful fishing, lumbering, planting, and congenial courtship. Taken to achieve spiritual objectives, tobacco facilitated vision quests and spirit consultations, introduced trance states, and aided in psychiatric curing. All of this early information given by chroniclers, missionaries, soldiers, travelers, and scholars was amply confirmed and significantly elaborated upon by later ethnographic reports of the colonial and modern eras.

At this juncture, and before detailing the various traditional methods of native tobacco consumption, I should note that what follows has been informed by hundreds of bibliographic sources spanning nearly five hundred years of South American ethnography (Wilbert 1987:xv). Accordingly, doing full justice to the historical reference of each and every source would necessitate switching back and forth between the past and the present tenses, resulting in a snarled and perhaps confusing piece of writing. To avoid this I have cast this chapter largely in the so-called ethnographic present, regardless of whether a particular tobacco practice still exists, has changed, or has been discontinued. Although this stylistic device conveys a feeling of constancy, the methods of traditional tobacco use may in reality have undergone considerable change. Thus, for instance, although religious and medicinal customs pertaining to the drug still prevail in many societies, general indulgence in tobacco for secular reasons has become widespread and often exists side by side with traditional practices of tobacco shamanism within the same local group. Yet, many of the methods detailed below have as their ultimate purpose the ecstatic trance in which shamans experience themselves as traveling, or projecting their souls, to Otherworlds.

METHODS OF TRADITIONAL TOBACCO USE

In terms of traditional methods of tobacco use by South American Indians, three features stand out as particularly characteristic: (1) the plurality of methods of tobacco ingestion, (2) the intake of large quantities of tobacco, and (3) the transcendental purpose of tobacco ingestion. Short of intravenous injection, South American Indians take tobacco through practically all humanly possible routes of administration (gastrointestinal, respiratory, or percutaneous) and in a large variety of forms. They chew tobacco quids, drink tobacco juice and syrup, lick tobacco paste, administer tobacco suppositories and enemas, snuff rapé powder, inhale tobacco smoke, and apply tobacco products to the skin and the eye.

METHODS OF TOBACCO INGESTION
1. Gastrointestinal Administration

Tobacco chewing. The chewing, or, more precisely, the sucking of tobacco quids has wide distribution in South America and the West Indies. It occurs in the Lesser Antilles and eastern Venezuela and ranges from northwestern Colombia and the upper Amazon sporadically through locales from the Montaña to the Gran Chaco. A few scattered incidences are also found in eastern Brazil. In North America tobacco chewing was practiced mainly by Indians of the Northwest Coast, to whom tobacco may have been introduced by early Russian traders.

Indians prepare wads or rolls, about ten centimeters long, from green tobacco, sometimes dusting the wet leaves with ashes or salt and mixing them with certain kinds of soils or honey. They also knead finely chopped green tobacco leaves mixed with niter-containing earth into a dough from which tobacco pellets are prepared. Similar pellets are obtained by simply mixing finely crushed tobacco leaves with ashes and wetting the powder with water to produce a smooth paste. Guianese Indians bake a cake of fresh tobacco leaves the size of a cartwheel and two centimeters or more thick on a griddle over a slow fire. In the process, the cake is sprinkled with salt or with a surrogate obtained from *oulin* (*Mourera fluviatilis* Aubl.), a podostemaceous plant that grows in waterfalls on submerged rocks and ledges. The cake is cut up, and strips of it are kept in gourds with small openings. Additives to chewing mixtures other than salt and salt surrogates include lime from sea shells, caraña resin (*Protium hepta-phyllum* March.), pepper (*Capsicum fructescens* L. Willd.), and medicinal herbs, such as the acrid rind of *rosa amarillo*—an emmenagogic plant—among others.

Tobacco mastication frequently occurs simultaneously with other methods of administration, such as smoking and snuffing. And tobacco was sometimes observed to be chewed together with coca (*Erythroxylum*). Tobacco quids, rolls, or pellets are carried by the user in the cheek or the lower lip for protracted periods of time; sublingual application has not been reported. In contrast to coca and betel (*Piper betle*), nicotine does not require alkalizing agents for its liberation, although substances of this kind accelerate and intensify the action of the drug by increasing salivation (Hammilton 1957). Nicotine is readily miscible in the salivary secretions, and transportation of the solute proceeds rapidly. Also, the alkalizing of the buccal environment prepares the site for optimum absorption (Bray and Dollery 1983:274). As pointed out, Indians suck tobacco more than they chew it and swallow the trickling juices rather than expectorate them.

The far-flung distribution pattern of tobacco chewing is generally considered indicative of the great antiquity of this method of consumption (Zerries 1964:99–100). Furthermore, considering the naturalness of tobacco chewing, one feels inclined to agree with scholars like Sauer (1969:48) in their contention that chewing and taking it in liquid form represent the oldest methods of tobacco ingestion. With periodic fluctuations, tobacco has found wide acceptance among non-Indian societies.

Tobacco drinking. The distribution of tobacco drinking is similar to that of tobacco chewing, except for its absence in the Gran Chaco. The majority of tribes of Greater Guiana drink tobacco juice, as do a considerable number of societies of the upper Amazon and the Montaña of Ecuador and Peru. Some sporadic incidences of the practice have also been reported from northwestern coastal Venezuela, northwestern Colombia, and a few scattered places in Bolivia and Brazil.

In the Guianese region of distribution, tobacco juice is often a simple infusion of whole or pounded green leaves and water. The steeped or boiled leaves are strained and pressed by hand. Some tribes add salt or oulin ashes, mentioned earlier, to the brew. Other (unidentified) botanical materials used as ingredients by Guianese tribes include *ayung*, an emetic bark, and *quinquina*, a tree sap. Upper Amazon and Montaña tribes similarly steep, press out, and stir tobacco leaves in water, although they frequently mince or masticate the leaves rather than leaving them whole or pounding them. In this western region of distribution, however, Indians do not seem to add salt or ashes to their tobacco juice but occasionally do add pepper (*Capsicum* sp.). The boiling of tobacco leaves in water also occurs here more often than in Guiana, although the juice is not boiled down in the process as in the production of *ambíl* paste (discussed presently) but rather is left viscous enough to allow the product to be drunk.

Throughout its distribution area tobacco drinking is often practiced jointly with other methods of tobacco consumption and with the imbibing of alcoholic beverages. Several hallucinogenic or psychotropic substances may also be taken simultaneously with tobacco; examples include *ayahuasca* (*Banisteriopsis caapi*), coca (*Erythroxylum*), daturas (*Brugmansia aurea* Lagerh.; *huanto, Brugmansia* sp.; *maikua, Brugmansia* sp.), *parica* snuff (*Virola calophylloidea* Marcgraf), and *takini* latex (*Helicostylis tomentosa* [Poepp. & Endl.] Macbride or *H. pedunculata* Benoist).

Tobacco juice is imbibed by mouth or through the nose, using the cupped hands or gourds. In some instances the concentrate is also squirted directly from the mouth of a donor into that of a receiver. Outside South America, tobacco drinking has found little acceptance as a method of tobacco use.

Tobacco licking. Tobacco licking has limited distribution in South America. It occurs among tribes of the northernmost extension of the Andes in Colombia and Venezuela, in parts of the Northwest Amazon, and in a few spots of the Montaña.

Tobacco licking is very similar to tobacco chewing, but instead of sucking on a quid of tobacco leaves or a pellet of tobacco paste, licking tobacco entails the use of a syrup extract or jelly known as ambíl. In the Sierra Nevada de Santa Marta of Colombia, Indians prepare a thick, black gelatin by boiling tobacco leaves for hours and even days and by further thickening the extract by adding manioc starch (*Manihot esculente* Crantz) or arrowroot (*Maranta arundinacea* L.). Venezuelan tribes east of Lake Maracaibo used to mix *urao*, a sesquicarbonate of soda, into their ambíl, creating a mixture known as *chimó* (Kamen-Kaye 1971:43). Salt or alkaline ashes are used by Montaña tribes as part of their ambíl recipe. Very green leaves from the lower part of the tobacco plant are selected to be boiled down over a slow fire. Simultaneously, salts are obtained by some tribes by evaporation of water that has been poured over and drained through the ashes from parts of a large *Lecythis* tree, the shoots of *Bactris*, and the leaves of *Chamaedorea* palms. In other societies ashes are simply obtained by burning and sifting red cacao shells, green plantain peels, and yoco pods (*Paullinia yoco* Schultes & Killip). The salts are stirred into the ambíl before it concentrates into a thick syrup or paste (Schultes 1945:20–21). Pepper (*Capsicum* sp.) is also occasionally mentioned as an ingredient of ambíl, as are avocado seeds (*Persea americana* L.), crude sugar, *tapioca* or manioc juice, and the already-mentioned manioc starch. The paste is variously kept in leaf packages, bamboo tubes, nut shells, small pots, and, currently, glass bottles and tin cans. If properly preserved, ambíl keeps for several months before it is replaced with a fresh supply.

Ambíl is taken into the mouth by dipping a finger or extracting a small quantity on a spatula or fingernail and rubbing it across the teeth, the gums, or the tongue. Although taken alone, ambíl is at times ingested simultaneously with other tobacco products. Some tribes of the Montaña lick it in conjunction with coca (*Erythroxylum*), *ayahuasca* (*Banisteriopsis caapi*), and possibly other hallucinogens.

Enema. Enema syringes had wide distribution among American Indians (Nordenskiöld 1930:189, map 1). One type, consisting of a straight or funneled hollow bone or cane, was distributed from northwestern North America to the Peruvian Montaña. For application, practitioners blow the clyster by mouth through the tube into the body of the receiver (Gomara 1811:283; Nordenskiöld 1930:54, fig. 20; Davidson MS). A second type of syringe featured a bulb made of the bladder of an animal, leather, or rubber and a nozzle of bone or reed. Bladder or leather syringes were in use among Indians of western South America and Guiana (Roth 1916–1917:705, fig. 341). The rubber bulb syringe is a native invention and is in use among Indians of Amazonia (Nordenskiöld 1930:13, fig. 4). Syringes serve the purpose of applying medicinal peppers and antiseptic herbs. For intoxicating purposes, South American Indians apply clysters of *ayahuasca* (*Banisteriopsis caapi*), *Brugmansia* sp., *parica* (*Virola*), *willka* (*Anadenanthera colubrina* [Vell.] Brenan), and tobacco (*Nicotiana* sp.).

Tobacco is only rarely reported in connection with enemas and rectal applications in general. However, tobacco suppositories are in use as a remedy for constipation and helminthic infestations. Less well-documented cases of the association of tobacco with syringes come from prehistoric Bolivia (Wassén 1972), Surinam (Fermin 1775), and Brazil (Spix and Martius 1823–1831:3). A positively identified medicinal case is that of the Shipibo of Peru, who apply a mixture of tobacco juice and ginger as a vermifuge (Gebhart MS). Conclusive evidence for ritual tobacco enemas among the Aguaruna of the Peruvian Montaña has only recently been secured

(Davidson MS). No Caribbean, Central American, or North American cases of medicinal or ritual tobacco enemas have been observed.

In fact, the Aguaruna clyster consists of fresh tobacco juice mixed with the drawn head of boiling *ayahuasca* (*Banisteriopsis caapi*). Upon removing the mixture from the fire, crushed tobacco leaves are added to complete the reddish-brown brew. Prior to application, the recipient of the clyster purges himself with repeated and alternate swallows of *ayahuasca* and tobacco juice. The clyster is blown by an experienced practitioner into the rectum of a bent-over recipient, who is usually a young male between twelve and thirty-five years of age.

2. Respiratory Administration

Tobacco snuffing. Psychotropic snuffs are known sporadically from different parts of Central and North America (Bourne 1907:312, 313, 324, 328) but particularly from South America and the West Indies. From the days of Pané's (1974 [1511]) observation of chohobba (cohoba) snuff among the Taino of the Greater Antilles, powders were found to be prepared by Indians of the southern mainland from *Anadenanthera* beans, from coca leaves (*Erythroxylum*), from *Virola* spp. resin, and from a variety of nicotianas. The botanical sources of several lesser New World snuffs are as yet little understood (Schultes 1977:43–44; 1978:231–232), but rhinal absorption of intoxicants is widespread in South America. In fact, it is believed by some to be a peculiarly American form of drug administration that diffused, together with tobacco, to the Old World in post-Columbian times (Schultes 1967:292, 302–305).

Ethnographic sources document tobacco as a relatively common source of snuff among South American Indians. On the subcontinent, its five foci of distribution are the middle and upper Orinoco, the Northwest Amazon, the Montaña–Rio Purus, the Guaporé, and the Andean regions. Additional cases are mostly peripheral to this generally northwesterly and westerly distribution area.

To prepare tobacco snuff, the leaves of the plant are either wind dried in the shade or dried in the sun, over the fire, or on a hot cooking pot placed upside down on the embers. The dried leaves are crushed, pulverized, and often sifted. Nut shells and cooking pots may serve as mortars. Tobacco snuff is stored in containers made from bamboo, a calabash, or a snail shell.

Psychotropic powders, including tobacco rapé, may be snuffed directly from the hand or from a leaf. More commonly, however, powders are ingested by means of single-barreled, double-barreled, forked, or angular snuffing tubes made of cane or hollow bone.

Relatively short single-barreled snuffing tubes are used as inhalators for self-administration. As mentioned previously, the earliest example of this type in South America is the bird-bone inhalator Junius Bird found with a snuff tablet carved from whalebone at the preagricultural site of Huaca Prieta, on the coast of Peru, dated c. 1600 B.C. These implements were presumably used for *willka* (*Anadenanthera colubrina*), not powdered tobacco. When tubes one meter long or even longer serve as insufflators, intoxication requires two partners; one blows the powder with a sharp puff into the nostrils of the other. This form of administration has been well documented, for example, in print and on film, among the Venezuelan Yanomamö. They too, however, prepare their intoxicating powder not from tobacco but from the inner bark of the *Virola* tree. The receiving end of some of the long insufflators are provided with plain or carved conical nosepieces.

Double-barreled snuffing tubes measure about twenty centimeters in length and commonly feature at the proximal end of each tube a nosepiece fashioned from a round perforated nut or a bulbous ring of wax to facilitate application to the nostrils. Snuff is absorbed through double-barreled insufflators from the palm of the user's hand.

Forked snuff tubes are Y-shaped and relatively short. They allow self-administration of powders through both nostrils simultaneously.

Angular snuff tubes are V-shaped; short ones are for self-administration, and longer ones, measuring twenty to thirty centimeters, are for mutual administration between cooperating partners. The snuff is placed at the nasal end of the angular insufflator and blown from the buccal end with a sharp puff into the nostrils of the receiver.

Tobacco rapé may be inhaled from the surface of a small table, but snuffing tablets commonly employed in connection with hallucinogenic powders have not been reported specifically for tobacco snuffing. Actually, tobacco snuff, compared with hallucinogenic powders, is of secondary importance in South America, possibly because the former contain less "spirit power" than the latter. This may explain why the snuffing accessories for tobacco rapé are so much more rustic than the artistically elaborate paraphernalia used in association with *parica* or *ebena* powders, for example.

Tobacco snuffing has found wide acceptance in the non-Indian world as well, although the practice has gone in and out of fashion several times over the centuries.

Smoking. The practice of smoking is the most prevalent form of tobacco consumption in native South America. It is particularly common in greater Guiana, the upper Amazon, the Montaña, Yungas, Matto Grosso, and the Gran Chaco. But it was also reported in many intervening and peripheral areas, such as central and northern Colombia, along the middle and lower Amazon, the coast of Brazil, and Patagonia and southern Chile.

The Indians smoke tobacco in the form of cigars, cigarillos, cigarettes, and in various forms of pipes. Sun-dried or wind-dried tobacco leaves are crushed before being rolled into wrappers of different origins. Sometimes, whole tobacco leaves or pieces thereof are used for this purpose. More often, however, the Indians employ tree foliage of various kinds, palm stipules, banana leaves, and maize husks. A very common cigar or cigarillo wrapper is made of the whitish inner bark of the tree *Couratari guianensis* Aubl., of the Lecythidaceae family.

To prepare a perfectly white and tasteless *tauari* wrapper, the inner portion of the bark is separated from the trunk, pounded with a mallet, and exposed to the air for several hours. The naturalist H. W. Bates (1975:162) described how one may obtain "sixty, eighty, and sometimes a hundred layers from the same strip of bark." Guianese Indians cut a two-meter or three-meter-long and fifteen-centimeters-wide piece of preferably black bark from the *Couratari guianensis*. To separate the layers, one end of the strip is beaten with a stick and the resulting laminae tied together in a bundle to prevent them from coiling up. The bundle is dried in the sun (Ahlbrink 1931:475–477, 128). Similarly, fine, paperlike layers of inner bark suitable for cigarette wrappers are obtained from the bark of the Sapucaia (*kakareli* [*Lecythis ollaria* Loefling]), a tree of the same natural order as the *Couratari* (Im Thurn 1883:317; Roth 1916–1917:241). Usually, men roll their own cigars; in several Indian communities, however, women are expected to perform the task. They also light the cigars and take a few puffs themselves before handing them to the men. Generally, wrappers add a peculiar flavor and odor to the tobacco, and in some instances observers have remarked that the cover leaves may enhance the narcotic effect of the cigar (Weyer 1959:114).

To give the cigar or pipe a particular odoriferous component, Indians of Guiana and Amazonia add different kinds of herbs or the resin of

Protium heptaphyllum, a tree of the myrrh family, or Burseraceae. Known as caraña, the hard, translucent, and whitish resin has a distinctly pungent odor, similar to frankincense. Caraña powder or granules are mixed with tobacco (or coca) to give it a balsamic savor but not to heighten or lessen its narcotic effect (Schultes 1980:55). In Patagonia, calafate shavings (*Berberis* sp.) are mixed into the tobacco to give it an acrid taste and to allow it to burn with a very blue smoke.

Smoking is often accompanied by the ingestion of hallucinogens such as *Banisteriopsis caapi, Brunfelsia grandiflora,* and *Virola* and of such psychoactive beverages as yoco or guaraná (*Paullinina cupana* H.B.K. var. *sorbilis* [Mart.] Ducke) and cassiri.

North American Indians, with the exception of the Pueblos and certain Californian tribes, were exclusively pipe smokers (Linton 1924:14; Robicsek 1978:9–11). But despite this predominance of the pipe, and notwithstanding the flowering of formal variations of pipes in North America, pipe smoking in South America still has considerable distribution throughout the subcontinent. Here it is practiced with tubular, monitor, and elbow pipes made of reed, bamboo, wood, dry hard fruit shells, bone, clay, or stone. Pipe smoking is prevalent primarily in two focal areas; the Marañon-Huallaga-Ucayali region and the Gran Chaco. More sporadically it occurs along the north coast and the Guiana hinterlands, along the Amazon, and in coastal Brazil. Farther inland and north of the Gran Chaco focal area, pipes occur in central and southern Bolivia and on the lower Araguaia. South of the Chaco pipes are found in middle and southern Chile and in Patagonia.

As in North America, pipe smoking is of prehistoric origin in South America, and of the three major types of pipes previously mentioned, the tubular form is perhaps the oldest. It occurs in Central and North America, and its main distribution center in the southern subcontinent is located in the Gran Chaco. Sporadically, however, the tubular pipe is found from the Andes through the Gran Chaco and central Brazil to the Atlantic coast, as well as in Colombia and Surinam, a distribution so far-flung that it corroborates the claim for the great antiquity of this pipe in the New World.

The monitor pipe is rare in South America, occurring only among the Araucano-Huilliche Indians and the Tehuelche of central and southern Chile and Patagonia, respectively.

Finally, the elbow or angular pipe is the most common type of all South American pipes. Probable pre-Contact pipes are known from archaeological sites (Cooper 1949:527). The modern distribution of the elbow pipe coincides with the maximum distribution area given in paragraph 6 of this section. Angular pipes may be of one piece or of composite manufacture with a conico-tubular bowl and a detachable stem. Characteristic types include the cone-bowled pipe of the Montaña and the cylinder-bowled or spool-bowled types of the Gran Chaco. Chaco pipes may also be in the form of effigies featuring anthropomorphic and zoomorphic designs, as seen in a good number of widely scattered archaeological examples from Venezuela, Ecuador, Peru, northern Argentina, and southern Brazil (Cooper 1949:531).

South American Indians usually smoke by means of deep inhalation and hyperventilation but rarely by retaining a puff of smoke in the mouth before expelling or swallowing it. Inhalation is described as taking the smoke of a cigar with "great sucking gasps" into the lungs, "working the shoulders like bellows" (Huxley 1957:195). Giant cigars measuring nearly one meter in length and two centimeters in width are smoked with hyperventilation by the Warao of the Orinoco and by several other tribal societies, such as the Indians of the Vaupes. The latter cigar, according to the naturalist A. R. Wallace (1972:195, 206), "is eight or ten inches long and an inch in diameter, made of tobacco pounded and dried, and enclosed in a cylinder made of a large leaf spirally twisted. It is placed in a cigar-holder about two feet long, like a great two-pronged fork. The bottom is pointed, so that when not in use it can be stuck in the ground."

A peculiarly South American method of respiratory absorption of nicotine is by inhalation of free tobacco smoke in the atmosphere. As previously mentioned, this occurred on the east coast of Brazil, where religious practitioners blew tobacco smoke from canes and funnel-shaped cigars onto the heads and into the faces of dancing warriors. The men of this same society also inhale the smoke of tobacco they set to burn inside effigy rattles representing a human head. Cuna elders of Panama have tobacco smoke blown into their faces from an inverted cigar, and Jivaro men of Peru blow tobacco smoke through long tubes into the open mouth of a partner.

3. Percutaneous Administration

Administration to the skin. The administration of tobacco products to the intact or abraded skin has widespread distribution in native South America and includes the practice of general and directed smoke blowing; spit blowing with tobacco juice, nicotine-laden saliva, and tobacco

powder; saliva massages; juice ablutions; rapé and leaf plasters; and compacts. Tobacco use in this context invariably serves therapeutic purposes.
   Ocular administration. Tobacco smoke and juice are applied to the
eye for nicotine absorption from the conjunctiva of the inner surface of
the eyelid and the forepart of the eyeball. The main purpose of this
application is magico-religious.

INTAKE OF LARGE QUANTITIES OF TOBACCO

   The principal goal of traditional tobacco consumption in South
America was, and often continues to be, the speedy achievement of
acute intoxication. Although social tobacco consumption in modern times
is increasingly indulged in more for the mere enjoyment of the stimulant
effect of the drug, traditionally the Indians mainly sought the toxic and
organoleptic effects of nicotine. Accordingly, Western observers tend to
be aghast at the large quantities of tobacco aboriginal practitioners are
prone to ingest.
   In Guiana, for example, shamans make their students drink liters of
tobacco juice to take them to the very brink of death. Several cups of
tobacco pulp are ingested in rapid succession, and a large bowl of liquid
tobacco is force-fed through a funnel into the mouth of a swooning candidate. Elsewhere, fasting and purged novices are reported to rush—driv-
en out of their minds—into the forest, where they remain for days. One
who fails to vomit part of the brew is expected to go into convulsions,
become chronically ill, or die. Among the Tupinamba of Brazil, novices
were repeatedly and on successive days fed tobacco juice through a funnel until they would swoon and vomit blood. Similarly, Aguaruna vision-
seekers of Ecuador take tobacco enemas to die repeated deaths.
   As I discuss later, the attainment of a deathlike state in the form of
transitory respiratory arrest is the ultimate goal of tobacco initiation and
practice. In addition to using tobacco juice and enemas for this purpose,
South American shamans are known to ingest up to five three-foot-long
cigars (while simultaneously chewing tobacco) in the course of a single
seance. During an all-night performance, a Yaruro shaman of the
Venezuelan llanos region was observed to have smoked forty-two com-
mercial cigarettes in addition to approximately one hundred native cigars.
Furthermore, participants in certain rituals and shamanic curing seances
on the Guaporé (Brazil) were observed to take dozens of insufflations of
tobacco powder in the course of three hours; one credible source men-

tioned as many as sixty doses of rapé in this context. Examples of this kind of elevated tobacco consumption are frequent in the ethnographic literature on South America and are symptomatic of the magico-religious objectives of tobacco consumption in native context as opposed to the hedonistic purpose of tobacco indulgence in Western society.

TRANSCENDENTAL PURPOSE OF NATIVE TOBACCO USE

In view of the described unpleasantness and the health-threatening and life-threatening nature of tobacco praxis in South America, one wonders why the drug attained such overriding importance in the religious and ritual life of the Indians. Undoubtedly tobacco, like other psychotropic substances taken by humans, provides a means of escape from the conditions of life and from stress. Nicotine addiction and sociocultural considerations have played additional roles in this respect. More important, shamans, in order to maintain their credibility and effectiveness as religious practitioners and healers, must demonstrate their spiritual empowerment to themselves and to their community on a continuing basis; tobacco, because of the effects of nicotine on the human body, assists them in accomplishing that goal.

It is essential for tobacco-using shamans (as for shamans in general) that, although human, they be considered, and consider themselves to be, supernaturally endowed. This natural-supernatural duality is attained during initiation when the novice dies as a normal human being and is reborn as a person with otherworldly powers. By taking increasing amounts of tobacco, shamans manifest a state of illness through nicotine-mediated nausea, heavy breathing, vomiting, and prostration. Progressively, through tremors, convulsion, or seizure, they lie in agony until, in acute narcosis, they suffer transitory respiratory arrest and apparent death for all to witness. The initiatory masters' experience is crucial for the success of this status change. Inducing literally a situation of life or death—measured in seconds of acute poisoning—they depend for the success of this essential change upon the normally accelerated biotransformation process of nicotine in the human body (Larson 1952:279; Larson, Haag, and Silvette 1961). But during the initiation of their students, as well as in the course of their own professional lives, they repeatedly risk the underlying pharmacological conditions of progressive blockade of impulse transmission at autonomic ganglia and central stimulation. Nothing could convince them more of their otherworldly status than the experience of this continuum of biphasic nicotine action within themselves as a journey of the soul out-side the body. On this celestial path, they have been enculturated to choose well at the crossroads, clear dangerous passages, escape death-dealing blows, and face eventual dismemberment, skeletonization, and rebirth.

The ingestion of tobacco in this process on a quasiperpetual basis makes shamans aware of their new bodies. As a consequence of heavy smoking, for instance, they and their peers will take note of their changed voices, which have become hoarse and guttural as they experience the typ-ical distress symptoms of a "smoker's throat" because of local action of cer-tain chemical agents in tobacco (Stevenson 1933). Shamans who chew, smoke, or drink tobacco are expected to develop characteristic guttural and low-timbered singing voices that are held to be more fitting than the human voice for discourse with supernaturals. Mature shamans have been known to lose their voices altogether. To further aid in accomplishing this change of voice, shamans like to mix caraña resin (*Protium heptaphyllum*) into their tobacco, not only to perfume the smoke but also to coat their vocal cords and thereby heighten the desired effect.

Nicotine-induced paranormal sight is a particularly impressive acqui-sition of the shaman, which is noticed first during initiation and subse-quently throughout tobacco praxis. Under conditions of advanced nico-tine intoxication, the shaman's eyesight is best in crepuscular light (rather than in the glare of the day), permitting him or her to discern moving game animals or approaching enemies in the twilight (Mendenhall 1930:408). The symptoms of tobacco amblyopia (Larson, Haag, and Silvette 1961:591–610), which shamans are likely to suffer as a consequence of advanced intoxication through smoking (Hedges 1955), snuffing (Duke-Elder and Scott 1971:146), and chewing (Meyerhof 1921), are totally over-whelming. This condition allows the practitioner not only to see in the dark but actually to live in the dimness that results from the condition, primarily because of neural changes in the retina and, only secondarily (if tobacco consumption is not curbed), because of damage to the optic nerve. Accordingly, tobacco amblyopia is reversible through abstention from nicotine, so that the shaman may enter and leave the darkness of the Otherworld at will. In sum, nicotine is experienced by shamans as a sight-altering and vision-altering drug that enables them to see the hidden and the future, an ability that allows them to function as diviners, prophets, and interpreters of dreams.

Shamans are often considered to be masters of fire and to have become insensitive to heat by assimilating the magical heat of their sacred cigar. Nicotine-induced increased perspiration and the liberation of norepinephrine with a resulting drop in skin temperature may assist them in performing such heat-defying feats as extinguishing a cigar against their naked bodies, walking over live coals, or swallowing embers.

South American Indians consider tobacco to be a food, and in some societies shamans are actually referred to as "tobacco eaters." There is general recognition of the similarity that exists between the intake of regular food and the ingestion of tobacco products. As reasons for this relationship, we can point to a number of effects of nicotine on the gastrointestinal tract because of parasympathetic stimulation. Similar to food, tobacco (nicotine) tends to diminish or even abolish hunger pangs by inhibiting hunger contractions of the stomach (Daniélopolu, Simici, and Dimitriu 1925), which in turn are caused by stimulation of the sensory nerve endings in the mouth and the stomach mucosa (Carlson and Lewis 1914). The desire to eat is also curbed by the dulling effect of nicotine on the taste buds (Marti and Matasaru 1964), as well as by nicotine-induced higher blood sugar levels, which cause the liver to release stored carbohydrates (Wachholder 1948). Nicotine may also function, other than through its parasympathetic effects, as an appetite inhibitor because of direct or indirect action on the hypothalamus (Walker 1953). And nicotine-triggered epinephrine release depresses hunger because its action excites the central nervous system. Thus, nicotine intake, like the ingestion of food, appeases the feeling of hunger, just as the cessation of nicotine consumption, like the abstention from food, brings back the gnawing of the stomach and a feeling of emptiness (Chessick 1964).

The use of tobacco as an anorectic agent has been reported for South American Indians from the earliest to the most recent historical times. Shamans pine for tobacco as ordinary people hunger for food. We can project this longing of the shaman into the supernatural realm, in which spirits are believed to consume tobacco as appropriate fare. From South America to the woodlands of North America, shamans have fed the Great Spirits with the tobacco food they lack in the spirit world. Fully aware of the coercive power of the drug, they have employed tobacco as a bargaining asset to obtain favors from above.

Shamans are universally expected to function as healers. From the time of their initiation, shamans' breath is believed to be endowed with supernatural properties, and their most commonly employed therapeutic technique is that of blowing over the afflicted body part of patients. Tobacco smoke dramatically manifests their otherwise invisible life-giving pneuma, and shamans blow thick clouds of smoke over their patients. They capture the smoke under their cupped hands to make it linger on the ailing body part; they direct it over open wounds; they blow it into the patient's face, eyes, nose, and mouth and massage the patient with it for protracted periods of time. Smoke is also administered to a hollow tooth and to the open wound of a tooth extraction. The fumigated patient experiences a reduction of pain and fever and, in some cases, feels cured.

As already pointed out, in addition to smoke, shamans blow nicotine-laden sputum, tobacco powder, and juice on their patients. They administer saliva massages, juice ablutions, and rapé and tobacco leaf plasters and compacts—that is, therapeutic techniques that involve the respiratory, gastrointestinal, and dermal routes of nicotine administration and that deliver the nicotine in large enough amounts to be locally and systemically effective.

Application of tobacco to open wounds, bites, and stings presents no passage problem, because nicotine reaches the exposed subcutaneous tissues unencumbered by epidermal barriers. The application of tobacco liquids, powders, and plasters to the intact skin is conducive to nicotine absorption. Administration of tobacco smoke to the unabraded skin is less effective, unless the nicotine in smoke is retained by perspiration on the patient's body. Nicotinic media in the form of solutes, such as saliva and infusions, can be applied with more intensity than smoke and are highly effective, especially because the therapeutic dose of a tobacco decoction is as low as 1 percent for lotions (Gutiérrez Muro 1934).

Even more effective than smoke and lotions are local applications of plasters of tobacco powder and wet leaves. Snuff plasters have long been shown to be effective analgesics (Somervail 1839). Plasters of tobacco leaves deliver enough nicotine locally to cause relatively acute poisoning (Weizenecker and Deal 1970). Green tobacco plugs or nicotine-laden cotton balls inserted into a hollow tooth function like sustained-release preparations and deliver enough nicotine in situ, promptly, and over a protracted period of time to serve as analgesics and potentially even to cause severe nicotine poisoning (Chapman 1880). Absorption of the alkaloid even in small quantities, however, stimulates the sympathetic release of norepinephrine from skin tissues with local effect, and the resultant reduction in skin temperature has a soothing effect on the patient and may temporarily relieve his or her pain.

In concluding, I should perhaps point out that shamans are combative protectors of their societies. They blow tobacco smoke and spittle against atmospheric enemies such as thunder and lightning and against a host of adversaries that threaten human existence. In many societies they exercise their power in the form of aggressive were-jaguars, a shape-shifting condition they accomplish with the aid of tobacco ingestion. To activate their aggressiveness, nicotine first provokes a number of physical changes, which include night vision like that of the nocturnal jaguar, a deep, raspy voice, a furred tongue, and a fusty body odor. Second, cholinergic preganglionic fibers of the sympathetic nervous system stimulate the adrenal medulla to discharge the arousal hormones epinephrine and norepinephrine, mobilizing the shaman's body for emergency reaction (Schievelbein and Werle 1967:82). Third, the generalized arousal induced by nicotine is interpreted by the properly enculturated shaman—who generally has a special relationship with the jaguar, as specific to jaguar-men—to be expressed as anger, hostility, and sexual aggressiveness. Thus, nicotine-mediated physiological changes, similarly triggered epinephrine release with its concomitant emotional and psychological changes, and appropriate enculturative conditioning allow shamans to enact characteristic jaguar behavior and to experience an essential feeling of "jaguarness" that confirms their shamanic status and role.

What becomes apparent through these examples is that American Indians used tobacco as a faith-confirming—that is, a life-ordaining—drug. The shamanistic beliefs of the nontobacco-using Paleo-Indian hunters, the high value they placed on the ecstatic trance, and the special experiences and attributes ascribed to the shaman as specialist in the sacred all provided a value-resonant background onto which tobacco shamans of Neo-Indian agriculturalists were able to project their drug experience with remarkable compatibility. In contrast, the disenfranchised cultural environment of the modern drug scene is often devoid of transcendental values, so that scenarios of pseudoimagery must be conjured up (by means of advertising) to make the use of tobacco plausible on purely hedonistic grounds.

REFERENCES

Ahlbrink, W.
1931.   *Encyclopaedie der Karaïben, behelzend taal, zeden en gewoonten dezer Indianen.* Amsterdam: Verhandelingen der Koninklijke Akademie van Wetenschappen te Amsterdam. Afdeeling Letterkunde n.s. 27, I.

Anghiera, P. M. d.'
1912.   *De orbe novo: The Eight Decades of Peter Martyr d'Anghera.* 2 vols. New York: G. P. Putnam's Sons [1511].

Bates, H. W.
1975.   *The Naturalist on the River Amazon,* 4th ed. New York: Dover Publications.

Benzoni, G.
1967.   *La historia del mundo nuevo.* Biblioteca de la Academia Nacional de la Historia, 86. Caracas: Academia Nacional de la Historia [1565].

Bourne, E. G.
1907.   Columbus, Ramon Pané and the Beginnings of American Anthropology. *Proceedings of the American Antiquarian Society* n.s. 17:310–348 [1906].

Bray, W., and C. Dollery.
1983.   Coca Chewing and High-Altitude Stress: A Spurious Correlation. *Current Anthropology* 24, 3:269–274.

Carlson, A. J., and J. H. Lewis.
1914.   Contributions to the Physiology of the Stomach. XIV. The Influence of Smoking and of Pressure on the Abdomen (Constriction of the Belt) on the Gastric Hunger Contractions. *American Journal of Physiology* 34:149–154.

Cartier, J.
1545.   *Brief recit, & succinte narration . . . de la nauigation faicte es ysles de Canada, Hochelage & Saguenay & autres.* Paris: P. Roffet and A. Le Clerc.

Chapman, F. R.
1880.   Effects of Tobacco. *Lancet* 1:388.

Chessick, R. D.
1964.   The Problem of Tobacco Habituation. *American Medical Association Journal* 188, 10:932–933.

Cooper, J. M.
  1949.   Stimulants and Narcotics. In *Handbook of South American Indians*, J. H.
          Steward, ed. Vol. 5:525–558. Washington, D.C.: Smithsonian Institution,
          Bureau of American Ethnology, Bulletin 143.

Daniélopolu, D., D. Simici, and C. Dimitriu
  1925.   Action du tabac sur la motilité de l'estomac étudié, chez l'homme, à l'aide de
          la méthode graphique. *Comptes Rendus Hebdomadaires de la Société de
          Biologie et de ses Filiales* 92:535–538.

Davidson, J.
  n.d.   Fieldnotes on Tobacco Use Among the Aguaruna. MS.

Dickson, S.A., and P. H. O'Neil, comps.
  1958–1969.
          *Tobacco: A Catalogue of the Books, Manuscripts and Engravings Acquired
          Since 1942 in the Arents Tobacco Collection at the New York Public Library
          From 1507 to the Present.* New York: New York Public Library.

Dillehay, T. D.
  1984.   A Late Ice-Age Settlement in Southern Chile. *Scientific American* 251,
          4:106–119.

  ———.
  1989.   *Monte Verde: A Late Pleistocene Settlement in Chile.* Washington, D. C.:
          Smithsonian Institution Press.

Duke-Elder, S., and G. I. Scott.
  1971.   Toxic Amblyopia. In *System of Opthalmology*, S. Duke-Elder, ed. Vol. 12,
          Neuro   Opthalmology. London: H. Kimpton.

Fermin, P. D.
  1775.   *Philipp Fermins ausführliche historich-physikalische Beschreibung der Kolonie
          Surinam.* 2 vols. in 1. Berlin: Joachim Pauli, Buchhändler.

Furst, P. T.
  1976.   *Hallucinogens and Culture.* San Francisco: Chandler and Sharp.

  ———.
  1989.   Review of *Peyote Religion: A History*, by Omer C. Stewart. *American
          Ethnologist* 16, 2:386–387.
Gebhart, A.
  n.d.   Fieldnotes on Tobacco Use Among the Shipibo. MS.

Gomara, F. L. de
  1811.   *Conquista de Méjico.* Madrid.

Goodspeed, T. H.
  1954.   The Genus Nicotiana: Origins, Relationships, and Evolution of Its Species in
            the Light of Their Distribution, Morphology, and Cyotygenetics. *Chronica
            Botanica* 16, 1–6. Parts 1–5 T. H. Goodspeed; Part 6 T. H. Goodspeed,
            H. M. Wheeler, and P. H. Hutchinson. Waltham, Mass.: Chronica Botanica.

Gutiérrez Muro, F.
  1934.   *Tabaquismo. Clínica y Laboratorio* 24:217–230. Zaragoza.

Hammilton, D. W.
  1957.   The Use of Alkaline Admixtures With Narcotic Plants. Cambridge, Mass.:
            Manuscripts, Library of Economic Botany, Harvard Botanical Museum.

Hedges, H. S.
  1955.   Eye Damage by Tobacco. *Virginia Medical Monthly* 82:544–545.

Huxley, F.
  1957.   *Affable Savages: An Anthropologist Among the Urubu Indians of Brazil.* New
            York: Viking Press.

Im Thurn, E. F.
  1883.   *Among the Indians of Guiana: Being Sketches Chiefly Anthropologic From the
            Interior of British Guiana.* London: K. Paul, Trench.

Kamen-Kaye, D.
  1971.   Chimó: An Unusual Form of Tobacco in Venezuela. *Botanical Museum
            Leaflets* 23 I:1–59.

Larson, P. S.
  1952.   Metabolism of Nicotine and Nature of Tobacco Smoke Irritants. *Industrial and
            Engineering Chemistry* 44, 2:279–283.

Larson, P. S., H. B. Haag, and H. Silvette.
  1961.   *Tobacco: Experimental and Clinical Studies: A Comprehensive Account of the
            World Literature.* Baltimore: Williams & Wilkins.

Léry, J. de.
  1951.   *Viagem à terra do Brasil.* Translation of *Histoire d'un voyage fait en la terre du
            Brésil,* 2d ed. São Paulo: Livraria Martins [1578].

Linton, R.
   1924.   *Use of Tobacco Among North American Indians.* Anthropology, Leaflet 15.
           Chicago: Field Museum of Natural History.

Marti, T., and J. Matasaru.
   1964.   Prophylaxie des intoxications au tabac. *Praxis* 53, 24:828–835.

Mendenhall, W. L.
   1930.   *Tobacco.* Harvard Health Talks. Cambridge: Harvard University Press.

Merxmüller, H., and K. P. Buttler.
   1975.   Nicotiana in der afrikanischen Namib—Ein pflanzengeographisches
           und phylogenetisches Rätsel. *Mitteilungen aus der botanischen
           Staatssammlung* 12:91–104.

Meyerhof, M.
   1921.   Beobachtungen über Tabakbeschädigungen der Sehnerven im Orient und in
           Deutschland. *Klinische Monatsblätter für Augenheilkunde* 66:107–111.

Nordenskiöld, N. E. H. von.
   1930.   *Modifications in Indian Culture Through Inventions and Loans.* Gothenburg:
           Comparative Ethnographical Studies, Vol. 8.

Oviedo y Valdés, G. F. de.
   1851–1855.
           Historia general y natural de las Indias, islas y tierra-firme del mar océano,
           J. Amador de los Rios, ed. 3 parts in 4 vols. Madrid: Imprenta la Real
           Academia de la Historia [1549].

Pané, R.
   1974.   *Relación acerca de las antigüidades de los indios: El primer tratado escrito en
           América.* Version original 1511. Version nueva, con notas, mapa y apéndice
           por J. J. Arrom. México City: Siglo 21.

Plowman, T.
   1979.   Botanical Perspectives on Coca. *Journal of Psychedelic Drugs* 2, 1–2:103–117.

Robicsek, F.
   1978.   *The Smoking Gods: Tobacco in Maya Art, History and Religion.* Foreword by
           M. D. Coe and B. A. Goodnight. Norman: University of Oklahoma Press.

Roth, W. E.
1916–1917.
An Introductory Study of the Art, Crafts, and Customs of the Guiana Indians.
38th Annual Report of the Bureau of American Ethnology. Washington, D.C.:
Smithsonian Institution.

Safford, W. E.
1916. Identity of Cohoba, the Narcotic Snuff of Ancient Haiti. *Journal of the
Washington Academy of Science* 6, 15:547–562.

Sauer, C. O.
1966. *The Early Spanish Main.* Berkeley: University of California Press.

———.
1969. *Agricultural Origins and Dispersals: The Domestication of Animals and
Foodstuffs.* Cambridge, Mass.: First M.I.T. Press.

Schievelbein, J., and E. Werle.
1967. Mechanism of Release of Amines by Nicotine. *Annals of the New York
Academy of Sciences* 142, 1:72–82.

Schultes, R. E.
1945. El uso del tabaco entre los Huitotos. *Agricultura Tropical* 1, 9:19–22.

———.
1967. The Botanical Origins of South American Snuffs. In *Ethnopharmacologic
Search for Psychoactive Drugs*, D. H. Efron, B. Holmstedt, and S. Kline, eds.,
pp. 291–306. Washington, D.C.: Public Health Service Publications, No. 1645.

———.
1977. The Botanical and Chemical Distribution of Hallucinogens. In *Drugs, Rituals
and Altered States of Consciousness*, B. M. du Toit, ed., pp. 22–55.
Rotterdam: A. A. Balkema.

———.
1978. Plants and Plant Constituents as Mind-Altering Agents Throughout History.
In *Handbook of Pharmacology*, Vol. 2, L. L. Iversen, S. D. Iversen, and
S. H. Snyder, eds., pp. 219–241. New York: Plenum Press.

———.
1980. Coca in the Northwest Amazon. *Botanical Museum Leaflets* 28, 1:47–60.

Somervail, A.
1839.   On the Use of Tobacco in Certain Cases. *American Journal of Medical Sciences* 23, 46:518.

Spix, J. B. von, and C. F. P. von Martius.
1823–1831.
Reise in Brasilien, 3 vols. Munich.

Staden, H. V.
1557.   *Wahrhaftige Historia und Beschreibung*. Marburg: Andres Colben.

Stevenson, H. M.
1933.   Acute Nicotine Poisoning as Noted in the Manufacture and Use of Nicotine Insecticides. *California and Western Medicine* 38, 2:92–95.

Thevet, A.
1928.   *Les singularités de la France Antarctique, autrement nommée Amerique: & de plusieurs terres & isles decouvertes de nostre temps*. Paris: Chez les Heritiers de Maurice de la Porte [1557].

Wachholder, K.
1948.   Zur hungerstillenden Wirkung des Rauchens. Rauchen und Blutzucker. *Naunyn-Schmiedesbergs Archiv für Experimentelle Pathologie und Pharmakologie* 205, 1:115–128.

Waldseemüller, Martin.
1907.   *The Cosmographiae Introductio of Martin Waldseemüller in facsimile*, Charles G. Hebermann, ed. New York: United States Catholic Historical Society [1507].

Walker, J. M.
1953.   Physiological Effects of Smoking. *Proceedings of the Nutrition Society* 12:157–160.

Wallace, A. R.
1972.   *A Narrative of Travels on the Amazon and Rio Negro* (2d. ed. of 1889 edition. London: Ward, Lock). New York: Dover.

Wassén, S. H.
1972.   *A Medicine-Man's Implements and Plants in a Tiahuanacoid Tomb in Highland Bolivia*. Etnologiska Studier, Vol. 38. Gothenburg: Göteborgs Etnografiska Museum.

Weizenecker, R., and W. B. Deal.
    1970.   Tobacco Cropper's Sickness. *Journal of the Florida Medical Association* 57, 12:3–14.

Weyer, E. M.
    1959.   *Primitive Peoples Today.* New York: Doubleday.

Wilbert, J.
    1987.   *Tobacco and Shamanism in South America.* New Haven, Conn.: Yale University Press.

Zerries, O.
    1964.   *Waika. Vol. 1: Die kulturgeschichtliche Stellung der Waika-Indianer des oberen Orinoco im Rahmen der Völkerkunde Südamerikas.* Munich: Klaus Renner.

4

WALKING ON TWO LEGS: SHAMANISM IN SANTIAGO ATITLÁN, GUATEMALA

ROBERT S. CARLSEN AND MARTIN PRECHTEL

Every living and healthy religion has a marked idiosyncrasy. Its power consists in its special and surprising message and in the bias which that revelation gives to life. The vistas it opens and the mysteries it propounds are another world to live in; and another world to live in—whether we expect ever to pass wholly over into it or no—is what we mean by having religion.
—Santayana, *Reason in Religion*

At the Juan Franklin Church in the town of Panajachel, Guatemala, members delight in recounting the story of the religious conversion of a Tzutujil Maya "witch doctor" from the neighboring town of Santiago Atitlán. This conversion was one of the earliest in the long and illustrious career of the church's now retired founder, U.S. missionary John Franklin. Although conversions have been common at that Assembly of God Church—the adjoining seminary turns out nearly one hundred newly ordained Indian pastors per year—the nature of this particular incident was exceptional enough that Franklin's flock even made a movie about it. Movies such as this are a favorite fare of the church's largely Cakchiquel Maya congregation, known regionally for its bouncy electric guitar music and the ecstatic rapture of its Pentecostalist members when possessed of the Holy Ghost.

For reasons that will become clear, accounts of the Atiteco witch doctor's conversion (Atiteco is the common name for the people of Santiago Atitlán) invariably assume a classic good-and-evil structure. Countering the intrinsic evilness of the indigenous religious expression is the unqualified goodness of the fundamentalist Christianity as embraced by Franklin. References to idolatry and witchcraft, even to Satanism, pepper the account. In the story, evilness inevitably gives way to the power of the Holy Spirit, and the old Maya converts to

Franklin's religion. But who was this "idolatrous witch" from Atitlán? Shorn of the Satanized context of the story, his position is quite unlike that into which the faithful cast him. In fact, the protagonist of this account was an *aj'kun,* a Tzutujil Maya term that many would translate as shaman.

THE PROBLEM WITH "SHAMANISM"

As is indicated in the witch doctor's conversion story, accounts of shamanism often confront a primary concern of anthropological description: the question of the emphasis on culturally specific information. Basic to this type of description, and to the present volume, is the comparability of data. Yet, too much cultural information inevitably reveals difference, hence muddling data compatibility. As a result, in order for such data to be made comparable, some cultural information must be ignored. Returning to the example cited above, there is much that separates an Atiteco aj'kun (in whose culture, incidentally, a Christian concept of Satan is lacking) from a witch, who is often characterized by pacts with the Devil and with antisocial behavior. At times, however, the observer (we are thinking here of the anthropologist and the missionary alike) finds it useful to ignore such cultural idiosyncrasies, electing instead to sacrifice cultural information to gain data compatibility.

Related to this is another concern—the issue of narrative perspective. Specifically, in the presentation of accounts of other cultures, a decision must be made as to whether to emphasize a vantage in which the participants in the considered society have access or a perspective in which only the observer engages. In the jargon of anthropology, the first type of research perspective is called *emic* and the second type *etic.* As an example, emic analysis of the preconversion religion of the witch doctor in the earlier account would likely consider its underlying meaning, what gods the associated rituals are designed to affect, and so on. In other words, particular weight would be given to explanations the old Maya himself might have given for his actions. Etic analysis, however, might consider the functional relationship of Atiteco shamanism with local birth rates. In Atitlán, as is explained later, one shamanic role (*nabeysil*) requires celibacy, hence lowering the community birth rate.[1] Nonetheless, the shaman involved would deny engaging in his craft for this reason and in fact would be unaware of its etic reality.

This type of etic concern lies in the exclusive domain of the social scientist, which brings us to our point.

Strictly speaking, shamanism is specific to certain religions of the Ural-Altaic peoples of Northern Asia. The category *shamanism,* however, has gained scholarly (and popular) acceptance as having application for the description of religio-cultural phenomena observed throughout the world; hence, the comparability of those phenomena has been raised. Mircea Eliade's book *Shamanism: Archaic Techniques of Ecstasy* exemplifies this type of cross-cultural approach. In his study, Eliade favorably considers Willard Park's definition of shamanism as being "all the practices by which supernatural power may be acquired by mortals, the exercise of that power either for good or evil, and all the concepts and beliefs associated with these practices" (1972:298). Although Eliade adds that "we should prefer to emphasize the ecstatic capacity of the shaman as opposed to the priest, and his positive function in comparison with the antisocial activities of the sorcerer" (1972:299), conflicting data force him to acknowledge the problems in making such distinctions. As Eliade notes, some shamans engage in sacerdotal activities, and others engage in "sorcery" (Eliade defines the latter as "black" shamanism). We show later that both priests and sorcerers are encountered within the realm of Atiteco shamanism.

The Park definition of shamanism, and the dilemma to which it gives rise, resonates with the witch doctor's conversion story and exposes several significant implications. First, the overarching category *shaman* allows room for the Juan Franklin congregation's association of aj'kun and witch. Interestingly, however, according to this definition the descension of the Holy Ghost onto Franklin's Pentecostalist flock, and the resultant glossolalia of those anointed by the Spirit, identifies that group as also being shamanic. (We confess to delighting in the idea.) From the vantage of the social scientist, both of these associations may be valid; however, the identifications must be etic. In both cases, those involved would be blind to them and, in fact, if confronted would certainly object. (Undoubtedly, the aj'kun would be nearly as adamant in rejecting association with a witch [*aj'itz, aj'tzay, q'isom*; see the Appendix to this chapter] as the Pentecostalist would be with the aj'kun.) What these examples seem to indicate is that a cross-cultural analysis of shamanism requires a thinning of attributes in the manner described earlier. Yet, those attributes the observer chooses to ignore may be those the actual participants in the native traditions hold as most important. In other words, to those participants, more importance may be attached to what distinguishes their tradition from another than to how those traditions might be similar. And what distinguishes such traditions is the quintessentially emic category of *meaning*, an element that is easily lost when the traditions are removed from their native contexts.

This situation gives rise to fundamental epistemological concerns. Specifically, is an observer justified in ignoring certain cultural attributes in order that some desirable element of similarity might be encountered? In some cases, the answer may be yes. Those anthropologists of the cultural materialist school, for instance, argue that material factors, such as a given society's modes of production, tend to assume higher precedence in explaining that society's culture than do nonmaterial factors, such as its religious belief system (Harris 1980; Price 1982). Hence, in consideration of more significant material factors, emics are typically accorded scant priority. The potential dilemma of shamanism, however, stems from a quite different operation. In this case we are confronted with an attempt to employ an essentially etic concept—shamanism—in order to penetrate highly emic phenomena, the religious beliefs and practices of the considered indigenous societies. The results are to be seen in the association of Pentecostalism with shamanism or even with witchcraft, associations that, in the words of Clifford Geertz (1973:11), are "logically equivalent but substantially different."

So where does this leave us? To be sure, there are various elements of similarity in the shamanic traditions of the world, as is evident in a comparison of the chapters in this volume. But where there are similarities, there are also significant differences. This is so even if, as per Eliade's desire, the roles of the priest and sorcerer are discounted. It is for reasons of the uniqueness of the various shamanic traditions that, in the presentation of ethnographic data pertaining to shamanism, we are drawn to the work of Geertz. According to him, the idiosyncrasies of cultures can be more important than any associated universals. He notes (1973:43) that "it may be in the cultural particularities of people— in their oddities—that some of the most instructive revelations of what it is to be generically human are to be found." Geertz maintains that the way to gain entrée into this realm is not by "arranging abstracted entities into unified patterns" (1973:17) by cultural thinning. To the contrary: Geertz advocates what (following Gilbert Ryle) he calls "thick description."

In the remainder of this chapter, we offer thick description of the shamanic traditions of Santiago Atitlán. Specifically, our efforts are directed toward describing the place of those Atiteco religious special-ists, generically called shamans, within the context of their own culture. This is not to say, however, that we abandon entirely a comparative approach, because we give some attention to contrasting Atiteco culture in general with Western culture. After a brief description of the environ-ment of Atitlán, we consider key distinctions of Atiteco culture, espe-cially its worldview. In this way a platform is established from which to commence analysis of local shamanism as a specialized subcategory of Atiteco culture. We then focus on the place of Atiteco shamanism with-in the local culture. In the course of this discussion, we give particular attention to one type of Atiteco shamanism—*aj'kuniel* of the *rxin way ya* ("food-water") and the *rxin ch'oj* ("lust-insanity") traditions. To best convey a sense of the meaning behind shamanism in Atitlán, and there-by to allow a glimpse into the imaginative universe in which the Atiteco shaman walks, we conclude where we began—with consideration of the Juan Franklin Church. Specifically, the rigid good-and-evil dualism so characteristic of the flock at that fundamentalist Christian church is contrasted with the system of shifting binary opposition that defines aj'kuniel. An appendix describing the different types of Atiteco religious specialists that fall under the rubric of shamanism is included at the end of the chapter.

THE ATITECO WORLD:
CULTURAL GEOGRAPHY AND COSMOS

The highland region of Guatemala includes some of the most pro-nounced microgeographic diversity to be found anywhere in the world (McBryde 1947). Santiago Atitlán serves as a case in point. Within just a few miles of the town, high mountain plains give way to deep river val-leys, three volcanoes—the highest of which towers 11,590 feet in eleva-tion—drop steeply to Lake Atitlán (5,115 ft. elev.), and cloud-producing rain forests of the mountain tops grade quickly into pine forests and then into the tropical vegetation of the lower elevations. Perhaps most important to our present discussion is the region's climate of pro-nounced wet and dry seasons.

The geographical diversity of the area is directly reflected in its cul-tural diversity, with the rugged terrain restricting easy cultural intermix-ing (McBryde 1947). Scattered throughout Guatemala's highland region are numerous towns and hamlets, most reachable only by dirt roads.

Community location—including local geography, climate, and proximity to Hispanic centers—directly affects local economics, including types of production and the degrees of integration with the national economy (Smith 1984). The population to the east of the country's capital, Guatemala City, is predominantly Hispanic, and the great majority of those living in the highlands to the west are Indian.[2] Many of the Indian communities are noted for a distinctive localized style of costume, often woven on back-strap looms by women in the individual households (O'Neale 1945). The cultural diversity of the region is also demonstrated linguistically, with more than twenty different Indian languages, in addition to Spanish, being spoken. In the immediate Lake Atitlán area alone, three different Indian languages are spoken. The primary language of Santiago Atitlán is Tzutujil (literally "Flower of the Corn Plant"), the language of most of the indigenous population inhabiting the south and west shores of Lake Atitlán. Yet, even among the seven Tzutujil-speaking communities lexical, phonological, morphological, and syntactic variations exist (Dayley 1985:3). Atitecos claim that only they speak Ktz'oj'bal ("the Language"), the indigenous name for Tzutujil. Even within the approximately two-square-kilometer town, moreover, there are sublocal linguistic variations. Although the indigenous languages spoken in Guatemala are of the Mayan family, most are mutually unintelligible.

Although much of the variation in regional cultural geography is ancient, one aspect is fairly recent and reflects the gradual opening of the area to the outside. Until a few decades ago, the indigenous population was numerically dominated by followers of the traditional religion, a group that is generally called *costumbrista,* or "followers of the old customs." However, such factors as civil war, rapidly deteriorating economic and ecological conditions, increased Western education, and massive Protestant missionization (exemplified by the Juan Franklin Church) have combined to effect the decline of this sector in all of the country's Indian communities. In Atitlán, for example, Robert S. Carlsen's (n.d.) research determined that slightly over 35 percent of the approximately twenty thousand inhabitants are Protestant. Although the remainder are divided between Catholics (*catequistas*) and costumbristas, a sharing of traits between those two factions prevents convenient demarcation.[3] For the present study, unless otherwise noted our discussion is of costumbrista worldview and religion.

In a literal sense—hence justifying the otherwise flagrant tautology
—costumbrista worldview is based on the world in which the Mayas
live. To the present day, many highland Mayas deify the world, often
calling it in Spanish *Dios Mundo*, which literally means "World God."
This belief receives perhaps its clearest articulation in Atitlán, where the
Atitecos speak of the world using the Tzutujil name *Ruchiliew*, which
means "Face of the World." Accordingly, the world's surface is understood to be the literal face of an ancestral deity (see O'Brien 1975).
Although this deity is now dead—in fact, it is sometimes understood to
be a skull (*Tzimai Awa*)—its essence continues to sustain the living. It
is particularly significant that Atitecos speak of having an "umbilical"
relationship with the world. Much as the infant in the womb is sus-
tained by its mother, this manner of speech reflects an awareness that
all sustenance is ultimately derived from the ancestral world deity.

Indicative of the predominantly agricultural local and regional economy, the Atiteco beliefs embedded in this understanding are often
expressed using metaphors based on vegetation. For instance, E. Michael
Mendelson (1956:65) cites an Atiteco who called the original life essence
palabra del mundo and said that "it is the root (*raiz*) of the world, it is
ancient . . . The village cannot go on living without it because it is an
original thing: it is tied to the beginning of the world." Similarly,
Nathaniel Tarn and Martin Prechtel (1986:176) cite an informant who
says that "each object in the world had a different father, but an umbilical linked them to this single large womb-root, which he also called a
tree root." Implicit is adherence to a concept of a cosmic tree at the
world's center, what Eliade (1969) calls the *axis mundi*.[4]

Central to this conception is a continual death to life and back to
death progression of binary opposition, which brings this discussion
back to where it began, to the highland Guatemalan natural environment. As mentioned, that environment is characterized by pronounced
wet and dry seasons. During the rainy season, the area around Atitlán is
blanketed with lush green vegetation. With the end of the rains, however, the area quickly transforms into a brown dust bowl. It is easily
understandable that local Mayas associate the dry season with death
and the wet season with life. As we have shown elsewhere, in Atitlán
this structure of binary opposition is expanded to include other logically consistent elements (Prechtel and Carlsen 1988). During the rainy
season, for instance, the path of the sun across the sky is to the north
of the equinox, and during the dry season it is to the south. Hence,

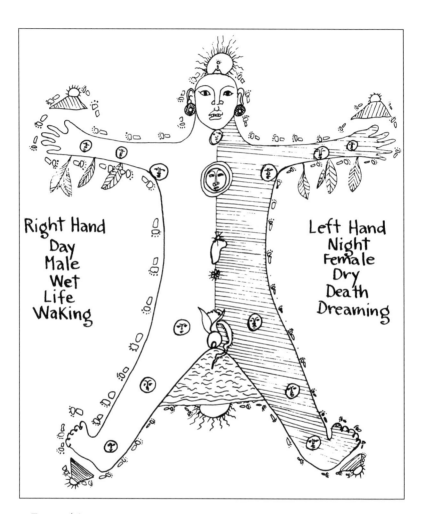

Right Hand
Day
Male
Wet
Life
Waking

Left Hand
Night
Female
Dry
Death
Dreaming

FIGURE 4.1

The worldview of Atitecos incorporates understandings of both the world and the human body as a tree. Atiteco shamanism extends these beliefs to include a concept of the world as body. According to these understandings, the middle of the body is associated with the middle of the year, the equinox. This division serves to define a set of binary opposites that characterize both the human body and the world itself. The above schema also depicts, in the form of footprints, the path the sun takes in its annual traverse across the sky. Atitecos call this path *R'kan Sak R'kan Q'ij,* or "Footpath of the Dawn, Footpath of the Sun." (Drawing by Martin Prechtel) north joins the association of wet with life, and south is equated with dryness and death. As depicted in Figure 4.1, other elements that fit into this scheme are right and left, male and female, waking and dreaming, night and day, and the moon and the sun. It merits notation that in this structuring of binary opposites, the Atitecos are consistent with what has been identified (Coe 1984:152) as "the Mesoamerican philosophy of dualism, the unity of opposite principles."

In summary, the varied symbolism described here constitutes a fairly simple and sensible indigenous expression. It was mentioned that at its basis is the world, particularly an Atiteco recognition of the world's primal ancestral quality, that quality being associated with death. This understanding is consistent with the focus of the traditional Atiteco worldview that is backward; back to the original, undifferentiated life force, the "Father-Mother" of all that is. According to Atiteco understanding, the primal ancestral life force is the element that continues to sustain the living. A death to life and back to death transition is evident and is consistent with a more encompassing Atiteco focus on dualism. Finally, we should add that according to the worldview we describe, the "living" include numerous elements Westerners consider to be inanimate, including segments of time and, as is explained later, geographical places.

RELIGIOUS SPECIALIZATION IN SANTIAGO ATITLÁN

FOOTPATH OF THE DAWN, FOOTPATH OF THE SUN

In Santiago Atitlán the paradigm explicated earlier provides a basis for local religious specialization, in which context the associated symbolism receives considerable elaboration. The primary realm of Atiteco religiosity is the semisecret organization known as the *cofradía* system. That system, often referred to in the literature under the rubric "cargo system," consists of a number of individual cofradía houses, each characterized by a ladder of hierarchical positions held for a minimum of one year (DeWalt 1975). Each cofradía is located on a year-by-year basis in the house of its highest ranking member. For much of the post-Conquest period in the Guatemalan highlands, Indian participation in this institution was locally mandated by formal and informal regulations. Nearly fifty years ago, however, national legislation mandated that cofradía participation be voluntary, and the institution has subsequently undergone gradual erosion. Although in various communities cofradías have disappeared altogether, in Atitlán, despite diminished participation, the institution remains important.[5]

Although the cofradía is of European origin, soon after its introduction into colonial Guatemala in the sixteenth century, the Indian population began to refabricate it into a distinctly native institution.[6] The result was a syncretistic Maya-Catholic cofradía religion, with considerable local and regional variation. As we have shown elsewhere, in Atitlán the Catholic elements have largely been incorporated into the local religion according to identifiably pre-Conquest Mayan paradigms (Carlsen and Prechtel 1991). Most cofradías in Santiago Atitlán are named after and dedicated to a Catholic saint (Santa Cruz is a notable exception). In reality, however, such "saints" are a far cry from their Catholic namesakes. For instance, San Juan is actually a god of wild animals, Concepción is a goddess of impregnation and planting, San Francisco is a lord of death, and San Nicolás is associated with *aj'kuna* (plural of *aj'kun*) or "shamans" (Mendelson 1956:45–48; Douglas 1969:66–90). We should add that each of the local cofradías is used by shamans in the performance of rituals. As a system, Atiteco cofradías and their rituals are designed to assist the sun (*Kdta*, "Our Father") in its traverse across the sky (Prechtel and Carlsen 1988). This function is called *R'kan Sak R'kan Q'ij* ("Footpath of the Dawn, Footpath of the Sun"), which is the closest the Atiteco cofradía system has to a formal name. Consistent with the logic that permeates Atiteco culture, costumbristas believe this function fuels the continual transition of opposites, such as night to day, dry to wet, and death to life.

It is particularly relevant that only two of the approximately one hundred cofradía positions are shamanic. The first of these is the nabeysil (Figure 4.2), which is one of the most interesting cofradía positions in Guatemala. In short, nabeysils are Mayan priests in charge of the ritual maintenance of sacred bundles. Their priestly status is underscored by the fact that they must remain celibate for as long as they hold the position, which is generally for life. Importantly, because the bundle cult can be demonstrated to have existed in the Mayan area from at least the Late Classic period (c. A.D. 600–900) and into the Post-Classic period (A.D. 900–1524), some form of the nabeysil position almost certainly existed long before the Conquest. Although various cofradías in Atitlán house sacred bundles, at present only the cofradías

FIGURE 4.2
The position of nabeysil is sacerdotal; it is always held by an aj'kun and is held for life. The nabeysil must be unmarried and must remain celibate. In the center foreground of this photograph is Aklax (Nicolás) Chiviliu, the nabeysil of the cofradía San Juan, dancing the very sacred Martín bundle. In procession behind him is the leader (alcalde) of the cofradía. The Martín bundle is danced only a few times a year. It is never taken outside the cofradía and can only be danced when all doors and windows are closed tightly. Should these restrictions be violated, it is thought that a great wind would destroy the world. The god Martín, who is usually referred to using secret names, is associated directly with the original life essence of the world. (Photograph by Paul Harbaugh, 1990)

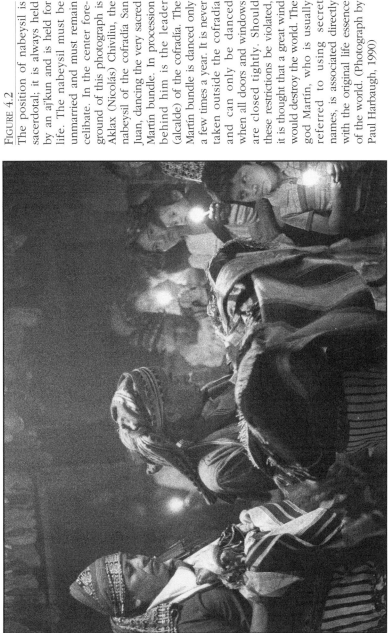

San Juan, Ch'eep San Juan, and San Antonio have nabeysils. More is said later about the role of the nabeysil.

The other of the two shamanic positions in the town's cofradía system is the *telinel* (Figure 4.3). Although that position is held for only one year at a time, and few *aj'kuna* are ever telinel more than once, Atitecos insist that the role is sacerdotal (McDougall 1955:65). The word *telinel* comes from the Tzutujil *telej,* which means "to shoulder." In fact, a telinel's single most important duty during his year on the job is to carry the deity Mam (a.k.a. Maximón) on his shoulder during Holy Week festivities. Throughout the rest of the year, the telinel works as the resident shaman in the cofradía Santa Cruz, where Mam is generally located.[7] Although there is no remuneration while on the job, after his tenure an ex-telinel usually profits from his enhanced reputation. And although there is no formal association or hierarchy of aj'kuna, those that have been telinel enjoy a special status among their peers.[8]

The cofradía system provides an excellent context in which to define the place of the shaman in Atiteco society. As mentioned, the system is structured around a ladder of ascending positions. The higher a person ascends in the system, the greater his or her prestige and respect in the community.[9] In contrast, it is informative that prior to the relatively recent decline in the demand for cofradía positions, shamans were actually discouraged from entering the system. Unlike cofradía members, who are accorded respect for their service to the community, shamans are individualistic and largely self-interested and hence, in a community-oriented society such as Santiago Atitlán, are categorically distrusted. In Atitlán, depending upon the type of shamanism in question (see the Appendix to this chapter), public acceptance ranges from simple distrust to violent rejection.

Despite this sentiment, many aspects of shamanism are accepted by Atitecos as being necessary; in fact, at times even Protestants use their services. William Douglas, in a 1969 study on Atiteco medical practices, found that although Atitecos tend to use Western medicine, most believe some afflictions require treatment by shamans. According to Douglas (1969:332), Atitecos tend to use Western medicine (most often relying on the advice of local pharmacists) in the treatment of the "illness condition" but use shamans in the treatment of the "illness situation." For instance, an Atiteco with tuberculosis would probably use Western medicine in the treatment of the disease symptoms, but he or she might use a shaman to figure out "why" the disease was contracted

FIGURE 4.3
The telinel is one of two positions associated with the Santiago Atitlán cofradía system that must be held by a shaman. Unlike the other position, the nabeysil, the telinel is not an official member of the system. This photograph is of the former telinel Axuan Ixbalam and his wife, Yaluor (Dolores). (In this depiction, Axuan is wearing the headcloth [*x'kajkoj zuñ*] of a cofradía member because of his prior membership in the system.) As part of this job, the telinel maintains the deity María Castelyana (the female counterpart to the god Maximón). This goddess is located—on her back with a cigar in her mouth—in the open case behind Axuan. (Photograph by Paul Harbaugh, 1986)

and then to correct its underlying cause. Douglas observed that the "why" of the disease typically involves a person's unbalanced relationship with the world. Hence, "the use of a native treatment specialist is directed at re-establishing the individual in the social order through appeal to the supernatural powers in the universe" (1969:314). Importantly, he concludes that "Western medicine has not been incorporated [into Atiteco culture] as an alternative system of treatment but rather as an extension of an already existing system" (1969:326). We might add that aj'kuna often bless medicines obtained from a pharmacy, hence converting them into something that in the patient's eyes is functionally equivalent to the shaman's herbs.

Douglas's conclusion exposes a process of local medical syncretism much like the highland Mayan religious syncretism cited earlier. In both cases, accepted Atiteco models of the world's vital operations have pulled nonindigenous intrusions into conformation with the culture system. This process also helps to explain how core paradigms have come to permeate multiple components of the local culture, including shamanism. In the remainder of this chapter, the contextual relationship of such Atiteco paradigms with one type of local shamanism, aj'kuniel, is probed. This exercise demonstrates how aj'kuniel is influenced by Atiteco paradigms. Moreover, in explaining the aj'kuna's manipulation of the accepted paradigms and, hence, that groups' challenge to "normalcy," an understanding of the place of shamanism within Atiteco society can be gleaned.

THE "WAY OF THE HUNTER"

The Tzutujil word that most closely approximates "shamanism" is aj'kuniel. Yet, this word literally means "the way of the aj'kun" and refers specifically to one type of shaman, the aj'kun. The word *aj'kun* comes from the Tzutujil verb *kumxic,* which means "to go out and find." (In its infinitive form, *kun* becomes *kum.*) Aj'kun can be glossed to mean "hunter." We should note, however, that this definition stands in contrast to the earliest references we have found. The Coto dictionary (Cakchiquel) (c. 1650) defines *ah cun* as *médico,* or "doctor" (Coto 1983:339). And around 1700 the Dominican friar Francisco Ximenez defined it as "healer" (*curandero*) (1985:63). In both cases, these early definitions are based on interpretations of *cun* as meaning "medicine." The word for medicine in Tzutujil, however, is *aq'uom,* an *aj'q'uom* (*aj'q'umanel*) being an herbalist (see the Appendix to this chapter). Hence, either the Tzutujil aj'kun reflects etymological differences from the ah cun, as defined by Coto and Ximenez, or the meaning has evolved over the past three hundred years. (See *aj'mes* in the Appendix to this chapter for an example of this type of lexical evolution.) Whatever the history of the term, contemporary Atiteco aj'kuna hold the kumxic derivation to be correct.

There are far more aj'kuna in Santiago Atitlán than any other type of shaman. Although male aj'kuna outnumber females, both sexes are represented. Establishing an accurate figure for the total number of aj'kuna, however, is difficult. Douglas (1969:185) reported fifty-one active aj'kuna in Atitlán for the year 1966. Carlsen established that the number had not declined in 1990. Yet because of the status of shamanism, aj'kuna are reticent to openly discuss their participation in aj'kuniel. Even in arranging the employment of an aj'kun, a client will typically avoid direct mention of the craft, electing instead to say something like "you have your content." Further complicating the establishment of the exact number of aj'kuna is the fact that there are both professionals and amateurs, with the latter group especially secretive about its shamanic activities.

The professional aj'kun differs from the amateur both by customarily charging fees—which vary according to reputation and competence—and by being trained and formally initiated by a master. (Amateurs will sometimes hire a master for their initiation.) The aj'kun's initiation almost invariably entails ceremonies at thirteen sacred locations in and around the town. These places were once demarcated by stone crosses, which were removed several decades ago by Catholics. Most often, further initiatory rites are held at some of the town's cofradías and sometimes in caves near the neighboring hamlet (*aldea*) Cerro de Oro. In all cases, depending upon the procedures utilized by the master, there is considerable variation in the initiatory rites.

Perhaps the best way to approach the specific understanding of aj'kuniel is by way of the common denominator of traditional Atiteco culture, the world. The aj'kuna relationship to the "Face of the World" marks an area of membership in this culture, yet it also serves as a point of departure. Aj'kuna adhere to the general costumbrista understanding of the world's deified nature. Recounting what was stated earlier, that understanding holds the world to be the vital remains of the most primal entity, the Father-Mother of all that is, and is identified with the World Tree. It is that ancestral entity, a "womb-root," that sustains the living. Accordingly, humans maintain an "umbilical" relationship with the world and, hence, with the original primal ancestor. At this juncture, however, the aj'kuna jointly depart down a road that is uniquely shamanic. The Atiteco understanding of a deified world, and of humans who are linked to it in an umbilical relationship, is carried to its logical conclusion in aj'kuniel. Specifically, in spite of the many differences that characterize aj'kuna, they are unified in an understanding that the human body is a projection of the world itself.

In Tzutujil, the world is spoken of using the verb *lexic*, which means "to be derived from," and not with the verb *banic*, "to be created." In other words, the world, Ruchiliew, is a "born" being, not a "created" thing. Accordingly, it has a mind (the sun), breath (wind, the word for which is *xlajuyu*, "breath of the mountain"), a heart (located at the earth's core), and blood (sometimes likened to tree sap). Basic to this understanding is that the world's "derivation," its birth, came long before that of humans. As such, according to aj'kuniel, humans are made in the image of the world. In this, aj'kuniel is consistent with shamanic traditions in other Mayan towns.[10] For instance, citing a study by James Boster of Q'eqchi' shamanism, Barbara Tedlock (1982:137) notes that "the main pulse points, located at the wrists and ankles, are called the 'four sides of one's being' (*caxcuitl acue*), analogous to the four sides or corners of the milpa, home, and world." In her own study of Quiché shamanism (*k'ijloxic*) in Momostenango, Tedlock (1982:3) writes that the diviner's "body is conceived as a microcosm filled with movements that reflect the past and future events of the macrocosm."

Accepting that humans are made in the image of the world, Atiteco aj'kuna understand that phenomena of the natural environment have counterparts in the body. This understanding is evident on a general level, in which the left side of one's body is associated with south, the Guatemalan lowlands, and female and the right side of the body with north, highlands, and male. In addition, times of the year are associated with moods and afflictions. By way of example, sadness is related to the dry season. Or consider the names of the afflictions "residue from the time of cold" (*rxtibul tiew*), "lightning blood" (*kaypa' kik*), and "rainbow blood" (*xkunq'a' kik*). On a more specific level, the epistemology of aj'kuniel recognizes a correspondence between body parts and primary elements in nature. Among these are an association of the head with the sun, the chest with the moon, genitals with the center of the day, bones with rocks (also ancestors), intestines with the inside of the earth, the gall bladder with the stars; very importantly, the umbilicus is associated with Santiago Atitlán itself. It is Atitlán, the *R'muxux Ruchiliew*, the "Umbilicus of the World," that serves as the conduit between the primal "womb-root" and the "Face of the World."

The introduction of Santiago Atitlán into the body-as-world association exposes a different level of this relationship, one that incorporates specific geographical locations. Aj'kuna conceive of a system of twelve concentric geographical places, all of which surround a thirteenth locale, Santiago Atitlán itself. Each of these places corresponds to a point in the body. Suggestive of the Boster study cited above, these points are located at the pulse areas of the armpits and groin, the elbows and knees, the wrists and ankles, and the body center. Each of these points is called *r'ximik* ("knot"), or sometimes *r'kux* ("heart"), and is conceived of as the locus of an individual circulatory system. Importantly, the geographical counterparts of the body's knots are mountains or volcanoes. And just as the individual knots of the body are thought to be semiautonomous systems, so are their corresponding geographical locations.

Perhaps the most important aspect of those geographical place-systems is what is variously referred to in the literature as its *dueño,* or "owner" (Mendelson 1956:44), *ahau,* or "lord" (Douglas 1969:70), or *nawal* (O'Brien 1975:43).[11] In the present study, we elect to use the Tzutujil word *rajawal.* All of these terms have been employed to refer to a group of sometimes twelve and sometimes thirteen deities who are associated with rain-making and who are believed to inhabit various Guatemalan mountains. Linda O'Brien (1975:43) says of these deities, "From their mountain domains they control the forces of nature, the rain, the fertility of the earth, the wild animals, and the destiny of men." She adds that they are so closely "identified with the forces of nature that they are called in songs, 'the lightning-men, the mist-men, the rain-men, the earthquake men.'" Consistent with the Atiteco concept of duality explained earlier, the male rajawal are paired with female rajawal. We have written elsewhere of the association of these goddesses with weaving implements (Tarn and Prechtel 1986; Prechtel and Carlsen 1988). Importantly, this association is indicative of a much wider relationship of both male and female rajawal with a variety of elements. For instance, each is associated with a particular mountain, a type of lightning, a segment of time, a type of herb, and so on.

It is appropriate to mention that rajawal are prone to incarnate, in which form they are called *nawal achi* (nawal-men). These avatars of Atiteco religion are recognized by identifiable characteristics. For instance, the incarnate form of one of the rajawal is invariably discovered inside a gourd, another walks on the lake, another is found on a garbage heap, and others have characteristic physical deformations. Although the most important of the modern nawal achi was Aplas Soguel, who according to legend walked back into the sky shortly after the beginning of this century (see Mendelson 1956:49), others, such as Maxuan Quieju (who died in 1974), have lived much more recently. In fact, they continue to incarnate (see Figure 4.4). Most often, however, the modern representations are said only to have "nawal blood," which is lesser than being an actual nawal achi. We should note that the nabeysils, as described above, are usually Atitecos with nawal blood. Importantly, although a nabeysil is invariably an aj'kun, nawal achi are not. To be sure, these avatars possess great powers; however, as is explained presently, unlike the aj'kuna who seek such powers, in many cases the nawal achi actually constitute the desired power itself.

HUNTERS OF THE RIGHT AND HUNTERS OF THE LEFT

The general blueprint of the body-as-world is the common ground of aj'kuna. Yet, it also provides a stage for those shamans' peculiarities, their individualism. First, there is considerable variation among aj'kuna on the specifics of the body-as-world configuration. For instance, although most aj'kuna would recognize that the *klantun* (datura) plant is an aspect of the deity named María Castelyana (depicted in Figure 4.3), there would be disagreement on other characteristics of that goddess. Or, as Mendelson (1956:46) notes, Atiteco shamans generally do not know the names of all the rajawal. In short, the specifics of the body-as-world configuration differ from aj'kun to aj'kun, with unanimity on the details being absent.

No doubt, one reason for this variation is that aj'kuna are not particularly concerned about it, which points to another level of aj'kuna idiosyncrasy: specifically, no aj'kun attempts to work equally with all aspects of the body-as-world configuration. A characteristic of aj'kuniel is that each shaman has a special relationship with some aspect of the system. In fact, that aspect is the source of a shaman's power. Most often, it first comes to the aj'kun in a dream, which may even constitute

FIGURE 4.4
The term *nawal achi* is generally used in cases of individuals who have already died. Before dying, the future nawal achi is called *k'as rwa* (literally, "his head lives"), which can be glossed as meaning "immortal." This photograph is of Atico (Diego) Soguel, a contemporary k'as rwa. As an infant, Atico exhibited signs (*rejtal k'as rwa*) that identified him as the incarnation of a rajawal. According to custom, during his upbringing Atico was never allowed to go outside his house, nor were his feet allowed to touch the ground. Instead, he was always carried. Only when his mother died when he was an adolescent did Atico begin to venture into public. (Photograph by Paul Harbaugh, 1988)

the shaman's "calling." For instance, an Atiteco who is sick (or who knows someone who is sick) might dream of a woman (typically of unearthly beauty) who, in some manner, suggests a type of herb. According to the reality we are describing, the female in the dream is a deity, and the herb is one of her attributes. In this example, should the herb lead to the person's healing, and should the dreamer become an aj'kun, that aj'kun would have a special relationship with the deity, with the associated herb, and, hence, with a component in the body-as-world configuration. That aj'kun would then be employed for curing of his or her specialty affliction.[12]

Importantly, according to this system of curing, it need not be either the aj'kun or the herb that actually effects a cure. Instead, in many cases, the shaman's ritual is designed to direct the deity (in her herbal form) to the location of the affliction in the patient's body. The deity then effects the cure.[13] However, not all aj'kuna practice this path of curing. Although aj'kuna generally begin and end their curing cere-monies in much the same manner—by burning candles, offering incense and liquor, and using similar prayers—what they do in between can vary. The particular methodologies of individual aj'kuna reflect a most important division of aj'kuniel. Some aj'kuna attempt to cure by summoning spirits, as just described. Alternatively, there are those that attempt to expel the affliction (an attribute of a deity) by fighting it. The first branch of aj'kuniel is called rxin way ya, which means "food-water way." The second comes from the expression ch'ojrik, or "lust-insanity," and is called rxin ch'oj. Similarly, the first type is known as "right-hand-ed" aj'kuniel and the second as "left-handed" aj'kuniel. Accordingly, the right-handed aj'kun, the *aj'way ya,* is allied with the attributes associat-ed with the right side (see Figure 4.1), especially the sun. Conversely, the left-handed aj'kun, the *aj'ch'o,* is allied with the moon, femaleness, the night, and so on.

In order to understand the implications of this division, we must realize that although Atitecos hold the various attributes of the right-left construction of binary opposites to be integral and necessary, equal value is not accorded to those attributes. Quite simply, the left grouping is considered to be dangerous, and, as necessary as it might be, it is mistrusted. This is not to say that it is considered to be "bad" but that it is "delicate." As such, it might seem that Atitecos would be more accepting of aj'way ya than of aj'ch'o, which, to an extent, is true. Nonetheless, there is a general sentiment that all aj'kuna cultivate an abnormal familiarity with the left, which is also partially true. On one level, the dream world, a definitively left component, is in many ways the aj'kun's workshop. Basic to aj'kuniel, and to Atiteco culture in general, is the understanding that a person's dreams reflect his or her physical condition. (See Douglas 1969:107–111; Barbara Tedlock [1981] notes certain similarities in Quiché dream interpretation.) Not only do aj'kuna diagnose diseases through dream interpretation, but they often venture into the dream world to remedy a patient's affliction. Similarly, when aj'kuna gaze through a crystal during divinations, it is to observe the state of the patient's "fire soul" (*q'aq'al*) in the dream world. On a more specific level, all aj'kuna, whether they be aj'ch'o or aj'way ya, maintain a formal relationship with the left. This relationship is very important and requires particular consideration.

Aj'kuna typically begin their ceremonies by praying to each of the twelve sacred mountains and places surrounding Santiago Atitlán, as well as to the "Umbilicus of the World" itself (see Mendelson 1956:40–41, 46). According to many aj'kuna, the surrounding locations are organized into concentric circles, with Atitlán at the center. Some aj'kuna pray first to a point on the outside and then to single points on each descending ring until they reach Atitlán. Then they pray to the next point in a counterclockwise direction on the outside ring. Repeating the process, they move consistently inward until all the places have been acknowledged. As such, although all aj'kuna operate from a position of centrality, the entire world, including both its left and right sides, is remembered and is honored. Hence, in varying degrees, all aj'kuna embrace both the left and the right. Importantly, this relationship is also constituted on a very significant formal level. When conversing, aj'kuna often drift toward discussion of the various "roads" that each possesses. Behind this rather cryptic terminology is the understanding that aj'kuniel entails thirteen different technical specialties, which aj'kuna refer to using the Tzutujil word *be,* or "road."[14] Six roads lie to the left, six to the right, and one is the common ground of each. The left roads lie in the realm of the aj'ch'o and the right roads in that of the aj'way ya. The center road allows each side entrée to the other side. In addition, several techniques are common to aj'kuna, such as divining with *tz'aj'tel* seeds and crystals.

In this system, all aj'kuna know between two and seven roads. The minimum number includes the common road and one other. The maximum entails the common road plus the six of either the left or the right side. Aj'kuna learn new roads either through dreams, by being taught by another aj'kun, or by a combination of the two. We should note that given the secrecy that surrounds aj'kuniel, we cannot state with certainty that there are exactly thirteen. Considering the freedom from organization that characterizes aj'kuniel, we suspect variance in the actual number.

In concluding this discussion, we cite the example of one aj'kuniel road, the definitively left technique of bloodletting. This technique, called in Tzutujil *yol chay* ("giving the obsidian"), is most often used to cure the "bad blood" of one of the pulse areas. Although there is some variation in technique, aj'kuna who perform bloodletting first use either an obsidian or a glass point to make several small punctures. In most cases, the point is hafted to a small, forked stick. The puncture is made by flicking the point at the skin. The blood is then collected in a gourd (*akbal*). Incidentally, we disagree with Douglas's assertion that the use of a gourd in this bloodletting is an optional technique. According to Douglas (1969:157–158), "A piece of cotton, soaked in *aguardiente* [liquor] or kerosene is dropped into the gourd and ignited. The akbal [gourd] is then applied to the patient, mouth first, at the site of the 'bad blood.' A vacuum is created and when the gourd is removed, by puncturing the small hole in the base and breaking the vacuum, a large welt is left which is then punctured." Although we cannot categorically state that this technique is never used, in the great majority of cases, the aj'ch'o uses the gourd, in much the manner described by Douglas, *after* the punctures have been made. The purpose of this technique is to suck the blood into the gourd. In most cases, bloodletting is performed in the patient's house; at times, however, it is done in the cofradía San Nicolás. In his capacity as patron deity of aj'kuna, San Nicolás oversees bloodletting.[15] In fact, that "saint" is sometimes referred to simply as Chay, which means obsidian. After the actual extraction of the blood, the assisting aj'ch'o transfers it to another gourd. Traditionally, the blood was removed to a location near the back edge of the town, where the aj'ch'o then poured it into the mouth of a stone image, what Mendelson (1956:43) identified as the "stone of the brujos." However, because this image was stolen several decades ago by Catholics, a cave located behind the town cemetery has served for the disposal of the bad blood.

DISCUSSION AND CONCLUSION

This chapter began by considering the evil of aj'kuniel, as perceived by the flock at the Juan Franklin Church. Although this assessment perhaps reveals more about the flock than it does about Atiteco shamanism, it offers a useful device for the interpretation of aj'kuniel. In the course of this chapter, the role of binary opposition in the Atiteco worldview has been explored. However, as is evident in the good-versus-evil focus of the Juan Franklin congregation, Atiteco costumbristas are not alone in their incorporation of binary opposition into a view of the world's essential operations. In the perception of the church flock, evilness is a result of original sin, as triggered by Eve, and hence is a semipermanent condition of the world. Only in the world to come will goodness reign. It is significant that in the worldview of the Juan Franklin flock, key components of the Atiteco "left" symbolic complex are associated with evil. Among these are death, darkness, sexuality (conception), and femaleness (after all, who first ate the apple?). The doctrine taught at the church segregates these sorts of components, categorizing them as unnatural, as conditions of the fallen, and as stationary symptoms of evil. In the Atiteco system, however, they are dynamic and integral elements of the world, hence of the human condition, and are forever prone to change.

According to the core paradigms of Atiteco culture, the right without the left is abnormal, even pathological. In Atitlán, to be crazy, to be "unbalanced," is to exhibit this type of pathology. One of the primary gods of the Atiteco pantheon is associated with "insanity" (*ch'ojrnak*, literally "split in half"). It is significant that this god has only one good leg and hence is sometimes called Lame Boy. In Atitlán, crazy people (which, incidentally, includes individuals that in Western culture would be said to be in love) are said to stand on one leg (*ch'ey*). Conversely, to be healthy is to stand on two legs (*jik atpaala*), to walk with a balance of the left and the right sides. Yet Ruchiliew, the Face of the World, is an unbalanced platform on which to attempt to stand and to walk. Costumbristas understand that the continual transformation of opposites allows the world its modus operandi and, hence, that the nature of the marriage of its left and right sides is fickle and given to change. The combined effects of the world's disposition to transform, coupled with its awesome power, inevitably result in expressions of danger and, hence, of human peril. It is the nature of the Face of the World to rip away its familiar face and glare back with the strange stare of another. As such, most Atitecos can at some time expect to explore the precipitous and fragile edges of their existence, ignobly dumped there by the world's inconstancy.

The perilous nature of human existence, as perceived by Atitecos, provides for the aj'kun's livelihood. The fact that those specialists demand financial compensation is a source of community distrust. Even more distrusted is their familiarity with the world's dangerous personality. Nevertheless, at times Atitecos find it necessary to seek out a guide intimately familiar with this personality, to hire someone who "has a content." Since a time that exists only in myth, Atitecos have employed aj'kuna to navigate courses through the sometimes perilous realities of the world on which all humankind must attempt to stand and to walk.

APPENDIX: A TYPOLOGY OF ATITECO SHAMANISM

We have mentioned that in Atitlán, different occupations fall under the category *shaman*. Importantly, however, the culture lacks a concept of *shamanism*. To be sure, there are Atitecos who, wanting to denigrate the *costumbres* (the old ways), lump all aspects of the Old Religion under the Spanish heading *brujería*, or "witchcraft." Or, at times, Atitecos use the Arabic-to-Spanish loan word *zahorín*, which translates as "diviner." This word, however, as with the Tzutujil aj'kuniel, refers only to shamanic subgroups. The only way to accurately assess the role of shamanism in Atitlán, including its acceptance and utilization, is to approach Atiteco shamanism through its component parts. Toward that end, this section considers the different types of Atiteco shamans. We should note that because we have already given attention to aj'kuniel, that type of shamanism is not considered here.

1. Iyom. Until recently, it was normal for the first face seen by an Atiteco upon birth to be that of a shaman. Although the growth of nontraditional religion in Atitlán has affected this somewhat, it remains true for much of the local population. The shamanic role we refer to is the *iyom*, a Tzutujil term that means "midwife." Several earlier studies are particularly useful in the identification of the shamanic nature of the Atiteco midwife.[16] Mendelson's work on Atiteco religiosity is explicit in its association of the *iyoma* (pl. of iyom) with the aj'kuna (1956:21). Mendelson identifies the Atiteco association of iyoma with the deity Yaxper. Similarly, Douglas (1969:145) cites the relationship of the iyoma with "Spirit-Lords and Guardians," particularly with the thirteen "Marias." Douglas observes that iyoma are utilized for a number of tasks related to pregnancy, child bearing, and children's illnesses. He adds that they are used to divine the sex of the child before its birth and even to change the sex of the unborn child. Both Tarn and Prechtel (1986) and Prechtel and Carlsen (1988) emphasize the distinctly female nature of the Atiteco mid-wife symbolic complex, including its association with weaving, the night, and the moon. Although this corpus of work is clear in its identification of the iyom as shaman, one key aspect goes unmentioned. Specifically, it is most important that during a birth, the assisting iyom is thought to actually become possessed by her patron deity or even by the moon (*Ek*) itself. We might add that iyoma often supplement their midwifery with aj'kuniel and in that capacity refer to themselves as aj'kuna.

2. Aj'q'umanel. From the very important and clearly shamanic role of the iyom, we go to what is perhaps the most marginal of the Atiteco shaman types, the *aj'q'umanel.* This term is derived from the Tzutujil word *aq'uom,* which means "medicine" and in English would be trans-lated as "herbalist." Douglas (1969:134) calls these specialists *ajkomanel,* for which he offers the "literal" translation "master curer." (Incidentally, he offers the same translation for aj'kun, p. 146.) The correct literal trans-lation for ajkomanel, however, would be "he of the medicine way." Douglas, in differentiating this category of specialist from what he defines as "prayer-makers" (a category under which he includes all of the other types of Atiteco shamans), discounts the herbalists' shamanic side. In fact, he lumps them with osteopaths and pharmacists as purvey-ors of Western medicine (1969:332). Although this interpretation is partly correct, it ignores important aspects exhibited by many aj'q'umanel, not the least of which is that in fact, they commonly incorporate specialized prayers into their treatments, hence challenging Douglas's master-curer versus prayer-maker distinction. Quite simply, many Atitecos will not accept medicine that has not been transformed through prayer.

3. Aj'q'ij. The term *aj'q'ij* is derived from the Tzutujil word *q'ij,* which variously means sun, day, or time. Most often this term is trans-lated as "daykeeper" (Colby and Colby 1981; B. Tedlock 1982) and arguably is the predominant type of shaman found in highland Guatemala. In fact, Barbara Tedlock (1981:314) writes that nearly ten thousand of this type of shaman are living in the Quiché-speaking town of Momostenango alone. Writing around 1725, the Dominican friar Ximenez noted that before the Conquest, aj'q'ij (*abquih*) utilized the sun and seeds of corn, or *tzajtel* (*tzite*), in their divinations, hence attesting to the pre-Columbian origins of the craft (1977:88). As well, the ancient Mayan text *Popol Vuh* discusses similar shamanic rituals (D. Tedlock 1985:81). In around 1715, the Franciscan friar Francisco Vásquez documented the presence of aj'q'ij (ahquih) in Santiago Atitlán (1938 2:28). Whereas Ximenez (1985:63) defined aj'q'ij (ajquih) as a "diviner," the Coto dictionary (1983:74) defines it (*ah 3ih*) as "*brujo*," or witch (resonations of the witch doctor's conversion story).

Much as described in these early primary sources, the contemporary Atiteco aj'q'ij typically utilizes implements, most often tzaj'tel seeds, corn grains, and small rock crystals, in order to divine a course of action a client might utilize in the resolution of some problem. At the basis of this type of shamanism is the ritual use of various manifestations of the ancient Mayan calendar, most commonly the 260-day divinatory calendar but also the solar cycle. As Mendelson (1956:27) noted nearly forty years ago, however, although the ancient calendar is still present in Atitlán, its utilization "is relegated to the background." Similarly, in 1965, Douglas observed that in Atitlán, the aj'q'ij role had largely been integrated into that of the aj'kun.[17] Although the role of the Atiteco aj'q'ij has clearly been important, currently most Tzutujil-speaking aj'q'ij are from the coastal area, particularly around San Antonio Suchitepequez. (Various of these aj'q'ij customarily come with their clients to the cofradías of Santiago Atitlán to perform costumbres.) Nonetheless, in 1990 several shamans in Atitlán claimed to be aj'q'ij.

4. Aj'mes. The aj'mes is a type of shaman most commonly associated with the Quiché-speaking area of the Guatemalan highlands. Writing about the Quiché community of Santiago El Palmar, Benson Saler (1964:31) calls this type of shaman *aj nagual mesa*. Barbara Tedlock (1982:74) cites the same title for Momostenango. Both of these scholars contend that *mesa* comes from the Spanish word for "table," and they translate the term as "worker with the spiritual essence of the table." Duncan Earle (personal communication 1991), who has spent considerable time studying aj'mes, says that in most Quiché communities, the "a" in mesa is dropped; nonetheless, he says the association with tables remains. In all reported cases, the most notable characteristic of Quiché aj'mes is their spiritist capacity.

In reference to Atitlán, Douglas (1969:159) offers a translation similar to Saler's, calling the aj'mes "Master of the Table." However, contrary to Douglas's arguments, in Tzutujil the term *aj'mes* has nothing to do with tables; instead, it literally means "sweeper." Incidentally, we suspect that the Quiché etymology is the same but that in Quiché the meaning of the word has evolved. At the basis of our suspicion is the Ximenez dictionary (c. 1700), which incorporates Cakchiquel, Quiché, and Tzutujil. Importantly, Ximenez (1985:65) defines *ahmez* as "sweeper." According to contemporary Atiteco aj'kuna, the aj'mes sweeps one's "road," one's path in the dream world. Douglas, however, claims that an aj'mes is primarily an aj'kun who counteracts witchcraft. In fact, the Atiteco aj'mes is not a type of aj'kun but is a spiritist pure and simple. It is worth noting that in Yucatecan Maya, *mis* means "sweep," an *ah misib* being a "sweeper" (R. Quizar, personal communication 1990).

At present, there are at most three practitioners of the craft in or around Santiago Atitlán. A reason for the paucity of Atiteco aj'mes is that the work is grueling—so much so, in fact, that according to Atitecos, aj'mes tend to die within a few years of taking up the profession. Atiteco aj'mes can be either male or female.

5. Lsay ruki kumats and *ruki kik 'om.* The *lsay ruki kumats* and the *ruki kik 'om* are bite specialists. The first type works with snake bites and the second with spider bites. Both occupations are exclusively male. The most common path to becoming either a snake bite specialist or a spider bite specialist is through a "calling" in dreams. This calling often includes the transmission of special prayers; other times it comes after the person himself has been bitten.

Primary to both specialties is the use of highly esoteric prayers. Generally, these prayers include antiquated usages of the Tzutujil language in conjunction with secret words. For instance, some ruki kik 'om refer to spiders as "walking obsidian." And lsay ruki kumats call certain varieties of snakes "the one who has it written across its eyes." The prayers also commonly incorporate codified references to the sun. The purpose of the bite specialists' treatments—including their prayers, incisions with obsidian blades, and the application of poultices—is to extract the power of the animal that inflicted the bite. This power is often conceived of as having a relationship to rainbows. The use of esoteric and antiquated language in the curing ceremonies of bite specialists contributes to the distrust of these shamans, especially by Protestants. Nonetheless, these types of specialists are most often the first choice of Atitecos who have been bitten.

6. Q'isom, aj'tzay, and *aj'itz.* Finally, we consider the several occupations that might appropriately be categorized as witchcraft. The first is the q'isom, what Saler (1964) translates as "transforming witch." Mendelson (1956:67) calls the q'isom (*isom*) "the bad *ajelbal* [see footnote 11] of the witch." In fact, according to Atiteco belief, the q'isom is the animal transformation of a "witch." According to accounts cited by Mendelson (1956:68), "Their main pastimes included the killing of their enemys' animals, the invasion of their houses, undressing sleeping people and flinging them to the floor, and the bestial affairs which they had with q'isom of the opposite sex." Belief in these sorts of phenomena is historically deep in the Guatemalan highland region. For instance, the English Dominican priest Thomas Gage (Thompson 1958:273–277) noted several cases of it in and around Mixco during the first quarter of the seventeenth century. As recently as 1987, a purported q'isom was killed in Atitlán. This incident, which was reported in Guatemala's major newspapers, occurred when, after several nights of harassment, the residents of a house in Atitlán cornered an animal. Upon killing it with their machetes, the animal transformed into the bloody corpse of one of their neighbors.

The aj'tzay is the most malevolent of the Atiteco shamanic types. The Coto dictionary (1983:163) defines the word as *Diablo,* or "Devil." However, as mentioned earlier, traditional Atiteco culture lacks a Christian concept of Satan. In reality, aj'tzay is derived from the Tzutujil world *atzam,* which means "salt." An aj'tzay is a "witch" who symbolically salts the victim's road. We must realize that salt is associated with dryness, which, as we have explained, to Atitecos is related to death.

Unlike the q'isom or the aj'tzay, who utilize specific techniques, the term *aj'itz* applies to a more generic occupation. The term itself comes from the Tzutujil word *itzil,* which means "bad." In fact, the habitual application of any of the shamanic occupations or activities described earlier for the exclusive purpose of causing harm would qualify a person as being an aj'itz. No Atiteco, unless quite inebriated, would claim to be an aj'itz, or, for that matter, either a q'isom or an aj'tzay.

NOTES

1. We use the example of the nabeysil only to make a point. There are too few of these individuals to significantly alter birth rates.

2. Since the early 1980s, Guatemala's indigenous population has been victimized by a bloody civil war. Between fifty thousand and one hundred thousand persons have been killed and many more displaced. As part of its counterinsurgency, the country's army has destroyed several hundred Indian communities. During the writing of this chapter, a

▼

massacre in Santiago Atitlán was responsible in part for the U.S. government's decision to terminate all military aid to Guatemala (see Loucky and Carlsen 1991).

3. To be sure, the end points of a continuum based on the religious behavior and beliefs of Catholics and costumbristas would be quite distinct. Nonetheless, many Atiteco Catholics continue to embrace a number of cultural attributes anchored in the "Old Ways," the costumbres. For a cogent analysis of Guatemalan Protestantism, see Stoll (1990).

4. The fact that this primal element is sometimes called *Ti Tie Ti Tixel* (Father-Mother) is indicative of the understanding that its origin lay in a distant unity that existed even before the differentiation of the sexes. The logic that underwrites this conception forms a paradigm that permeates Atiteco culture. We have written extensively on this paradigm, showing that it informs such diverse aspects of Atiteco culture as myths, conceptions of lineage, weaving, and economic production (Carlsen and Prechtel 1991).

5. There are ten public cofradías in Santiago Atitlán. In addition, there are four private cofradías (cofradías that belong to a particular family), one Catholic cofradía, and one Ladino (non-Indian) cofradía.

6. Foster (1953) offers perhaps the best analysis of the historical relationship of European and Mesoamerican cofradías. MacLeod (1973) explains the process by which the region's indigenous population transformed the institution. Cortés y Larraz (1958) describes in detail the distinctly non-Christian character of cofradías as they existed in the diocese of Guatemala in the late eighteenth century.

7. Mendelson's pioneering investigation in Atitlán focused on the god Mam (Maximón) and remains the most important body of work on the associated cult (Mendelson 1956, 1959, 1965). O'Brien (1975) adds considerable important data.

8. Despite this fact, in recent years the vicissitudes of the local political violence have been such that an unusual paucity of aj'kuna have been willing to take the position. Specifically, in February 1990, as he was walking home from the cofradía, then telinel Axuan Ixbalam was approached by three hooded men and shot down. In October of the same year, a masked man burst into the cofradía and assassinated Axuan's successor, Martín Kik, even as he was seated next to Mam. In that incident, Mam's nose was shot off. According to the members of the cofradía, however, his nose subsequently grew back. Many Atitecos, including the members of the Cofradía Santa Cruz, assign that shooting

to the army and attribute recent military setbacks in Atitlán to the fact that Mam was shot.

9. Whereas this prestige and respect used to be accorded by the local population as a whole, the inroads of nontraditional religion, especially fundamentalist Protestantism, have affected this. As exemplified in the witch doctor's conversion story, the new religions have attempted to "Satanize" most aspects of traditional culture, including what Atiteco Protestants sometimes refer to as the "old religion."

10. This understanding may at one time have been pan-Mesoamerican. In a 1984 study of the Nahuas, Lopez Austin cites the ancient Mexican correlation of the human body with the universe (see particularly Vol. 1, Chapter 11). In this correlation, Lopez Austin recognizes the ancient Nahua concept of the World Tree and an association of the human body with vegetation.

11. Of these terms, the closest to being correct is the Spanish word *dueño*. Both ahau and nawal are too general to be of much use. For instance, ahau can be used in reference to the head of a household. And, according to costumbristas, virtually everything has its nawal, its pure spiritual reality, even the ink that forms these words. In this sense, nawal is used almost as an adjective, as in *nawal tinte* ("the nawal of ink"). Further confusing the use of the term *nawal* (*nahual, najual, nagual*) is that most often it is considered by scholars to be a human being's alter ego. This entity generally inhabits the body of an animal but may also be associated with plants or even inanimate objects. This interpretation seems to emanate from ancient Mexican culture (for instance, see Lopez Austin 1984). Although the concept exists in Atiteco culture, in Tzutujil a person's alter ego is called *jelbal*, not nawal.

12. See B. Tedlock (n.d.) for a detailed description of the role of dreams in contemporary Mayan culture.

13. Douglas (1969:159) says that "*aj'kun* [sic] frequently absolve themselves of the responsibility of a specific treatment by accounting for its origin through dream revelation . . . it is prescribed by a higher authority and I am only acting in the role of intermediary in giving you this knowledge."

14. This construct was first explained to Prechtel by the aj'kun Matzikai, who likened it to the sun. Matzikai said that from a solar center, six rays emanate toward the left, six toward the right, and one rises upward along a middle path.

15. O'Brien argues that the god Mam (Maximón) is especially associated with shamanism. She calls him "the shaman-god" (1975:5), as well as the great and the first of the shamans (1975:242). Although we realize that a shaman-god is not the same as a god of shamans, we would argue that he is neither. Recalling the earlier cited definition of shamanism as "the practices by which supernatural powers may be acquired by mortals," we must keep in mind that Mam is a god and not a mortal. Moreover, he is definitely not the primary god of shamans (aj'kuna). That distinction belongs to Aclax (San Nicolás).

16. In addition, Paul and Paul (1975) have written in some detail about the iyom of San Pedro la Laguna, a neighboring Tzutujil-speaking community of Santiago Atitlán. Much of what the Pauls observe for San Pedro applies to Santiago Atitlán.

17. Douglas (1969:116–117) includes a table depicting a divinatory calendar he saw in Santiago Atitlán in 1965.

REFERENCES

Carlsen, Robert S.
    n.d.   Bibles, Bullets, and the "Great Doctor": On Conquest and Adaptation in a Highland Mayan Town (manuscript in preparation).

Carlsen, Robert S., and Martin Prechtel.
    1991.   The Flowering of the Dead: An Interpretation of Highland Maya Culture. *MAN* (n.s) 26:23–42.

Coe, Michael D.
    1984.   *The Maya* (3d. ed.). New York: Thames and Hudson.

Colby, Benjamin N., and Lore M. Colby.
    1981.   *The Daykeeper: The Life and Discourse of an Ixil Maya Diviner.* Cambridge: Harvard University Press.

Cortés y Larraz, Pedro.
    1958.   *Descripción Geográfico-Moral de la Diocesis de Guatemala.* Guatemala: Biblioteca de la Sociedad de Geografía e Historia (2 volumes).

Coto, Fray Thomas de.
    1983.   *Thesavrvs Verborv: Vocabvlario de la Lengua Cakchiquel V[El] Guatemalteca,*
            Nueuamente hecho y Recopilado con Summo Estudio, Trauajo y Erudicion.
            Mexico: Universidad Autonoma de México.

Dayley, Jon P.
    1985.   *Tzutujil Grammar.* University of California Publications in Linguistics,
            Vol. 107. Berkeley: University of California Press.

DeWalt, Billie R.
    1975.   Changes in the Cargo Systems of Mesoamerica. *Anthropological Quarterly*
            48:87–105.

Douglas, William.
    1969.   Illness and Curing in Santiago Atitlán. Ph.D. dissertation, Stanford University.

Eliade, Mircea.
    1969.   *The Quest: History and Meaning in Religion.* Chicago: University
            of Chicago Press.

————.
    1972.   *Shamanism: Archaic Techniques of Ecstasy.* Princeton:
            Princeton University Press.

Foster, George M.
    1953.   Cofradía and Compandrazgo in Spain and Spanish America. *Southwestern*
            Journal of Anthropology 9:1–28.

Geertz, Clifford.
    1973.   *The Interpretation of Cultures.* New York: Basic Books.

Harris, Marvin.
    1980.   *Cultural Materialism: The Struggle for a Science of Culture.*
            New York: Vintage Books.

Lopez Austin, Alfredo.
    1984.   *Cuerpo Humano e Ideología: Las Concepciones de los Antiguos Nahuas*
            (2d ed.). Mexico: Universidad Nacional Autónoma de México.

Loucky, James, and Robert S. Carlsen.
    1991.   Massacre in Santiago Atitlán: A Turning Point in the Maya Struggle?
            Cultural Survival Quarterly 15:65–70.

MacLeod, Murdo J.
　　1973.　*Spanish Central America: A Socioeconomic History 1520–1720.*
　　　　　　Berkeley: University of California Press.

McBryde, Felix W.
　　1947.　*Cultural and Historical Geography of Southwest Guatemala.*
　　　　　　Washington, D.C.: Smithsonian Institution, Institute of Social Anthropology,
　　　　　　Publication No. 4.

McDougall, Elsie.
　　1955.　Easter Ceremonies at Santiago Atitlán in 1930. *Notes on Middle American
　　　　　　Archaeology and Ethnology* 123:63–74. Washington, D.C.: Carnegie
　　　　　　Institution of Washington.

Mendelson, E. Michael.
　　1956.　Religion and World-View in Santiago Atitlán. Ph.D. dissertation,
　　　　　　University of Chicago.

————.

　　1959.　Maximón: An Iconographical Introduction. *Man* 59:57–60.

————.

　　1965.　*Los escándolos de Maximón.* Guatemala City: Seminario de Integracion
　　　　　　Social Guatemalteca, Publication No. 19.

O'Brien, Linda.
　　1975.　Songs of the Face of the Earth: Ancestor Songs of the Tzutuhil Maya of
　　　　　　Santiago Atitlán, Guatemala. Ph.D. dissertation, University of California
　　　　　　at Los Angeles.

O'Neale, Lila M.
　　1945.　*Textiles of Highland Guatemala.* Carnegie Institution of Washington,
　　　　　　Publication No. 567. Washington, D.C.: Carnegie Institution of Washington.

Paul, Lois, and Benjamin D. Paul.
　　1975.　The Maya Midwife as Sacred Specialist: A Guatemalan Case.
　　　　　　American Ethnologist 2:707–726.

Prechtel, Martin, and Robert S. Carlsen.
　　1988.　Weaving and Cosmos Amongst the Tzutujil Maya. *Res* 15:122–132.

Price, Barbara J.
　　1982.　Cultural Materialism: A Theoretical View. *American Antiquity* 47:709–741.

Saler, Benson.
  1964. Nagual, Witch, and Sorcerer in a Quiché Village. *Ethnology* 3:305–328.

Smith, Carol A.
  1984. Local History in a Global Context: Social and Economic Transitions
        in Western Guatemala. *Comparative Studies in Society and History*
        26:193–228.

Stoll, David.
  1990. *Is Latin America Turning Protestant: The Politics of Evangelical Growth.*
        Berkeley: University of California Press.

Tarn, Nathaniel, and Martin Prechtel.
  1986. Constant Inconstancy: The Feminine Principle in Atiteco Mythology.
        In *Symbol and Meaning Beyond the Closed Community: Essays in
        Mesoamerican Ideas,* Gary Gossen ed. Studies on Culture and Society,
        Vol. 1. Albany: Institute for Mesoamerican Studies.

Tedlock, Barbara.
  1981. Quiché Maya Dream Interpretation. *Ethos* 9:313–330.

———.
  1982. *Time and the Highland Maya.* Albuquerque: University of New
        Mexico Press.

———.
  n.d.   The Role of Dreams and Visionary Narratives in Mayan Cultural Survival.
        Ethos (forthcoming).

Tedlock, Dennis.
  1985. *Popol Vuh: The Definitive Edition of the Mayan Book of the Dawn
        of Life and the Glories of Gods and Kings.* New York: Simon and Schuster.

Thompson, J. Eric S.
  1958. *Thomas Gage's Travels in the New World.* Norman: University of
        Oklahoma Press.

Vásquez, Francisco.
  1937–1944.
        *Crónica de la provincia del Santísimo Nombre de Jesús de Guatemala de
        la orden de nuestra seráfico padre San Francisco (1714–17).* 4 volumes.
        Guatemala: Sociedad de Geografía e Historia de Guatemala.

Ximenez, Fray Francisco.

    1977.   *Historia de la provincia de San Vicente de Chiapa y Guatemala de la orden de Predicadores.* Volumes 1 and 2. Guatemala: Sociedad de Geografía e Historia de Guatemala.

————.

    1985.   *Primera parte del tesoro de las lenguas Cakchiquel, Quiché y Zutuhil, en que las dichas lenguas se traducen a la nuestra española.* Special Publication No. 30. Guatemala: Academia de Geografía e Historia de Guatemala.

"THE *MARA'KÁME* DOES AND UNDOES": PERSISTENCE AND CHANGE IN HUICHOL SHAMANISM

PETER T. FURST

I begin this chapter with an anecdote. It is a story that is both personal and professional. It is also a cautionary tale that serves two useful purposes.

First, it illustrates a vital aspect of shamanic ideology in general, and of its Huichol expression in particular. Second, it shows how easily one can become so overwhelmed by the drama and perceived universality of a shamanic performance that one forgets to ask questions—in this instance, questions of the right sort that might immediately, instead of nearly a quarter of a century later, have placed what one saw more securely into its culture-specific context. Yet, perhaps we may be forgiven, for what we observed demonstrated that—attenuated as Huichol shamanism may seem when compared to Siberia or the Pacific Northwest—Huichol specialists in the sacred continue to share some fundamental concepts of a generalized shamanic worldview.

I am speaking here of the concept of balance, or psychic equilibrium, as a precondition to the successful performance of those practical and magical arts the shaman has spent years to acquire and that in the traditional world, of which even today the Huichols remain very much a part, are considered essential for the maintenance or restoration of mental and physical health and mutually beneficial relations with the physical and metaphysical environment. The latter embraces not only the realm of the gods and the spirits of animals and plants but also the realm of the dead, who continue to influence the lives of the living and whose participation in the ceremonies Huichols hold to be essential to their proper performance and success.

In the summer of 1966, Ramón Medina Silva, a Huichol artist and then an aspiring shaman (Figure 5.1) and his wife, a remarkable woman named Guadalupe, or Lupe for short, asked us to take them to Ixtlahuácan del Rio, on the Santiago River north of Guadalajara. At the

FIGURE 5.1
Ramón Medina Silva with the "bow drum," the hunting bow as percussion instrument, which Huichols share with only a few other cultures in the world. (Photograph by Peter T. Furst, December 1968)

time the late Barbara G. Myerhoff, and my wife, and I were spending almost every day at their little rancho on the outskirts of Guadalajara taping Huichol myths—they called them *historias*—from Ramón's seemingly inexhaustible repertoire, often with crucial input from Lupe. They said we should take our tape recorder and plenty of tape, because after they did what they meant to do at the river, there would be lots of music and perhaps more historias for us to record.

One problem with taping at Ramón's rancho (Figure 5.2), located off the highway to Zacatecas, was the noise of passing traffic. It didn't interfere with the dictation of texts, but for music, Lupe's singing, and Ramón's chanting and playing his violin and guitar and flute—all homemade—it was impossible. Ramón and Lupe had suggested several times that we go into the country, away from the buses and trucks belching smoke on the road below, and now they said they needed to visit the river, a couple of hours or so to the north. For some days we had been watching them make sacred arrows and other ceremonial objects while we talked, and now they explained that these were offerings they meant to take to "a special place" on the Rio Grande de Santiago. From what Ramón said, this appeared to be one of the innumerable places in that part of Mexico that for Huichols are fraught with sacred meanings and to some of which they make periodic pilgrimages to deposit prayer offerings and petitions to the gods for favors.

We were all still very much neophytes at gaining some insight—however modest—into Huichol religion, ritual, and intellectual culture generally, but this was something we knew from Carl Lumholtz, the Norwegian pioneer ethnographer of the Huichols. Their "whole country," he wrote in one of his monographs for the American Museum of Natural History, "is full of what we might call natural fetiches [sic]" to which offerings of food, water, and ceremonial arrows must be made "because they are alive and their help is needed to protect the cattle and to bring rain and good-luck" (Lumholtz 1902:138–139). These "natural fetiches" are also scattered outside the boundaries of the Sierra Huichol, as are many kinds of power spots—from the Pacific Coast in the west to the northcentral high desert in the east and down to Lake Chapala, south of Guadalajara—that have acquired sanctity and potency through association with one of the nature deities or the doings of the divine ancestors.

It was also Ramón's birthday, or near enough to it, and afterward we could all go to another place, an oak grove near the Río Juchipila,

Figure 5.2
Sunup on Ramón's and Lupe's little rancho on the outskirts of Guadalajara. A thatch roof shields the out-door cooking area from the sun; the surrounding land is planted in maize, beans, squash, and a few tomato and chili pepper plants. At left, wild-growing castor beans, used for medicine. Husband and wife, at left and in foreground, respectively; a visiting Huichol family at right. (Photograph by Peter T. Furst, August 1966)

"very pretty, very pretty," not far from the small town of Moyáhua. There we could celebrate with a picnic and record Huichol music and stories. "All" on this promising occasion included Ramón and Lupe and a little girl I will call Francesca, and who we had seen them treat with such affectionate concern that we thought she was their biological child but who had simply been informally adopted. (At the time I did not know that Lupe was twelve years older that Ramón and thus, at fifty-two, considerably past child-bearing age.) The group included Barbara, then a doctoral candidate at UCLA who had already published solid anthropological research, who would write her doctoral dissertation and, later, a fine book on the Huichol peyote pilgrimage, and who would, in the years before her untimely death in 1985, become widely recognized as a distinguished anthropologist of aging. There were also a teenaged half-sister of Lupe's and her young Huichol friend, who were so determined to blend into the dominant mestizo culture that they refused to wear anything that marked them as Indian. (It didn't work out for them, though, and eventually they "returned to the blanket," to borrow a North American Indian expression.) There was also an older Huichol couple and, finally, my own small family. Ramón, with whom I had begun taping myths and other narratives—of which he had an astonishing repertoire—the previous summer, had expressed a wish for a .22 caliber rifle with which to hunt deer, and we had purchased one to give him on his birthday.

We arranged to come to the rancho at sunup the following morning. It was a fine, sunny day, and we took many color slides of Ramón and Lupe, making offerings on the river bank; of the Huichols anointing one another with water from the river; of Lupe dancing with two feathered *muviéris*, shaman's arrows, stuck in her headband to symbolize deer antlers; of Ramón performing a typically shamanic curing ceremony for the Huichol woman, who had some complaint in her abdominal region, followed by a similar massaging and sucking ritual for her husband; and of Ramón and his wife acquainting their little girl with the different colors and qualities of wildflowers and the shapes and feel of the leaves of oaks and cottonwoods (Figure 5.3).

We ate and drank, played with the little girl, recorded myths and music, photographed, and, at his insistence, tried out Ramón's new rifle. It was a very full and productive day.

We drove back in our VW camper. We had been traveling for perhaps an hour when Ramón suddenly asked me to pull off the highway,

FIGURE 5.3
Guadalupe, unable to bear a child of her own, and Ramón were the most loving and indulgent of adoptive parents to this little girl, who had been abandoned to their care. The natural and social environment was the only classroom she was ever to know. Never strong, she failed to respond to modern medicine, as well as to Ramón's considerable knowledge of shamanic healing, and she died the following spring. (Photograph by Peter T. Furst, 1967)

jumped out, and motioned for us to follow him. We went across the road and over a stretch of level, rock-strewn country spotted with brush and thickets of tuna cactus to the banks of a small, fast-flowing stream that occasionally widened into deeper water holes. A few Mexican families were picnicking there and children were playing in the water, and they stopped to watch this strange procession behind a Huichol man in full regalia, playing his little homemade violin and striding purposefully along. Lupe, singing in a high, falsetto voice, followed close behind him. The older Huichol man was carrying Ramón's *takwátsi*—the oblong, plaited shaman's basket in which he, like other Huichol shamans, kept his muviéris and an assortment of power objects (Figure 5.4). The takwátsi looks strikingly like its counterpart among the Papago and Pima; on this and other occasions, Ramón kept it wrapped in a large, red, printed bandanna. He called it not just takwátsi but "takwátsi Kauyumari." Kauyumari in the Huichol culture is the sacred Deer Person, chief helper of shamans and messenger between human beings and the gods. He thus made the shaman's basket into one of the many different aspects of the cultural hero.

According to Konrad Theodor Preuss (1908:386; 1932:445), Kauyumari is the Morning Star, Párikuta muyéka, "he who roams before daybreak." Preuss was the first ethnographer to note that, with all his sacred attributes and his absolutely essential participation in the rituals by the officiating shaman's side, Kauyumari—like many of the culture heroes of native peoples in North and South America—is also the puckish and mischievous character called Trickster in the anthropological literature.

A little while later we were close enough to the edge of the plateau to see the little stream, having forced its way through a jumble of giant water-worn boulders, fall hundreds of feet to the valley and the Río Santiago. It was spectacular country here at the rim of the plateau. We could see for miles across forest and cultivated fields far below and wooded mountainous country edged against the sky—none of the smog here that was already beginning to afflict the rapidly expanding city of Guadalajara.

Ramón still did not explain, except to say in Spanish that this *salto* (waterfall) was "especially for the mara'akáme." *Mara'akáme* is the Huichol term for the specialist in the sacred; without a precise English match it is loosely equivalent to shaman, shaman-singer, or shaman-priest. At the time I thought he meant shamans generally; as it turned

FIGURE 5.4
Huichol shaman's basket, *tak-uátsi*, with its assortment of power objects. (Photograph by Peter T. Furst, 1966)

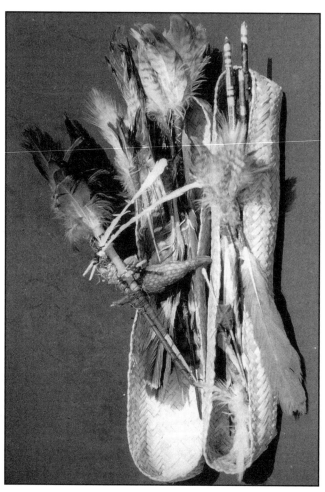

out, he was referring to *the* Mara'akáme, the aged fire god and First Shaman Tatewarí, our Grandfather, who is also the patron deity of shamans.

Ramón said something in Huichol we took to be a warning to walk with care, but Lupe was not to be deterred: holding the little girl in her arms, she ventured as close as she could to the edge of the escarpment, and some of the other Huichols followed suit (Figure 5.5). Then, led by Ramón, we all went back to a flat area, where he said we should stay and pay close attention. Thus commenced what was to be a truly breathtaking performance.

First Ramón unwrapped and, after removing its cover, reverently placed his takwátsi on a rock, with two ceremonial arrows sticking out in the direction of the waterfall. Next he unwound the long straps that secured his sandals to his feet and removed his footgear. Now barefoot, he picked his way past the giant boulders that lined the streambed until he was almost at the edge of the precipice. Lupe, chanting in rapid-fire Huichol, and our other Huichol companions were watching intently. Still not certain what was going on and why he had brought us to this scenic spot, we stood off to one side, Barbara asking that I be sure to get whatever was coming on film for both of us.

We watched with some trepidation as Ramón, now barefoot, clambered up one of the rocks, lifted his arms, spread them wide, and, after a moment's hesitation, proceeded to leap—"fly" might be more appropriate—from crag to crag, often seemingly landing only a few inches from the slippery edge. Or we would see him stand without moving for perhaps twenty seconds, arms stretched out, atop a monumental stone, then suddenly wheel about and make a great leap to the other side of the cataract. Sometimes he seated himself right at the edge, leaning slightly forward from the hips and shading his eyes against the sun as he peered down to the river far below and into the country beyond (Figures 5.6–5.11). He was not oblivious to us, for once or twice we saw him glancing in our direction, as though to assure himself that we were taking everything in. Now and again he disappeared from view for what seemed like an age, only to emerge suddenly from an unexpected direction. Barbara commented that he looked "like a bird, just like a big, colorful bird." Little did we realize at the time how close to the truth she was.

Unlike ourselves, never for a moment did he seem concerned about losing his foothold or his balance and falling into space. We,

FIGURES 5.5–5.11
Scenes from Ramón's breathtaking demonstration, in August 1966, of what he said were the balance and lack of fear of dangerous places required of one hoping, like himself, to "complete" as a shaman. What eluded the observers at the time was that this demonstration was also meant to drama- tize the part played by the bird-helper of shamans in the founding myth of the peyote pilgrimage of the divine ancestors. The river seen far below is the Río Grande de Santiago, which farther downstream becomes the Río Lerma and the locale of a substantial colony of Huichols who fled from the Sierra in the bloody aftermath of the Mexican Revolution and the Cristero Revolt. (Photographs by Peter T. Furst, August 1966)

FIGURE 5.7

FIGURE 5.8

FIGURE 5.9

FIGURE 5.10

FIGURE 5.11

however, were worried, and even a bit annoyed at what we took to be foolhardiness, fueled, we suspected, by the several bottles of beer he had consumed at the picnic. Lupe and the other Huichols were watching intently. Lupe especially appeared never to take her eyes off her husband. Once or twice she raised her right arm halfway and pointed toward him with a shout of encouragement. None of the others showed any apprehension, although the older man, in an aside to us in Spanish, said that he could never do this because he had a fear of falling, which had kept him from going on to "complete" as a mara'akáme himself.

The performance—which is what we took it to be, rather than some kind of mysterious ritual—ended as abruptly as it had begun. Nobody, Ramón included, provided an explanation. We dropped the Huichols off at Ramón's and Lupe's rancho, agreed to meet early the following morning for more interviews and taping, and went home. We were still wondering what it had all been about, whether what we had just witnessed was anything more than a bit of good-natured showing off on Ramón's part.

The next morning's taping session began, as usual, with an hour or so of eating *pan dulces* (sweet rolls) and drinking the heavily sugared *café con leche* we always brought along. Except for exclamations of appreciation from Ramón and Lupe at the fine taste of the sweet rolls and the coffee, nobody said anything significant, and we refrained from referring to the events of the previous day. Finally, Ramón inquired with a twinkle in his eyes if we thought he had been showing off. He said, "Perhaps you thought, 'Ah, Ramón is drunk with too much beer.' " Our expressions must have suggested that we had been thinking precisely that, because he continued, "But no, no. I took you there to show you what it means to have balance. So you could see and understand. Because when one crosses over as a shaman one looks below, and then one sees this great *barranca* filled with all those animals waiting to kill one. The mara'akáme does and undoes. If he does not have balance he is afraid. Those who do not have balance, they fall and are killed."

Barbara and I looked at each other and said, almost simultaneously, "Eliade!" Ramón had been trying to explain to us for some days that to become a shaman, to learn the arts of what he was fond of calling "doing and undoing"—another way of saying "transforming"—one had to be without fear, because sometimes one has to cross over narrow and dangerous places and doing that requires balance. What he said was strikingly reminiscent of what Mircea Eliade had written on this subject in his classic crosscultural work, *Shamanism: Archaic Techniques of Ecstasy* (1964). Eliade wrote from the point of view of the historian of religion rather than the anthropologist, but the book is must reading for anyone interested in the subject. In any event, balance, psychic equilibrium, is a theme that repeats itself over and over in traditional heroic, funerary, and shamanic mythologies.

Here is how it appeared to us: aware of the linguistic, cultural, and experiential gulf between us as this singularly gifted and perceptive Huichol artist and religious specialist had been almost from the first days of our relationship, Ramón had evidently been uncertain that we fully understood what he had been trying to tell us. How clever of him, we thought—not to say brilliant—to use dramatic performance to render intelligible something he feared our cultural experience might not have prepared us to comprehend. He probably did have too much to drink, but that was not the point. The same man who had never seen or heard of the very ancient X-ray style, or skeletonization, in shamanic art customarily employed it as a device to identify shamans and other sacred beings in his art (Figure 5.12) and had again shown us something we, though not he, knew to be universal. "Sometimes," he had told us, "when one goes traveling to these other places, when I dream these things with the peyote, I can see down there, far, far below in that barranca, the bones of that man, that woman, who tried to become a mara'akáme, this man or the other, but who had this fear. Fear gripped them in their hearts and they fell, fell, fell."

To repeat, I trust we can be excused if at the time the impact of all of this was so powerful that other questions did not occur to us. We did not consider that there might have been something more to Ramón's waterfall than a convenient stage for him to translate a metaphysical concept into action, into dramatic reality. Performance, verbal and theatrical, is everywhere a vital aspect of shamanism. And Ramón, who was then what, for want of a better term, can be called an apprentice shaman, was ever the shaman as performer, frequently dramatizing sacred stories he was sharing with us—not only in his yarn paintings but by acting out the parts of the different characters (Furst 1978:24–26). We did not realize that he was doing just that in this case as well.

I published a brief description of the waterfall incident in 1972 and mentioned it again later as a particularly fitting conclusion to an essay

FIGURE 5.12
Yarn painting by Ramón Medina, depicting a shaman, skeletonized and with antler-like votive arrows on his head, lower right, embarking on a path into the sky that will lead him past numerous obstacles, including a fiery curtain of solar rays, to a rock crystal, here depicted as a shining star. The rock crystal is conceived as the physical manifestation of a deceased ancestor who sent an illness to the shaman to signal his wish to return as his and his family's guardian spirit. After capturing the crystal, the shaman will place it inside a reed and attach it in a little sacred bundle to an arrow, hence its name, *urukáme*, from *uru* (arrow). (Photograph by Peter T. Furst, 1970)

on universals through time and space in shamanism in the special issue of the Canadian magazine *Artscanada* devoted to that topic (Furst 1973:152–53; 1974:33–60). For Barbara Myerhoff, who returned to Los Angeles at the end of the summer to resume teaching at the University of Southern California and complete her doctoral studies at UCLA, what she had seen Ramón do at the waterfall was particularly significant because it seemed to throw light on some peculiar and (like Ramón's) unexplained antics of a Luiseño shaman named Domenico. She had gotten to know this interesting man, one of the last of the old Indian shamans in southern California, during summer fieldwork on the Rincon Reservation near San Diego, in which we had both participated as graduate students (discussed later). In December 1966, at Ramón's invitation, she returned to Mexico to participate in the first peyote pilgrimage to have been witnessed by anthropologists. In the doctoral dissertation that resulted from her participatory observation of that event, she mentioned the waterfall experience to illustrate some of the essentials of the shamanic vocation (De Mille 1990:336–354).

A book followed—*Peyote Hunt: The Sacred Journey of the Huichol Indians* (1974)—her sophisticated and sensitive analytical treatment of Ramón's and Lupe's 1966 peyote pilgrimage and of deer, peyote, and maize as a unified religious symbol complex central to Huichol religion. In her book she used the waterfall incident as a graphic demonstration of shamanic balance, a universal topic in which she had first become interested while working with the Luiseño (Myerhoff 1966:60–72).

Whether it was because she had thought more about the event or simply because she was more sensitive than I to subtle nuances, she clearly could not quite shake off the feeling that there had been something more to it than just a display of equilibrium for our benefit—that there might even have been a ceremonial or ritual component to which we did not at the time have access. As she put it: "I could not be sure whether Ramón was rehearsing his equilibrium or giving it public, ceremonial expression that day. . . . Whether seen as a practice session or as a ritual, the events of the afternoon provided a most demonstrative assertion that Ramón was . . . like all authentic shamans, a man of immense courage, poise and balance" (Myerhoff 1974:46).

In a subsequent essay on shamans as mediators between the known and unknown worlds, she returned once more to Ramón's performance because, she said, it had helped her to understand a "peculiar piece of behavior" by the California shaman Domenico that had long puzzled her. This Luiseño shaman was widely renowned for his curing skills, she wrote, with an extensive clientele that included not only Indian people from his own reservation but also Anglos, Mexicans, and Indians from other tribes. He practiced only on weekends, his patients arriving on Friday afternoons with their bedding, prepared to camp out around his little shack. Early on Friday afternoons she would observe Domenico climbing to the roof of his shack and standing there quietly, "without moving for long periods of time while he gazed toward the road with one leg pulled up and curled into the crook of the other." She assumed at first that he was looking for his clients, but "even at the time it seemed odd that he risked life and limb by standing on the fragile, tar paper–roofed little structure when he could easily have walked up a little hill behind his house for a better vantage point." In retrospect, and with Ramón's dramatic demonstration in 1966 in mind, "it seems clear that he was demonstrating his mediating capacity by showing himself to be a specialist in balance" (Myerhoff 1976:101–102).

For the Nahuatl scholar Willard Gingerich (1988), Ramón's remarks about balance and the danger of falling into chasms fit into a much wider, and clearly pre-Conquest, Mesoamerican ideological framework. As he points out in an essay on the Nahuatl discourses generally (but erroneously) known as the *huehuetlatolli*, exquisite balance between chasms as ideal behavior was very much a part of the Nahua ethic generally and not just in relation to the work of the shaman. Gingerich notes that the same imagery as that evoked by Ramón Medina in Myerhoff's writings can be found again and again in the discourses scattered throughout Book VI of Fray Bernadino de Sahagún's *Florentine Codex*. As one example he cites this admonition by a mother to her adolescent daughter: "On the earth we walk, we live, on the ridge of a mountain peak (sharp as a harpoon blade, *chichiquilli*?). To one side is an abyss, to the other side is an abyss. If you go there, you will fall, only through the middle one can go, or live" (Sahagún 1969:101). And again in Chapter 22: "They [the elders] used to say that on the earth we walk, we live, on the ridge of a mountain peak. Here is an abyss, there is an abyss. Whenever you deviate, wherever you go astray, there you will fall, you will plunge into the depths" (Sahagún 1969:125).

The doctrine of the middle way, then, was a central principle in formulating and interpreting this ethic. But this middle way is decidedly not the Golden Mean of the Aristotlesian ideal. This thoroughly indigenous conception, of indeterminate antiquity, has its roots in the shamanic complex which Eliade suggests underlies all religious activity and which retained its original vitality throughout many regions of the Americas, even today providing the essential pattern for ritual in a number of cultural areas. (Gingerich 1988:523)

As for Ramón's explanation of what he had been doing at the edge of the waterfall, Gingerich (1988:523) comments that "we almost feel he must have been reading Sahagún's *tenonotzaliztlatolli* discourses, so explicit is his reference to balance between abysses 'this way and that.' " He hadn't, any more than he knew of Eliade, for like most adult Huichols, this gifted Huichol intellectual had never learned to read or write. But Gingerich is right: Ramón's behavior was not idiosyncratic but was part of a much wider, and very old, indigenous ethic. The fact that the Huichols, like the Aztecs (and the Luiseño), are members of the Greater Nahua, or Uto-Aztecan, family helps, but I suspect much the same ethic exists among many, if not most, Native American peoples.

In any event, Myerhoff used these two examples of shamanic balance from her own observations in Mexico and southern California to examine the role of shamans generally as mediators who gain power each time they travel to "the edge of the social order" and beyond, always facing and conquering the possibility of loss of balance as they stand "at the juncture of opposing forces" and face the perilous task of moving between and reconciling these opposites. "The passage," she wrote, "is a dangerous one fraught with peril," and she thought both Domenico, the shaman of Rincon, and Ramón, the Huichol shaman-in-training, had displayed their mediating capacity by showing themselves to be specialists in balance.

They had indeed. But in the Huichol case, this was not the whole story, after all. On June 27, 1989, nearly a quarter of a century after Ramón's waterfall performance, I was sitting with his widow, Lupe, in the front yard in one of the barrios of Santa Fe, New Mexico.[1] I learned from Lupe that since Ramón's tragic death at around age forty-five in 1971 (as discussed later), life had not been easy. In recent years especially there was often not enough to eat, and she and members of her family were beset by illnesses all too obviously linked to malnutrition. Her eyesight was failing, and the rheumatoid arthritis in her knees sometimes made walking, and especially dancing, awkward and painful. Yet, not only had she established herself as an accomplished artist and artisan in several media, especially the storytelling yarn paintings in the style pioneered by her late husband, but in her late sixties (she is not sure of her exact age), and as undisputed matriarch and spiritual mentor of a large family, she was training to become a full-fledged mara'akáme in her own right—curer, singer, and spiritual leader of her own small band of young and old relatives. She has also become an enthusiastic and, despite her physical limitations, seemingly indefatigable traveler: by 1989 she had visited not only Indian pueblos and Anasazi ruins in the Southwest but new Anglo friends on the West Coast, Plains Indian communities, and Indian villages on James Bay in northern Quebec—some so remote they could be reached only by small plane. (This latter adventure had been facilitated by the Quebec authorities. The Cree elders were hoping that meeting with Indian people from Mexico who were steadfast in their commitment to the old traditions might counteract the alienation that had developed among some of their young people.)

On this occasion we chatted for a bit, and she reminisced about our time together in Mexico so many years ago and about Ramón. He had so much knowledge, she said with a deep sigh, he knew all the ceremonies and the ancient historias (their term for the myths). So much knowledge and wisdom had made some people envious, she said, even relatives. And such people had used witchcraft and sorcery against her and her family. She was convinced that this was the reason they often did not have enough to eat and became sick. But now, with this new market for their crafts in the United States, she and her family could save money to buy land, and life was better. As often happens even now when she speaks of Ramón, Lupe became weepy, brushing away tears, although her life with him had had its share of ups and downs, including a period of off-and-on separation during the final years of Ramón's life.

We talked about our two peyote pilgrimages together and about Barbara's death and my wife's death in 1974 ("So many friends dead," she said, her eyes wet with tears, "Ramón, Barbara, Dee, all dead, all dead"). I told her I had been thinking about the waterfall incident, too. Did she remember it? Yes, yes, she said eagerly, obviously happy to get away from so sad a subject; it was Ramón's birthday, when he showed you how the mara'akáme is not afraid of anything, even of falling, way, way down into the barranca. And she, whose memory is sometimes a bit vague but more often is astonishingly acute and detailed, repeated pretty much what Ramón had said about the shaman not being afraid of falling.

And did she remember where this waterfall was located? Did it have a name? "*Sí, como no?*" she said, yes, of course. "It is called Salto de Temajar, Salto de Temajar." Does it have a Huichol name? "Aitá," she said. "In Huichol it is called Aitá. Salto de Temajar in Spanish, Aitá in Huichol." And how did Ramón know where this salto was? (We had wondered about this even at the time, because it had not been visible from the road.)

And Lupe launched into a story, or parts of a story, in Spanish, with some untranslatable Huichol terms thrown in, about the first peyote hunt of the *kakauyaríxi*—the ancient, ancient ancestors who were gods and who followed the Mara'akáme Tatewarí on the first hunt for the divine Deer Peyote in Wirikuta, where they now live in the rocks and mountains. The tradition of this primordial hunt is the charter myth of the Huichol peyote pilgrimage, which is a major event in the annual ceremonial cycle (Furst 1972, 1976; Myerhoff 1974).[2]

When the ancestors went to Wirikuta, Lupe said, they visited many places, and where they stopped the Huichols who go to the peyote today leave offerings to ask for their favor. One of these sacred places was Aitá.

This was a new and unexpected twist to the story. I asked Lupe to tell me more. "They came down, tired, tired, from the Cerrito de Picachos, where there are many, many pinnacles, very steep, very hard. And then they came to Aitá," she said. "There they took their rest."

They wanted to climb down from there, she continued, and they did not know how. Then they saw a little bird, a bird who could fly down there on its wings, "catching the wind on its wings, so"—and she stretched her arms wide, as we had seen Ramón do twenty-three years earlier—"and sailing, sailing, down. They were looking for it to show them the way. But they could not fly, they had to go down purely on their feet. And Ramón, he was showing how this little bird spread its wings and flew from those rocks, how it showed those ancient, ancient ones the way one gets down those big stones, from Aitá, which is the same as Salto de Temajar."

And what was the name of this bird? Its name is *uitzi*, a "tiny, tiny little bird," black all over, Lupe told me, and only the mara'akáme, the shaman, or one who is learning to be a shaman can see it.[3]

She sighed and added that Huichols are no longer able to go by way of Aitá, because "they say all those places are pueblo now." That sounded as though since 1966, when the country near the waterfall was uninhabited, the population explosion has caught up with this beautiful and, at least to some Huichols, sacred place. (I have not been back there, but those were Lupe's words.)

This elaboration by Lupe on Ramón's dramatic demonstration in the summer of 1966 was quite an eye-opener. It explained why he had known about the waterfall, why he performed as he did—jumping from rock to rock, disappearing and reappearing—and why he often seemed so like a bird: he was acting out his own lack of fear and, on the larger plane, shamanic balance. But he was doing it in a specifically Huichol context, the peyote tradition, just as he had acted out myths on other occasions. Lupe's addendum also clarified Ramón's cryptic remark in 1966 that the waterfall was "special for the mara'akáme," a statement by which I realized he meant not just shamans in general but, more specifically, the great Mara'akáme Tatewarí himself.

Was Ramón's Aitá the Aitá of the peyote myth, or are there other cataracts that fulfill that role? There probably are. By their very nature, waterfalls are apt to be landmarks in the sacred geography of many peoples. Ramón liked places that manifested what he called "a unity," that is, combined male and female principles. Waterfalls do that par excellence, at least in Ramón's personal worldview and probably that of other Huichols as well. Falling water is male, phallic; the still water into which the cataract empties is female, uterine, even as it transforms the male cascading stream from male into female. The symbolism and beneficial effect become even more powerful when the process of unifying male and female is repeated in several successive cataracts.[4] According to Ramón, who in so many ways exemplified Radin's *Primitive Man as Philosopher* (1927), it is the same with rivers: they are male where they flow fast and female in the quiet bends and eddies. In Ramón's worldview (and, I assume, that of other Huichol religious specialists) the complementary male-female symbolism attaches to water of celestial and terrestrial origin as well—the former, falling as rain, being male, the latter female—and to caves, whose level floor is female, whose vertical walls are male, whose vault is female, and that in totality are uterine entrances to the underworld. (The symbolism of water is even more complex, however, because as Ramón explained it, the male rain originates in the female caves, from which it rises as mist and clouds—female—to be transformed and returned to earth in the form of male raindrops. These conceptions about the origin of rain are shared by other Mesoamerican peoples, past and present.)

Had Ramón had some ulterior motive for not having told us of the mythic context of his waterfall performance in the first place? I have no reason to think so. More likely he assumed, as he had on other occasions (and as has been the experience of other ethnographers with their informants), that we knew and understood more than we did. So when he said the next morning that now we knew what he had meant by the need for the shaman to have balance, not to be afraid of falling into the barranca, he thought we surely knew the full story. Didn't everybody?

At this point I should explain something about Ramón and Guadalupe and our working relationship with them in the 1960s. As mentioned earlier, Ramón died in the summer of 1971. As deaths go among the Huichols, it was a particularly bad death, because after a cousin shot him several times in the back in a drunken quarrel said to have been over a woman who was Lupe's cousin (this was during one of his and Lupe's separations), he lingered on for a time in great pain while relatives tried to get him from his rancho across the swollen Río Santiago to the hospital in Tepic. The heavy drinking itself wasn't the bad thing, because it occurred in the proper context, which was a ceremony to celebrate the clearing of land of trees and brush for the new planting season. The bad thing was the violence that so often comes with drinking.[5]

For most of their lives before I met them, Ramón and Guadalupe had lived as poor peasant farmers in the rural Huichol refugee colony on the lower Río Santiago (also called the Río Lerma), outside the indigenous territory proper. Ramón's grandfather had been a shaman in the indigenous *comunidad* of San Sebastián. This community, and other parts of the Huichol territory in the Sierra Occidental, saw bloody fighting and major population dislocations during the Mexican Revolution and its aftermath, the Cristero Revolt of the 1930s, when San Sebastián especially was virtually depopulated. Along with hundreds of other Huichols, Ramón's family abandoned their rancho in the mountains and settled along the Santiago, setting up a rancho and growing maize. Ramón's mother, Doña Cuca, who had been raised among shamans in the Sierra and who lost her sight in the early 1950s because of untreated cataracts, became a mara'akáme after her husband deserted her and their children—for a time "the sole repository over a vast area of the myths and ancient rituals she had absorbed from infancy" (Benítez 1968:355–356). Ramón's sister Concha followed in her mother's footsteps, and later, when Ramón was far enough along in his self-training as a mara'akáme, he frequently assisted as her *segundo* in conducting the ceremonies (Figure 5.13).

According to Ramón, every year as far back as he could remember, the entire family migrated to the coast to work for pennies harvesting maize and tobacco for rich Mexican farmers. Every year there were times when there was not enough to eat. He and Lupe, who, born in the Sierra de Nayar, had likewise migrated to the Santiago, met while harvesting maize and, despite her considerable seniority in age, soon decided to live together as man and wife (they were never married in the legal sense). By the war-filled 1960s, they were tired of the hard life and constant poverty, so they packed their meager belongings and went to Guadalajara to try their luck.

When I met them, they were living in a little rancho they had established on a patch of empty land on the then still partly rural northern edges of Guadalajara. Maize is the mainstay of life for Huichols, their spiritual as well as ideological underpinning. Accordingly, that is what they had planted, along with beans, squash, chiles, and tomatoes. Their little *coamil* (a Huichol contraction of two Nahuatl words, *coa,* digging stick [literally snake] and *milpa,* maize field), on which they cultivated all crops alongside one another in the traditional Mesoamerican way, was within touching distance of a little one-room thatch-roofed hut, modest but well built, that they had constructed from found materials. Inside, along the interior back wall, was their *niwetári,* or altar, a simple wooden shelf holding an assortment of ceremonial objects, including a framed paper print of the Virgin of Guadalupe, the precious property of her human namesake. Hanging on the walls were other ceremonial paraphernalia, including some of Lupe's beautiful woven bags that were half filled with peyotes; the three-legged upright deerskin-headed shaman's drum the Huichols call *tepu* (another word derived from the Nahuatl); the traditional Chichimec-style short bow and arrow-filled deerskin quiver that today are used only in a ritual context, particularly on the peyote hunt; musical instruments; and an *'uwéni,* the high-backed, symbolically and technologically complex woven chair that is reserved mainly for shamans and rancho elders. I remember no furniture other than an old wooden trunk filled with clothing, a couple of little chairs, and two crude wooden pallets for sleeping. Close to the house were some large, wild-growing castor bean plants from which they extracted medicines. In front was an open

FIGURE 5.13
Ramón (wearing hat with white danglers) at his sister Concha's side, as she gestures in the four directions with her muviéri, a large compound arrow with hardwood top and bundles of hawk feathers at the butt end that serves shamans as staff of power. Concha, a shaman like her and Ramón's mother, Cuca, officiates at a ceremony in the Huichol colony on the lower Río Lerma, Nayarit. (Photograph by Dee Furst, summer 1967)

ramada of four posts, roofed with thatch. The open patio of hard-packed clay was relatively large—large enough for the ceremonies Ramón occasionally conducted for Huichol visitors. I estimated Ramón's and Lupe's little rancho to occupy perhaps less than a quarter of an acre, not enough to sustain them with maize and other vegetable foods for more than, at most, a few weeks, even in a good year, but more than enough for the ceremonies of the agricultural season. But they worked these modest food crops, from planting to weeding to harvest, with singular commitment and devotion, and I remember them making a ceremony out of roasting and eating the first ears of maize from the new harvest.

For much-needed cash income they both worked almost every day on folk art: yarn paintings on masonite or plywood, woven bags and sashes, beadwork and embroideries. They also made ceremonial objects for ritual use, for themselves and other Huichols. Through the Franciscans, who maintained a Huichol museum and crafts store at the Basilica de Zapópan, a popular way station for Huichols coming to the city, Ramón's unusual talents as a musician—he was equally expert on the homemade violin and guitar (instruments derived from the Spanish in the colonial period) and the indigenous reed flute—and his broad knowledge of Huichol myths and rituals were soon discovered, and he started to appear occasionally on radio, performing Huichol music and, more important, talking about the traditional culture and the trials and tribulations of the Huichol people at the hands of mestizos invading their lands. His appearances on the radio, with fervent pleas for economic and social justice for the Huichols, made him a man of stature back home on the Río Lerma; according to Benítez (1968:382), he was "regarded as a superior man and respected and admired by all the people on the Lower Lerma who had listened to him on the radio."

Occasionally, Ramón also performed with an Aztec dance group. More important, on the recommendation of Padre Ernesto Loera Ochoa, the priest in charge of the Huichol museum and crafts store, he was invited to talk about the Huichols, their religion, and their desperate needs at the University of Guadalajara. Having professors and students listen with rapt attention to the words and music of a Huichol, seeing all those books in the library, and being befriended and treated by men of learning with a respect and interest not usually accorded Indians left him with a very positive attitude toward the education he had never had and, by extension, toward anyone connected with a university—a fact that helped me in my initial contact with this interesting, intelligent, complex, and sometimes deeply troubled man.

I first heard about Ramón from the cultural attaché of the U.S. consulate in Guadalajara, who described him as a fine artist and an aspiring "medicine man." What piqued my interest was the fact that this medicine man was supposed to know many of the old stories. Where could I find him? Probably through the Franciscans at the Basilica de Zapópan, just outside Guadalajara. It was, in fact, through Padre Ernesto that I first met Ramón. The padre had spent two or three years at college in the United States studying sociology, and he spoke English well. He was also a talented photographer, having taken hundreds of pictures of Huichol life and rituals in the Sierra and of shamans who performed them; he also told me of one occasion when he was politely but firmly ejected from San Andrés Cohamiata, another traditional comunidad in the Sierra, after a mestizo woman kissed his ring and the Huichol authorities realized that, although he was not dressed as such, he was a Catholic priest. At the time, priests, even from the nearby Santa Clara mission, were decidedly unwelcome in San Andrés. Padre Ernesto readily confessed to having great admiration and respect for Huichol culture and religion ("The Huichol religion is so beautiful," he said once, "why do we want to change it?"), and he confirmed what I had already been told—that Ramón was not only a good artist and performer but that he was determined to become a mara'akáme, a shaman. (He actually said to Ramón on the occasion of our first encounter, "You had better become a good shaman, because you will never become a good Catholic. Or any kind of Catholic." Ramón smiled one of his characteristic mischievous smiles and agreed.)

I noticed the priest used the word *shaman,* pronouncing it shamán, a legacy of his anthropology courses at college in the United States. Ramón, believing it to be Spanish for mara'akáme, had picked it up.

Ramón was still three years—more accurately, three of the five peyote pilgrimages to Wirikuta he had pledged to his tutelaries Tatewarí and the Sun God Tayaupá—from "completing" as a shaman. We watched him complete, by the consensus of his *peyotero* companions—all relatives—at the conclusion of his fifth peyote pilgrimage. Even then, in 1965 and 1966, he enjoyed a reputation as a knowledgeable curer, counting among his clientele not only fellow Huichols but even an occasional middle-class Mexican whom modern medicine had failed and who turned in desperation to indigenous herbal remedies, the practical and psychosomatic therapies typical of shamans, and the special "knowledge" even otherwise racist mestizos tend to attribute to Indians.

And so, beginning in 1965, to add to his modest cash income from other sources, he now had one anthropologist and, by the summer of 1966, two, myself and Barbara Myerhoff. For the UCLA museum and ourselves, we purchased virtually every one of his striking storytelling yarn paintings—an innovation of which, as already noted, he was the pioneer and that even in his lifetime, and more so after his death, became standard fare for Huichol folk artists in this medium.

All of this attention could not help but reinforce Ramón's commitment to Huichol culture and religious ideology, his oft-expressed belief in the inherent superiority of "being Huichol," as he and Lupe understood it, and his determination to complete what he had started—becoming a practicing mara'akáme. I counted myself very lucky and privileged to have made contact with such a man and to have achieved a close relationship of mutual trust. As every ethnologist knows, this is not always easy to achieve.

After a few days of getting acquainted, during which Ramón must have decided we were all right, I met Guadalupe. She appeared one day at Zapópan to sell her splendid weavings and embroideries, some of the best I had seen, at Padre Ernesto's Huichol shop. She was obviously a woman of great strength and, although gregarious and always full of laughter, great dignity. Although like Ramón she had been distanced for most of her life from her birthplace in the Sierra Nayar and the traditional comunidades in the mountains, in every other respect she was very, very Huichol. Soon we stopped meeting at Zapópan and repaired to their rancho for our conversations—much to Ramón's relief, because, he explained, although he liked and was grateful to the good padre for his many favors, he did not quite trust him to not "steal our religion."

What impressed me from the start were the good humor and self-assurance with which Ramón and Lupe made Huichols traveling to and from the Sierra welcome, and how when these visitors—for the most part, obviously very poor and often only minimally conversant in Spanish—needed help in the mysterious ways of the bureaucracy, they extended it. He was even more gregarious than Lupe, generous, often self-serving, frequently exasperating. On two or three occasions, with money in his pocket from the sale of yarn paintings (we never paid him for his narratives), he disappeared for a day or two, sheepishly explaining upon his return that he had invited some Indians and mestizos, "muy amigos" (great friends) all, as his guests at the *pulqerías* (taverns). (Lupe eventually fixed that by asking that we pay her instead of him for his yarn paintings—to which she usually contributed the finishing touches.) He was completely indifferent to the time constraints under which people like ourselves often have to operate, so that, having kept us waiting for hours or even days, he would reappear with a little smile, as though to say, "I am here, aren't I?" Not infrequently, his sense of humor, like that of other Huichols I have known, was of the kind that laughs at someone else's expense—the sort Oliver La Farge called "Indian laughter" in one of his *New Yorker* stories (Caffey 1988:141–154).

Above all, Ramón had a strong sense of self as a Huichol in an alien world that came through clearly, especially as I watched him dealing with representatives of the dominant Mexican culture. He was no shrinking violet, and he had no feelings of inferiority as an Indian vis-à-vis the dominant society—quite the contrary. Unlike some other Indians (especially in highland Guatemala, where I once watched in dismay and anger as descendants of one of the great civilizations of the ancient world approached a minor Ladino bureaucrat on their knees, hats in hand), Ramón would without hesitation approach a Mexican policeman with his Huichol visitors in tow, introduce himself as a Huichol, and politely but firmly ask directions to some government office. And he would be given them, with grudging respect. On one of these occasions, the policeman insisted on personally escorting him to the desired destination. When I asked Ramón later what he had said to so impress the officer, Ramón replied, a big grin on his face: "I told him I was a Huichol, *puro Huichol de la Sierra, con sangre negro*" (a pure Huichol from the Sierra, with black blood). It was one of his favorite ways of defining himself, and he used it even as a signature for narratives he dictated into my tape recorder.

Precariously balanced as he was between two worlds, Ramón seemed to me the epitome of the culture broker. Yet, he was not a marginal man, in the accepted sense of that term, because although living on the edges of two cultures, he identified himself—without hesitation and with considerable force—with only one, his own.

Their immediate physical environment, their little Huichol rancho in exile, did not last. They were squatters, and without any title to the land they were cultivating and on which they had built their modest home, they lost it all to urban sprawl the following year. After staying with us for a few weeks, they returned to Ramón's maternal rancho on the lower Río Santiago. But while it lasted, with a constant stream of Huichol visitors—some of whom remained for a few hours, others days—with occasional domestic rituals for rain, crops, and health for themselves and relatives; with discussions of peyote pilgrimages and other ceremonial activities to come; with Huichol music and Huichol speech, their little enclave in Guadalajara was in many ways a world unto itself, transposed from another time and place into the improbable environment of Mexico's second-largest and still expanding city.

THE NEED FOR BALANCE

This, then, was the social context of Ramón's dramatization at the waterfall. Looking back on it now, in the final analysis—with or without the complete story as it eventually emerged thanks to Lupe's lively memory, and whether or not her Aitá was literally the waterfall in one of the many versions of the peyote myth or merely served Ramón as a geographically convenient equivalent—his performance loses none of its original import: that of the shaman as performer, putting on stage, making concrete the idea of the exquisite inner balance that is required to cross from one state of being to another, from one world to another. It is a given in the specifically Huichol form of shamanism, as in Huichol social and ceremonial affairs, that equilibrium must be maintained or, if it is disturbed, be re-established.

This fits with the assumption that the individual who lacks equilibrium cannot hope to complete as a mara'akáme. The very first peyote pilgrimage, as the myth that is its charter makes clear, was intended to cure the gods who had become sick and hence were out of balance, thereby restoring the ecological equilibrium. Indeed, as Preuss observed in 1907, one of the most important rituals in the Huichol ceremonial cycle is the curing of all of the gods. This is held only every few years rather than annually, like other ceremonies. According to this early-twentieth-century German ethnographer and linguist (and confirmed six decades later by Ramón), the ancestor gods are judged to be ill and out of balance if they have not been giving sufficient rain. The curing chant and its attendant rituals restore them to health and, implicitly, the world to its proper ecological balance. All this sounds very much like the winter ceremonials in North America that are intended to restore a world that has gone out of kilter or like "walking in beauty" in Navajo ritual: putting things and individuals that have become unsettled, out of equilibrium, within

themselves and, vis-à-vis their social, natural, and supernatural environment, back on the "Beauty Way."

What Navajos call the Beauty Way, Huichols know as "being of
one heart," and they apply it as much to the individual as to groups
engaged in some common sacred enterprise, such as the ceremonial
deer or the hunt for the peyote, which re-enacts the primordial hunt for
the sacred deer peyote by the ancestor gods under the physical guidance of the shaman and the spiritual guidance of Kauyumari, who himself is deer. Myerhoff (1974:102) makes the interesting point that even
the insistence upon proper placement of the participants in the peyote
pilgrimage and maintenance of this precise order throughout its con-
stituent ritual events—the repeated circling of the sacred fire, for example—are "closely associated with the Huichol sense of propriety and
balance." Elsewhere (1974:253) she notes that in religions dominated by
the personality of the shaman (which is true of Huichol religion),

> the special responsibility of the shaman is to return to *illud tem-*
> *pore* on behalf of his people, to make his ecstatic journey
> through the assistance of animal tutelary spirits and bring back
> information of the other realms to ordinary mortals. As mediator,
> the shaman travels back and forth and, with exquisite balance . . .
> His soul leaves his body during trance states and by means of a
> magical flight he rejoins that which was once unified—man and
> animals, the living and the dead, man and the gods.

The Huichol shaman does even more than that for his group, she
points out, because he shares with them all that existed before the
world began when he takes the pilgrims to *illud tempus*—they having
transformed into the ancestor gods by virtue of having taken their
names, functions, and original placement in the line, just as he assumes
the identity of the First Mara'akáme, the old fire god, who is addressed
as Tatewarí, our Grandfather. Fear of falling into the abyss to his death
metaphysically or in actuality, his failure to accomplish that crucial transition on the dangerous passage in his initiatory self-training, would
make assuming such great responsibility impossible. I might add that
incidents or threats of losing their balance and falling from high places
to their death or severe injury abound in Huichol accounts of attempted
seductions of people away from the proper path of life by sorcerers,
certain animals, or the spirit owners of psychoactive plants other than

the sacred peyote. No doubt the extremely rugged environment in which the Huichols live—with its high cliffs, cultivated fields clinging precariously to steep slopes, and canyons hundreds of feet deep—reinforces this imagery. But it is not just environmentally determined, because the same imagery of dangerous crevasses and yawning chasms exists in the mental geography of shamans who live in environments that are completely flat.

Examples of the need for fearlessness and balance in the initiatory shamanic journey can be found throughout the Indian Americas, no less than in Central or Eastern Asia. For the New World I limit myself to a pertinent passage from Johannes Wilbert's first published discussion of the Warao *wishiratu* shaman's experience when he travels to the world of the spirits in his tobacco-induced trance. The Warao have been making their homes in the delta of the Orinoco River for hundreds of years. This is a vast swampland, thickly covered by trees and mangrove swamps, traversed by innumerable *caños*, large and small, draining into the sea. Thus it lacks the fearsome gorges and mountains that populate the inner world of the shaman but that, for their invisibility to the ordinary eye, are no less real in the landscape of the mind.

What Wilbert's shaman informant told him of his initiatory experience is much more dramatic than any of Ramón's accounts of the dangers that await the novice Huichol shaman who lacks a secure grip on himself when he crosses a yawning barranca of the sort that really does exist in his natural environment. But the meaning is the same:

> Then the young *wishiratu* has to clear an abyss filled with hungry jaguars, snapping alligators, and frenzied sharks all eager to devour him. A vine hangs down over the abyss and, grasping it firmly, the novice swings himself across. But this is still not the end of his ordeal. Soon he reaches another obstacle. The path becomes extremely slippery, so that he can hardly keep his balance. To make matters worse, on every side are threatening demons armed with spears, waiting to kill him. (Wilbert 1972:64)

A "NATION OF SHAMANS"

According to Eliade, shamanism is pre-eminently, although by no means exclusively, a phenomenon of the hunting way of life. The fact that it persists to such a remarkable degree among the Huichols requires some discussion. How long they have been sedentary maize planters is a matter of dispute among ethnographers and ethnohistorians of the Huichols that is beyond the scope of this chapter, but we can at least agree that it has been many centuries. Yet, their religious life continues to be dominated by shamans and the shamanic worldview. Lumholtz estimated during his stay with them in the 1890s that least at a third of adult men were "doctors," that is, shamans. He even thought, mistakenly, that Wixarika (Wizrrarika), the Huichols' name for themselves, meant doctors ("Huichol" is a Spanish corruption and is not used except when Huichols speak Spanish).

Around seventy years after Lumholtz, the idea that with their high proportion of "doctors" the Huichols could rightly be called a nation of shamans, appeared at first improbable to those of us who started looking at aspects of their intellectual culture in the mid-1960s. Family band shamanism seemed incompatible with a well-integrated agricultural way of life, even one that retains a strong component of hunting ideology. But I soon came to see that Lumholtz was essentially correct, provided one discriminates between those shaman-singers—comparatively few in number—who are closely associated with temple organization and ritual and often enjoy high prestige, even outside their own immediate communities, and those many others who function essentially on the level of the extended family, the residential communities that constitute the widely scattered, semi-isolated Huichol ranchos or rancherías. In fact, it is precisely this widely dispersed settlement pattern that favors— even requires—the sort of family band shamanism usually found in hunting-and-gathering societies but that here is embedded in a sedentary horticultural context.

As noted, the Huichol landscape is extremely rugged. Many Huichol ranchos may be within shouting distance of each other yet be separated by many hours of strenuous climbing to the bottom of a steep gorge and up the other side. There are no pueblos and no villages, and the ceremonial and native government centers are virtually empty of people except on the several annual community-wide syncretistic ceremonials that became established, along with the comunidades themselves, when the Spanish won nominal control of the Sierra Indians in 1722. This is why rancho elders also frequently perform the functions of family shaman. Other male and some female members of the local group may also decide to become shamans.

However, here as elsewhere, shamanism tends to run in families, and it is my impression that individuals who numbered shamans among their forebears are more likely than others to hear and heed a supernatural call to embark upon the long and arduous path of the future mara'akáme.

THE SHAMAN AS DOCTOR

It is beyond question that, as Lumholtz recognized so long ago, many Huichol adults are sufficiently versed in the sacred mythology and the proper rituals for both agriculture and hunting deer, rabbit, or peccary, and in the native system of illness and curing, to function as singing and curing shamans, although usually not beyond their own extended family rancho compound. Most Huichol shamans today are still very much in the tradition of family band shamanism that is typical of nomadic or semi-sedentary hunter-gatherer societies and of northwest Mexican Indian cultures in general, and curing is one of their crucial functions.

There are basically two mechanisms by which, in the Huichol view (as in that of many Native Americans), people become ill and fall out of balance with their social and natural environment and the gods. One is soul loss, meaning that the soul—in particular that one of the several souls "owned" by a Huichol that resides in the top of the head—has become separated from its proper place (for more on this soul, see Furst 1967:51–56). The other is the sickness projectile or, in Huichol terms, the "arrow of sickness," that has been shot into the body from afar by supernatural means. These two principal agencies of illness function side by side, the second being seemingly more common than the first. In either case the cure is up to the shaman.

But before a cure can even commence, shamans must determine, by divination and other techniques, why the patient fell ill. For counsel they can also call on another kind of arrow, whose basic form is the same as that of hunting or magical arrows but to which is attached a very special kind of supernatural power—the *urukáme*, from *urú*, arrow. Because the shamans and the elders of the rancho community consult their *urukátes* (pl.) on many matters and follow their advice, the urukáte have enormous importance in the life of the rancho and even beyond. An urukáme is the soul of an ancestor that, after having manifested its desire to dwell once again among its relatives and give protection and advice to the elder or shaman in the manner of a family guardian spirit, has returned to the rancho in the form of a small, colored stone or quartz crystal. The idea of the urukáme, which outwardly looks like a little bundle attached to an ordinary arrow, whose existence was first noted by Lumholtz—who collected one or, apparently, the replica of one, for the American Museum of Natural History—has since been dealt with in greater detail by other investigators (Furst 1967; Perrin n.d.).

The subject is too complex and important to discuss here, but a brief description is useful. An urukáme may signal its wish to return from the other world by sending an illness, either to the shaman or to some member of his or her family, often a child. If divination determines an urukáme to be the cause, the shaman goes on a dream journey to look for the soul and bring it back in its concrete manifestation as a little stone. Because dead shamans are thought to travel with the sun, this may require that they pass through a fiery curtain of solar rays and through other obstacles of the sort familiar from the literature on what Eliade called "the paradoxical passage."

The little crystal embodying the ancestral soul is sealed inside a bamboo tube that, wrapped in a special little weaving, is tied to the shaft of a compound arrow. Over his or her lifetime a shaman or elder may acquire several urukáte as guardians and advisers. The urukáte are kept inside the *xiriki*—the family temple or oratory within the rancho that is set aside for the family altar, images of deities, stores of peyote, ceremonial paraphernalia, snares, and other equipment used in the ritual deer hunt and the like—and are consulted on important ritual and practical matters. (It is noteworthy that despite their power they are not treated with overt reverence; thus, on my first visit to his rancho, Nicholás Carrillo de la Cruz—known as 'Colas—the great mara'akáme of San Andrés Cohamiata [Figure 5.14], having seen me steal a glance at an urukáme stuck into the thatch of his xiriki next to my head, pulled it out, handed it to me, and urged me to take it apart to see what was inside the bamboo tube. It was a strange feeling, holding an ancestor of this grand old man in my hands. As casual and lighthearted as Huichols often seem to be about their sacred objects and events, and as curious as I was, I could not bring myself to follow his suggestion.)

Causes of illness include failure to fulfill vows made to deities, bad winds (the *mal aires* on which illness is blamed throughout rural Mesoamerica), displeasure by ancestors or different gods at having been neglected, sorcery, or a punishment by the souls of animals and plants or other phenomena of the environment that feel mistreated. According to Ramón, children are especially prone to loss or theft of

FIGURE 5.14

Nicholás Carrillo de la Cruz (d. 1974), whom everyone knew as 'Colas, was respected as the wisest and greatest of the shaman-singers and elders of San Andrés Cohamiata. Here, at dawn on the second day of the ceremony of the parching of the maize, he dips the feathers of his muviéri into a votive gourd bowl to spray water from a sacred spring toward the Land of Dawn to greet the sun god and help him ascend into the sky. (Photograph by Peter T. Furst, June 1967) their souls. Shamans dream the cause of illness over several nights, and during this preparatory time they are supposed to abstain from ordinary foods and sex. These restrictions are self-policed, because there is no authority—other than the gods themselves—to see to their enforcement. Yet, people around them can see what the shamans are up to, and not doing what is expected would soon cause their commitment and effectiveness to be doubted. Treatment is generally "supernatural," or what we would call psychosomatic, but we should not underrate the numerous herbal remedies in the shamans' practical pharmacopoeia. Unfortunately, the once extensive knowledge of the healing powers of plants is rapidly being lost. Whether the cause of illness is thought to be soul loss or sickness intrusion, both the underlying assumptions and the techniques by which Huichol shamans restore, or try to restore, their patients to health will, except for culture-specific details, be familiar to students of shamanism.

Let us first consider soul loss. Huichols proceed from the assumption that people have several souls, of which one, the *kupüri,* has its locus in the region of the anterior fontanelle.

Like native peoples generally, Huichols believe the soul, or life force, is separable from the body not just at death but at any time—voluntarily, accidentally, or by some forceful action of an adversary or supernatural. The kupüri may wander off during sleep and become lost, or it may be captured by a hostile sorcerer or an animal spirit. It may fall out in an accident and, unless it is quickly located and retrieved, may be devoured by malevolent animals under the control of sorcerers, which, of course, would mean death. Such a calamity may happen, for example, when a man stumbles and hits his head against a rock while clearing brush for a new maize field or while he is cutting firewood along a steep slope. Or stones may come loose and hit a woman on the head while she is collecting mesquite seeds. Let me quote Ramón:

> One falls there, and one hits one's head on a rock. Then that kupüri, that which is the soft spot on the head, the crown of the head which is the life of the soul, falls to one side. The kupüri falls and is frightened.
>
> One lies there and cannot think. One is not dead and one is not asleep. But one lies there, not moving. Then after a while one gets up from there, feeling bad. . . . One cannot think properly. One has no thoughts. One is out of one's mind,

as one says. One walks off-balance. It is because everything fell. One returns home, but one cannot do anything.

Then the relatives go to the mara'akáme. They say to him, "Well, this and that happened to our relative. This man fell. This one fell in such and such a place." (Furst 1967)

The shaman now goes to the injured man's rancho with his takwátsi, the basket that holds his power objects. In the curing ritual that follows, the shaman calls upon Kauyumari to come and assist him. So far the shaman only knows that his patient has fallen and hit his head. From the fact that he is unconscious or semiconscious, he may assume that the patient has lost his vital essence. But because the patient is still breathing, he knows that the fine, spider-silklike thread by which, according to Ramón, the soul is connected to the head has not been cut by a sorcerer or hostile animal spirit. If it has been cut and the shaman is unable to reconnect it, the patient will perish. In order to effect the soul's recovery, the curer must divine what or who made the patient fall. If the shaman finds that the accident was caused by a displeased deity or an animal that has been offended, he must tell the patient how the offense may be undone. If a hostile shaman—that is, a sorcerer— was responsible, the curer may turn the evil around by hurling his arrow of sickness in his enemy's direction.

When he has completed all of the requirements and, through Kauyumari, obtained agreement of help from the relevant deities, the curing shaman sets out to determine where "the life" has been dropped and what, if anything, happened to it as the injured man made his way home. According to Ramón, the shaman makes this search by sending out his muviéris, his ceremonial arrows, whose basic form is the compound, wooden-tipped hunting arrow but that has free-swinging feathers attached to the nock end—the notched end into which the bowstring would fit in practical use but that points forward when the arrow is employed ceremonially. At the shaman's behest the feathers travel through the air searching for the lost soul and listening for the high-pitched whistling sound it is said to emit. The shaman, or the feathers, emits a similar sound, which the soul perceives and to which it responds, its voice becoming ever louder the closer the shaman, or his feathered emissaries, comes to it. This idea that the soul emits a whistling sound and can be located or summoned by whistling is shared by some other contemporary Mesoamerican Indians. (Considering the demonstrable continuities between the Indian past and present, this seems to me the best expla-nation for the enormous number of anthropomorphic and zoomorphic whistles found in pre-Columbian burials.) To quote Ramón once more:

> The mara'akáme goes looking and looking, searching, listening and listening, until he arrives where that man tripped and rolled over into the barranca. And even if it is a perilous place full of sharp rocks, full of dangerous animals, with scorpions and snakes, the mara'akáme is not afraid. Even if there are dangerous animals there, he must not be afraid. . . .
>
> He comes closer and it begins to whimper. It hisses and whistles like a soft wind. It hisses softly, in the same manner in which Tatewarí hisses when he is first lit, when the wood that is his food is not dry.
>
> Then the mara'akáme listens to this sound with his feath-ers, with his arrows. Then he goes there very carefully, very slowly. He may find that life under a branch, or under a leaf, or under a small stone as he walks there on the ground. That life, it is only as small as the smallest insect, the smallest tick. That is how small it is. (Furst 1967:54–55)

Once the shaman has found the soul, he carefully raises it on the feathers of his muviéri and places it inside the hollow piece of bamboo that is the Huichol equivalent of the familiar soul catchers of carved ivory in Northwest Coast shamanism, seals off each end with a wad of wild cotton from the cottonwood tree, and secures it among the arrows and other power objects in his takwátsi. Then, says Ramón, he returns home with his feathered muviéris and reinstates the soul in its custom-ary place through "the soft spot in the head"—the anterior fontanelle (Furst 1967:52–56).

Even when soul loss is attributed to an accident, such as a fall, or someone cuts himself with a machete—events we would regard as accidents—the gods or some other supernatural agency are ultimately held responsible. Why did this man fall? Who tripped him? Why did the machete cut him? To illustrate: in 1967, when I was in San Andrés Cohamiata as codirector of a UCLA summer field school in indigenous health care, the son of 'Colas, a handsome young man who wore his hair long in the traditional way, came back one day from cutting brush with an ugly wound on his shin. The wound, he said, was made by his machete when it hit a stone and flew out of his hand. He and his shaman father conversed quietly for a moment, and then 'Colas explained to us that the machete had been angry because his son had forgotten to give it ceremonial food at the last Ceremony of the Feeding of the Tools. The machete's spirit had asked Tatewarí to give him a *golpe,* a blow, to remind him not to repeat so serious a violation, which was why it had turned on him. One of our medical students, delighted at the chance to demonstrate his skill on a real, live patient, cleaned and disinfected the wound, covered it with a bandage, and sent him on his way with instructions to return in a day or so for a checkup and a change of bandage. He was greatly disappointed to discover, upon unwrapping the now very dirty bandage, that the leg wound was still open and running, whereas another severe cut the young man had suffered on his arm at the same time, which had been covered by his sleeve and about which he had forgotten to tell the foreign *medico,* was already nicely healed with no trace of infection. The young man had treated this second wound himself with a poultice made of "some leaves." For our students it was a dual lesson: first, they witnessed the widespread belief among native peoples that not just humans and animals and all the phenomena of the natural environment but also the tools are sentient, endowed with a soul or life force, and must be treated accordingly lest they turn on you; and second, they saw that native remedies may be as effective or, as in this case, even more effective than those provided by Western medical science.

Most commonly, an intrusive sickness is thought to be sent by the gods, one of whom may have been offended by something the patient did or did not do or who may even have been prevailed upon by a hostile shaman to visit sickness upon an enemy. Lumholtz (1902:238) mentions the following among the things that might displease a god enough to cause that god to shoot an illness: failure to make sufficient sacrifices, not hunting deer sufficiently, or not performing a ceremony well. Forgetting a solemn vow is another serious offense. In cases in which a deity has been negatively influenced by a sorcerer, he writes, "it becomes a question of power among the shamans which of them can influence the gods more effectively—the bad one to make ill, or the good one to cure" (1902:238).

Sorcery is, in fact, a real problem for Huichols. I have heard shamans, including Ramón, insist vehemently that someone is a "sorcerer" rather than a shaman, only to hear the one so labeled say the same thing about the accuser. The truth is that a shaman who can cure can also cause sickness and that any shaman is capable of turning his or her arts in the wrong direction. Also, shamans who failed to complete are sometimes suspected of practicing sorcery. Needless to say, this knowledge tends to spur faltering novices on to finish what they started. According to Lumholtz, knowledge of sorcery or witchcraft may come to a shaman with age. No doubt, elderly shamans would indignantly reject such an idea (as I have heard one of them do), which is understandable, because persons charged with sorcery may suffer severe beatings or even forfeit their lives. In any event, according to Lumholtz, in order to do sorcery, an old shaman has to separate from his wife, abstain from salt, and obtain some physical part of his intended victim through the agency of the owl and the goatsucker. The sorcerer dreams the birds to the victim's head, where they pull a hair to bring back to him. When he wakes he finds the hair near his bed and puts it in a hollow reed, which he seals with wax. He then ties it to an arrow of the god to whose wrath he leaves the victim; if the god declines to help, the sorcery cannot succeed (Lumholtz 1902:238).

Goatsuckers, owls, and other nocturnal birds are especially efficacious for negative magic, or sorcery, and so are apt to be recruited as spirit helpers for nefarious purposes; among other birds, eagles, hawks, cranes, hummingbirds, and macaws and other parrots play that essential role for "good" shamans. Other potent animal helpers include various species of snakes, including the rattlesnake, as well as such reptiles as the venomous Gila monster, *Heloderma suspectum,* or its local variant, the Beaded lizard. A special ally of Tatewarí, and hence of his human counterpart, the mara'akáme, is the so-called horned toad, actually a small, spiny lizard of the genus *Phrynosora.* Huichols identify the horns on its head with those of deer and the bumps and line along its back and tail with the peyoteros' mountainous path to Wirikuta.

Whether the sickness was sent by a deity or a human sorcerer, to neutralize the sickness projectile and effect the cure the shaman hired by the victim or his or her family—against sometimes quite substantial remuneration in cash or in-kind—must not only discover its source through dreams but must determine what the patient must do to reconcile the offended god. That accomplished, he informs the patient and sets about the process of curing.

The way Lumholtz described the techniques parallels almost exactly what I saw Ramón do with a female participant in the 1968 peyote pilgrimage. The patient's illness consisted of not having been able to conceive. Ramón, who on the pilgrimage assumed the identity of Tatewarí and was so addressed by his companions (just as he addressed them by the names of the ancestor gods whose identities they had assumed), decided that the most favorable place for such a cure would be Tateimatiniéri, Where Our Mothers Dwell, the sacred water holes at the edge of a former lake in Zacatecas that are the manifestations of the eastern goddesses of rain and terrestrial water. He told his patient to lie flat on her back in front of the other peyoteros and bare her stomach. Squatting beside her, he sang for a while—shamans always begin their work by singing a chant that calls upon Kauyumari, whose home is at the eastern end of the world, to come to their assistance. That done, he began wringing his hands several times and cracking his joints, a gesture that, according to Lumholtz (1902:239), is meant to imitate "the crackling of the fire, the greatest of all shamans." He blew his breath and spat into his cupped hands, gestured toward the sacred world directions, and began to massage the patient's bared stomach and, while chanting, to squeeze and push from the four directions toward a central point. He also spat and blew his breath on her chest, head, and belly, and he repeated this with the smoke of a cornhusk cigarette made with the potent native *Nicotiana rustica* tobacco. Finally, he bent over her and, placing his mouth on the skin near her belly button, sucked mightily, at last spitting something we could not see into his hand. After holding up whatever it was close to her face for her to see and then displaying it in the direction of her attentive companions, he flung it with great force and a look of disgust to the ground, gesturing and waving it away as though he meant for it to be taken on the wind (afterward he explained that it was snatched up by a whirlwind only he could see and feel). He also spoke urgently to her, later explaining to us that Tatewarí had given him instructions for the offerings she had to make to render the cure effective. That done, the woman got up, rearranged her clothing, and resumed her ritual activities with the other peyoteros. However one chooses to explain it, I was told that a year later she became pregnant and gave birth. To her and her husband, this must have been proof that Ramón was indeed a powerful healer.

Huichols know that in overcoming illness in this way, the healer himself is subject to supernatural danger, for if he is dealing with a sorcerer, the latter may sneak up on him unseen from the back and shoot him with a sickness projectile. According to Ramón, one way for the shaman to protect himself is for his wife to protect his back, a custom that may explain the meaning of marriage pairs from ancient shaft and chamber tombs in Jalisco that have the woman seated directly behind, and slightly to the left of, the man. Another kind of peril lies in the fact that illness often manifests itself to the shaman in the form of a ferocious little animal, the *itáuki*, which only he can see and which he must kill by hurling—in song if not in fact—his feathered muviéri at it with great force, as though he were shooting an arrow from his bow.

Although some shamans work without singing, most rites—whether to recover the soul or extract a magical pathogen by sucking or to heal the natural or supernatural environment—require a lengthy chant. Preuss (1907, 1908) had the good fortune to witness a number of curing ceremonies and to record, on paper and wax cylinders, six major curing chants, including the preliminary prophylactic curing song in which Kauyumari interrogates the gods on behalf of Tatewarí and the singing shaman. One of these chants was for a serious illness, in which the gods tell the shaman, again through Kauyumari, who sent it and what is required for its cure; another was for the curing of livestock; yet another was for curing the earth when it fails to bring forth the fruits of life; one was for the curing of rain, which is intended to bring down the life-giving waters; and a very important chant was for the curing of the gods themselves, discussed earlier. I should mention that when a chant contains several speaking parts—Tatewarí, the gods, the shaman's own feathered muviéris, which are alive and able to speak, and Kauyumari—the singing shaman alone gives them voice, notwithstanding the presence of his assistants, who periodically repeat passages of the sacred song (Preuss 1909:43–44).

Significantly, almost all of the curing chants, which typically require an entire night to complete, involve the killing of the mythological animal, the itáuki. According to Preuss (1908:376–377), the dead itáuki is embodied in the foreign objects the shaman sucks from the patient or removes with his muviéris when the patient is the earth, rain, or the gods themselves. Preuss calls the killing of the disease-bearing itáuki "an arduous undertaking in which the singer falls shaking and vomiting to the ground. But this is done less in fact than in song." Preuss also saw a shaman start such a curing ceremony by first spitting all around the darkened patio, stroking different household items with his arrow and then hurling it in different directions in the hope of hitting and killing the dangerous itáuki, a mythic creature visible only to the shaman that reminds one of the *sisiutl* of the Northwest Coast.

HUICHOL SHAMANS AND MODERN MEDICINE

The shaman as curer, then, is alive and well among the Huichols as a vital link between people and what we would call the supernatural but that for the Indians, as guardians of the old knowledge and traditions, is an integral part of the natural world. But this should not be taken to mean that Huichols reject modern medicine, prefer the shaman to the medical doctor in every instance of illness, or invariably attribute every affliction to some magical or extrahuman cause. Not even shamans would do so. As an example: the mara'akáme 'Colas of the indigenous comunidad of San Andrés Cohamiata, where I had my introduction to traditional life and ritual in the Sierra Huichol, once told me that many illnesses from which Huichols suffer today did not exist before foreigners came to the Sierra. For these foreign scourges he had no songs. Thus, for some things—indeed, those that were most likely to prove fatal—the people had to turn to the foreign curers and their drugs. Such openness favors the introduction of Western medicine, provided the health professional approaches the Indians with the necessary cultural sensitivity, culture-specific training, and a healthy respect for native knowledge and experience.

In my experience, few do so, but I have fond memories of one such sensitive young doctor. I was invited by Salomón Nahmad, a Mexican social anthropologist who was then the director of the Cora-Huichol Center of the Instituto Nacional Indigenista (INI) in Tepic, to accompany him and Enrique Chávez, M.D., the INI medical officer, on a flight by bush plane to San Andrés Cohamiata. We landed just as the great mara'akáme 'Colas was conducting the "Parching of the Maize" ceremony (Furst 1967). Although it has other purposes as well, this ceremony can be understood essentially as a rain-calling ritual, because in it a young girl, who must be "new"—that is, not yet have begun an adult sex life—pops maize kernels of the popcorn variety on the fire into shapes that resemble and are meant to represent the billowing white rain clouds that herald the coming of the rains at the beginning of summer. The place of the all-day and all-night ceremony (during which a ritual clown kept people awake and attentive by drawing a bull penis dangling on a long stick across the face of those who fell

asleep, myself included) was the patio of 'Colas's rancho. It was followed at dawn with the presentation to the Sun Father and the first
naming of the old man's newest grandchild. Professor Nahmad's mission was to ask whether the community elders were interested in getting a gasoline-powered electric generator to provide light for the INI
store, the INI primary school, the *casa real* (used by the elected civil-
religious community officials for their deliberations), and perhaps even
the large, circular *tuki*, the indigenous temple. After deliberation by a
council of elders, presided over by 'Colas, the offer was rejected (things
have changed greatly since then). As 'Colas—whose prestige was such
that people in San Andrés Cohamiata regarded him as the embodiment
of Tatewarí himself—put it, Tatewarí, who is embodied in the sacred
fire, was sufficient to light up the night. The noise of the generator
would make it impossible to hear the animals and birds, and it would
even drown out the voices of the gods.

Dr. Chávez, whose first field experience was with the Huichols and
who, unaware of the symbolism of the popcorn, had earlier scooped
up a handful and popped it into his mouth (causing great hilarity,
rather than anger, among the very tolerant participants in the ritual),
fared better. He told 'Colas that he had brought medicines to cure the
chronic diarrhea caused by intestinal parasites and to immunize the
children against measles and other diseases that kill half of them before
age five. But, he added, none of his drugs and needles and other tools
of his trade had the power to heal unless and until 'Colas, the great
mara'akáme of San Andrés, asked his gods to put the power into them.
I was much impressed, because this showed respect, which is rare in
the medical profession, for native ways. It made 'Colas an ally and eliminated any chance that the powerful Huichol shaman would resent the
potential undermining of his own prestige as a healer. It was moving to
see a visibly pleased 'Colas put his arm around the younger man's
shoulders and tell him that from now on he was "Mara'akáme Chico,"
Little Shaman. Thereafter, Dr. Chávez had no problem doing what he
felt was needed for the health of his Huichol patients. If only all
Western medical doctors approached native peoples with such sensitivity and respect.

In early 1974, when 'Colas was seriously ill, a Mexican friend offered
to take him to Mexico City for diagnosis. 'Colas agreed but said he
would come on his own. How? his friend asked. By bus, 'Colas said. Sick
as he was, and in pain, he was as good as his word. He was examined

by specialists, and, anticipating their verdict, which was that his illness was terminal and surgery would do little good, he announced he was going home to see to his affairs and that he would die before the onset of the rains. He died before the first rain of the wet season fell and, on his own instructions, was interred in the floor of a house he had built many years before (Guillermo Espinosa, personal communication).

Like this grand old man, some shamans enjoy a greater reputation than others as singers of the sacred chants in the temple rites and also as curers; Lumholtz (1902:237) mentions one, a woman widely recognized as a singing shaman who was "frequently employed at the ranchos nearby both to sing and to cure." She was the only woman shaman he says he heard of during his stay in the Sierra, and "she is very chary with her patronage, and though the people have wanted her to sing in the temple, she has never consented to do so." The percentage of women among Huichol shamans is unknown, but there seem to be more today than there were in Lumholtz's time.

THE CALL TO SHAMANISM

How does a Huichol became a shaman? Lumholtz (1902:236) has provided this simple answer, which is as valid now as it was in his time, but it is still only part of the story.

Anybody who has a natural gift may become a shaman. Such a gift will be evidenced from early youth by a young person being more interested in the ceremonies and paying more attention to the singing than ordinary youths do. The feasts, where they acquire knowledge of the gods and their doings by listening to the songs of the shaman, are the only school the people attend. I have heard children no older than age five or six sing temple songs that are caught as the street children in our cities catch popular airs. In addition, a young person may ask an older shaman for information, but there is no regular system of teaching.

If anyone can become a shaman by his or her own volition, it is also a fact that, as noted earlier, family histories reveal that even though it may skip a generation, the vocation tends to run in families. It is self-evident that their mother being a practicing shaman had a decisive influence on the path taken by her son and daughter, Ramón and Concha. As Lumholtz observed, future shamans learn the shamanic arts primarily by watching and listening from an early age. They also do so through dreams—spontaneous and induced by peyote—in which they encounter the gods and hear from them how to predict the weather, locate the good places for hunting, call for rain, and properly conduct all of the rituals required to ward off misfortune and assure an abundant life for their people. There are also what Ramón called "secrets," which the novice can assimilate only from experienced and respected specialists. In most cases the informal mentor is an older relative. Ramón's real teacher was clearly, first, his mother. It was by watching and listening to her (who, along with other relatives of his or Lupe's, he frequently visited during our association) that he must have acquired much of the prodigious quantity of sacred lore and other esoteric knowledge that so impressed us and others who came to know him in the 1960s (cf. Benítez 1968).

Lumholtz surely did not mean to imply that becoming a shaman was easy, because as we saw with Ramón, and as other students of the Huichols—both in and out of the Sierra—have stressed, it is certainly not. The Huichol pantheon is crowded, and the inventory of sacred chants and rituals is extensive. Future shamans must acquire an enormous store of practical and esoteric knowledge—of the natural and supernatural environment, of animals and birds, of weather, of the sacred geography of this and Otherworlds, and of the many pitfalls that await one. As Ramón once put it with simple eloquence, "In this life one does not go lacking for something with which to get stuck in the eye."

Future shamans spend years taking on and fulfilling many obligations to the ancestor deities and acquiring different animals, including birds and reptiles, as spirit helpers. They must also demonstrate their knowledge, strength, and wisdom repeatedly if they are to earn and retain the respect and trust of their fellows. Ramón said he promised his tutelary deities, the old fire god Tatewarí and the Sun god, that he would learn everything well and that when he had done so, he would lead five peyote pilgrimages. Then, at the conclusion of the fifth, his "brothers"—that is, relatives—would surely accept him as a mara'akáme. This accords with what Robert Zingg found in the 1930s: "Peyote-hunting is necessary for all who would be shamans among the Huichols. This was established by Grandfather Fire. When the hunters of the Sun-father's party had all eaten peyote, it was *tatevalí*, the patron-god of shamans, who commanded, 'In five years you will know how to sing, cure, and be a shaman'" (Zingg 1938:305).

However, temple officers tend to double the number of peyote pilgrimages they should take to ten, and some older Huichols have made the arduous journey fifteen, twenty, and even thirty times. Ramón told me in 1966 that even though he had promised Tatewarí only five pilgrimages, he intended to go on many more and to keep on learning. By the time of his death in 1971, he had completed seven.

The point to remember is that regardless of the number of peyote hunts in which one has participated or that one has led, the right to call oneself a mara'akáme depends in the end upon consensus—the willingness of the shamans' community, their relations by blood or marriage, and the people they take to the peyote country to entrust to one of their members the business of conducting the rituals and dealing with the extrahuman forces. This consensus, and not merely his own conviction and satisfaction in having accomplished what as a young man he had vowed to the gods, is how and why Ramón—and others like him—could claim completion. Huichol life is precarious, and it is above all an effective mutual relationship of shamans with the nature deities, the proper performance of the many rituals of the annual ceremonial cycle, that assures the continuation of the cycle of life and hence survival for the community and health and well-being for the individual. And I cannot stress enough that these time-honored principles apply as much for the Huichols who were forced to flee and settle outside the Huichol territory as they do to those within its political boundaries.

SICKNESS VOCATION

Ramón once told me that his mother was ill when she had a revelation from the ancestors that she was to become a mara'akáme. This sounds and is much like the familiar "sickness vocation," a phenomenon of shamanic recruitment in which the future practitioner experiences a severe crisis. This crisis is taken as a summons from ancestor shamans or gods, and its cure may depend upon agreement to accept the call. I have heard too many such accounts from Huichols and other Mesoamerican Indians to doubt that a severe illness or similar personal crisis is here, as elsewhere, frequently involved in the call to shamanism. In Ramón's case, as a boy he was bitten on the leg by a coral snake while harvesting maize on a Mexican farm on the Nayarit coast. He nearly died, and for some months afterward he was paralyzed in both legs. This experience could be interpreted as a summons, because, as he told me, he regained full use of his legs only after a mara'akáme told him that Tayaupá, Sun Father, and Tatewarí, Grandfather Fire, wanted him to stay alive so he could become a mara'akáme.

The idea stayed with him, and he recalled that when he met Lupe while both worked for a rich Mexican farmer and she resisted his entreaties, he told her that one day he would become a mara'akáme. He said she was sure that he was boasting and told him to leave her alone. "She said she didn't like me at all, not one little bit," he told me. But a quarter of a century later, despite a severe—although temporary—marital crisis in the late 1960s, they were still a couple. And even though they were separated, in December 1968, Lupe readily participated at his side in the fifth of the five peyote pilgrimages he had vowed to lead with the goal of becoming a mara'akáme. And she stood at his side in the ceremony that marked his completion, loudly proclaiming that her husband was now a mara'akáme.

To be sure, although Benítez (1968:358) called him an *"aprendiz de cantador excepcional,"* an outstanding apprentice shaman-singer, and said that he was held in high regard and was admired as a superior person by all of the Huichols in the Río Lerma colony, who had heard him on the radio pleading for help to the Huichol people, no one would pretend—least of all Ramón himself—that this placed him on an equal plane with the great singers of the ceremonial centers in the Sierra. To a certain degree these men function, although never on a full-time basis, almost as much as priestly ritualists as they do as shamans in the traditional sense. So did Ramón, but he did so on the greatly reduced scale of the ranchos of the colony on the Río Lerma and the enclaves of Huichols living in urban centers rather than in the traditional comunidades in the Sierra.

Much of what constitutes "being Huichol"—the mother tongue; the pantheon of nature deities; the great stories of the mythic age; the old ceremonies, rituals, and sacrifices; the songs and dances; the fierce attachment to the land and the sacred crops; the deer-peyote-maize symbol complex; the myriad sacred places; and conscious and unconscious resistance against cultural and religious assimilation—has not only survived but is aggressively maintained and defended. Their defenders include not only those who still maintain themselves in the *comunidades indígenas* but some of those who, like Ramón's and Lupe's families, have moved away from the Huichol territory. Indeed, it is the diaspora Huichols who, if they want to maintain their cultural identity, need the knowledge and services of a knowledgeable shaman even more than their cousins in the mountains, whose physical isolation has helped to preserve cultural and religious integrity to so remarkable a degree after the Spanish, in 1722, finally achieved control—however nominal—over the rugged mountains of the Sierra Madre Occidental where the Coras and the Huichols make their homes.

THE SEXUAL TABOO

Like many other traditional peoples, the Huichols observe prohibitions against sexual activity before and during important rituals. Abstention from sex and salt (and also ordinary food and drink) is a prerequisite for the peyote pilgrimage. Lumholtz (1902) was the first to note a different, and much longer-lasting, sexual taboo for apprentice shamans. A man who has decided to become a shaman, he wrote, is expected to remain faithful to his wife for five years. Huichols will readily tell you that this is not easy, and few would probably do so were it not for the fear that the gods will exact punishment from anyone guilty of transgression: "If he violates this rule," wrote Lumholtz (1902:236), "he is sure to be taken ill, and will lose his power of curing. Not until the stated period of probation is passed may he have love affairs." It is generally agreed that this is still the case today. When a young man decides to become a mara'akáme and pledges himself accordingly to a tutelary deity, he must remain chaste for five years following his vow if he is unmarried or, if married, remain true to his wife. But what if he already has two or three wives? Polygamy, as Preuss noted at the beginning of the century, is acceptable to Huichols, and many such multiple unions exist in harmony. However, Huichols have told me that the sexual restriction may account, at least in part, for the fact that more men start out to become shamans than actually do so.

What makes things especially difficult for some shamans is that they may inherit vows made by a deceased relative who failed to complete before his death, even though they themselves have successfully passed through the long years of their own self-training (cf. Valadéz 1986b:30). Presumably, such a transfer of another's vow also requires a repetition of the five-year sexual taboo.

However seriously Huichol shamans take this restriction, the culture provides mechanisms to "undo" sexual transgressions. One is to make sacrifices, the nature of which is determined by the shaman through consultation with Kauyumari and the ancestor gods. Another,

more dramatic mechanism is purification through public disclosure near
the beginning of the peyote pilgrimage (Preuss 1908:384; Myerhoff
1974:131–138). In this ritual every participant in the forthcoming peyote
hunt—meaning not only those who will actually go to Wirikuta in
search of the sacred psychoactive cactus but also those who remain
behind and follow the sacred journey "in their hearts"—is expected to
divulge publicly by name every sexual partner other than his or her
spouse. Seated in a circle around the fire, the personification of
Tatewarí, peyoteros vigorously encourage one another to be frank and
open; to conceal anything would place the entire sacred enterprise in
jeopardy; the sacred deer (peyote) would not reveal itself; sorcerers
would deceive the peyotero into eating dangerously intoxicating plants,
such as *Datura*, or the "false peyote" (Furst 1969:31–39); and no rain
would fall on the maize. For each name and transgression, the officiating shaman ties a knot in a cord, which at the conclusion of this ritual
he consigns to the flames, with an appeal to the old fire god, the Great
Shaman "who does and undoes," to "burn it all away."

Yet, there is no dogma nor any religious or secular authority to
enforce conformity. Adherence to the rules comes solely from the conviction that the gods will punish the transgressor and will expect him or
her to pay them with sacrifices for the infraction. Thus, for example, a
shaman with the Huichol name Ulu Temay, Arrow Man, attributes a
long-lasting and serious illness he once suffered to the fact that during
his probationary period he had "sex with a new woman." The illness
resisted all treatment until some shamans dreamed that the stubborn ail-
ment was caused by his sexual transgression, and that the gods expected him to sacrifice a bull and make many offerings to regain their favor
and protection. When he did so, he was cured (Valadéz 1986a:19–20).

WOLF SHAMANISM

In certain cases the stricture against sex with someone other than
one's spouse can extend beyond the first five years to avoid arousing
the tutelary's jealousy. This may occur, for example, when the apprentice shaman has been chosen by the wolves or, more correctly, the
Wolf People, as one of their own and as recipient of the special power
believed to adhere to the wolf species. As noted earlier, shamans
acquire an entire range of animal and plant helpers during their
apprenticeship for curing, personal strength, artistic talent, swiftness

and sureness of eye in the deer hunt, and so forth. To obtain, say, a hawk or a parrot as a helping spirit, the future shaman hunts the bird, paints his or her cheeks with its blood, and plucks the feathers (Valadéz 1986b:34). But acquiring wolves as allies, or training as a wolf shaman, is much less overt and also more complex, arduous, and even dangerous than what is involved in the making of the ordinary Huichol shaman, a topic explored with much new information by Susana Valadéz, whose long-time shaman consultant, Ulu Temay, underwent this psychologically and physically demanding process (Valadéz, n.d.).

In assessing the historical and ethnological significance of this extraordinary, secretive, and evidently rare phenomenon of Huichol shamanism, we are at a disadvantage in not having comparable data from any other Mesoamerican Indian society, except for a few sketchy hints that something like this may once have existed among the neighboring Tepecan. The Tepecanos, southernmost of the speakers of Piman languages, are now almost completely acculturated, but judging from J. Alden Mason's field notes dating to 1912, their aboriginal ceremonialism—or those remnants of it and its underlying belief system that could still be found in the first decade of this century—shares some elements with that of the Huichols (Mason and Agogino 1972). In any event, Huichol wolf shamanism—wolves as sources of supernatural and shamanic power—sounds rather more North American Indian than it does Mexican.

PSYCHOACTIVE PLANTS IN HUICHOL SHAMANISM AND RITUAL

Sexual jealousy may also be involved where the future shaman has pledged completion to the plant spirit known as Kiéri, who is thought to be particularly possessive. The sacred cactus, peyote, *Lophophora williamsii*, is the primary agent for expansion or transformation of consciousness among the Huichols. They also employ it as a simple stimulant and restorative and as a medicine for various physical ills. But in the physical and spiritual universe of the Huichols, another psychotropic plant and its spirit owner also play a role. That plant is Kiéri. In his botanical manifestation, Kiéri is a species of *Solandra*, a solanaceous genus distinguished by spectacular, trumpet-shaped flowers that is closely related to *Datura inoxia* and its sister species (Furst 1976, 1989; Knab 1977; Schultes and Hofmann 1979).

Some Kiéri plants are shrublike, but others act more like vines and often reach heights of six to eight feet and more. Kiéri flowers are similar in form to those of *Datura* but are yellow instead of white (other hues have also been reported). The presence of two sacred intoxicants side by side—one the physiologically dangerous *Solandra*, the other the far more benign peyote, whose consumption, whatever the amount, involves none of the proven physiological risks inherent in the use of the *Solanaceae*—raises some interesting questions. These go beyond the scope of the present chapter, but we should remember that the Aztecs also used different psychotropic species in their rituals and that the contemporary Mazatecs employ both the sacred mushrooms and the psychoactive seeds of a morning glory.

There is no doubt that Kiéri is venerated by many Huichols as a plant spirit of great power to whom shrines are dedicated and offerings made and whose power to intoxicate is both recognized and feared. Likewise, the related *Datura inoxia*—which has a long history of use in ritual intoxication and medicine in Mexico, and which is still sacred to Pueblo peoples in the Southwest—is well known to, and treated with respect by, Huichols. At the same time, the little peyote cactus—which, in contrast to *Solandra,* is native not to the territory where the Huichols now make their homes but to the northcentral high desert around three hundred miles to the east—stands at the core of a symbol complex in which it merges with both deer and maize, a topic that, as noted, Myerhoff (1974) has explored with particular sophistication. It is *hikuri* (or *hikuli*) peyote, not Kiéri/*Solandra*, by means of which Huichol shamans and ordinary people dream themselves into the realm of the ancestor gods and spirits. To quote the shaman Ulu Temay, "When you go to the peyote desert, thinking only of becoming a mara'akáme, you will eat the peyote and speak to the deer and say, 'I come here to learn how to become a mara'akáme. I think only of this' " (Valadéz 1986b:34). And yet, by some accounts *Solandra* is occasionally used by some shamans for its psychoactive properties. It is certain that some regard this plant spirit as their tutelary and teacher.

Why this should be the case, and why there is a lingering concern with *Solandra's* cousin, *Datura*, and even *Brugmansia* when peyote is qualitatively equated by all Huichols with the deer spirit, when each year peyote draws Huichols to its distant desert home in re-enactment of the primordial deer-peyote hunt of the ancestor gods, are only some of the problems in the ongoing study of Huichol religion, shamanism, and ethnohistory that await future research. This much is clear: there is no denying or overlooking the many phenomena that make Huichol culture unique. They are at least as interesting and significant, if not more so, as cultural universals. Nevertheless, reflected in and reinforcing a remarkably intact aboriginal religion and ritual are elements of an archaic shamanic worldview and shamanic practices that have analogies elsewhere in the Indian Americas and that can ultimately be traced back to distant roots in Central and Northeastern Asia.[6]

NOTES

1. I had re-established contact with this redoubtable woman in 1988, seventeen years after her husband's death, when some old friends, on a visit to Nayarit, found her and her relatives in such obvious need that they arranged for them to be invited by the Heard Museum in Phoenix and then to come to Santa Fe to demonstrate and sell their arts and crafts. Not just Lupe but all of the adult members of her extended family group were proficient in the major Huichol crafts: wool yarn painting, backstrap loom weaving, beadwork, and embroidery. Indian people from some of the Río Grande pueblos saw them give a public dance performance and invited them to their own dances; one elderly Indian governor was so impressed that he went into the kiva and brought out sacred objects that had never been seen by outsiders. The Huichols were also accorded the singular honor of being invited to participate in the Pueblo dances. Not long afterward the entire group was invited to an Indian powwow in Oklahoma. Funds were collected to purchase a second-hand RV for them to travel in; a month later they had gone as far as Cree country in northeastern Canada. By the time they returned, they each had almost a thousand dollars—for them a considerable sum of money. But most important, during their stay in Santa Fe they ate better than they had for many years and quickly improved their deplorable state of health.

2. Just as no two peyote pilgrimages are entirely alike, so there are different versions of the myth that is the charter for the peyote hunt. Ramón and other Huichols I knew credited Tatewarí as the organizer and leader of the primordial peyote pilgrimage of the ancestor gods. Another version, held with equal conviction, states that the ancestors, some of whom still had the form of animals, were led by Maxa Kwaxí, great-grandfather of Deer Tail. The French scholar Léon Diguet (1899,

1911) has suggested that Maxa Kwaxí was actually a real person, a charismatic Guachichil-Chichimec shaman who introduced the ritual use of peyote to the Sierra Madre Occidental. He also proposed that Guachichil, rather than being extinct, as long thought, survives as the language of the Huichols. The Guachichiles (or Guachuchules, as they are called in early accounts and on Ortelius's map of 1579) were semi-nomadic hunter-gatherers of the high desert country of Zacatecas and San Luis Potosí, including that portion of the latter to which peyote is native; there is reason to believe that they are identical with the "Teochichimecas," or true Chichimecs, whose peyote rituals in the desert, as described in Book 10 of Fray Bernadino de Sahagún's *Florentine Codex,* were strikingly Huichollike.

3. This agrees with what Tim Knab learned when he visited Santa Catarina as a lingustic investigator in the late 1960s and again in the early 1970s. While in Santa Catarina, Knab, who was interested in Nahuatl borrowings in Huichol discourse, was taken to Teakáta, the most sacred place in the Sierra Huichol, to visit the shrines of the old earth goddess great-grandmother Nakawé (Lumholtz's "Grandmother Growth") and of Tatewarí. During a particularly steep descent, Knab says he was told by one of his Huichol companions, a shaman, that he need have no fear of falling because uitzi was there to guard them and help them down. Knab said he had the impression that the uitzi bird was essentially a helping spirit of shamans and peyoteros (Knab 1991, personal communication).

Although uitzi was not specifically identified as a hummingbird by Lupe, the name is clearly a Nahuatl borrowing, from *huitzilin,* hummingbird. The Aztecs had a number of spirit birds, of which the hummingbird was one of the most important. It was the *nagual,* alter ego and spirit companion of the sun and war god Huitzilopochitli, "Hummingbird of the Left." The souls of dead warriors reappeared in the form of hummingbirds (as well as butterflies), and because the Aztecs conceived of the hummingbird as passing the dry season suspended lifeless from a tree and coming back to life at the beginning of the rainy season, it symbolized the rebirth of vegetation. It is worth noting that the ethnologist Stacy Schaefer was told by one of her Huichol weaving teachers, who was a mara'akáme, that when a shaman wishes to acquire the hummingbird as a spirit helper and assimilate its powers, he or she catches one and eats its heart (Schaefer 1991, personal communication; see also Eger and Collings 1978:52).

4. The fact that there are other waterfalls with mythic connotations on the Huichol cognitive map, and that there have been for a long time, is also clear from the statement one of her consultants made to Stacy Schaefer (1990, and personal communication), whose doctoral research among the Huichols of San Andrés Cohamiata focused on the acquisition of the art and ideology of weaving as the woman's path in Huichol culture; as she learned from her weaving teacher at San Andrés Cohamiata, herself a shaman as well as a master weaver, the process of learning the art of weaving in crucial ways parallels and merges with the process of the shaman, as does that of the maker of canoes among the Warao of Venezuela (Wilbert 1976:303–358). Among the sacred places where the soul of a deceased Huichol stops on its westward journey to the land of the dead, she was told, is a waterfall. No precise location was given. However, in the early 1970s a colleague, archaeologist Stuart D. Scott, came upon a spectacular multiple waterfall that lies astride or near a Huichol pilgrimage route to San Blas on the Pacific coast of Nayarit, where Huichols locate the entrance into the land of the dead. Carved into the vertical walls of the cataract, Scott found unmistakably Huichol symbols, the most distinctive one being a rayed sun face at the base of a ladderlike stairway (Furst and Scott 1975:13–20). This was precisely the way in which Ramón, in a pencil drawing and a yarn painting illustrating the solar myth, had depicted the Sun god's ascent through the five levels of the underworld on the dawn of his fiery birth from a volcano in the east and his corresponding descent at dusk to begin his perilous journey through the underworld to the place of dawn. (One of the responsibilities of the leading shaman-singers of the different ceremonial centers in the Sierra, and also of the dead shamans whose spirits accompany the Sun on its daily round, is to make certain that this primordial cycle repeats itself without disruption. Shamans also "sing up" the sun at sunrise, as I saw the prestigious old shaman 'Colas do repeatedly at San Andrés (Figure 5.14) and Ramón do two or three times in his little rancho on the outskirts of Guadalajara and on the peyote pilgrimage.

5. Here it resulted in the death of a Huichol the Mexican author Fernando Benítez, who knew him in the period 1967–1969, remembered as a man of many talents and prodigious intellectual gifts. Ramón, he wrote in the last of the five volumes of his popular ethnography *Los Indios de México* (1968–1980), was not only an outstanding apprentice shaman and prodigious narrator of the sacred histories but

was also a great artist who, in the storytelling yarn painting he pioneered in the mid-1960s, created a new style based upon, but distinct from, traditional art. But he was also then a man positioned in the middle—Benítez used the Nahuatl word *nepantla*—that is, a man precariously balanced between two worlds (Benítez 1980:210).

6. The fact that Carlos Castaneda appropriated some of these shamanic universals for the fictional composite to whom he gave the name "Don Juan Matus," in what we now know to have been literary invention (more charitably labeled "allegory" by Richard de Mille [1976, 1990]) rather than ethnography, robs them of none of their validity; similar beliefs and behaviors in other Native American societies—North and South, as well as in Siberia and other parts of the world—are too numerous and too well-known to students of shamanism to require discussion here. Indeed, it is precisely because Castaneda did not simply invent but—if de Mille's meticulously documented and analytical characterization of Castaneda's writings as fiction rather than ethnography is correct (as many anthropologists, including myself, had come to suspect in the early 1970s, if not before)—borrowed and reassembled universals of the shamanic worldview, philosophical ideas and concepts from Buddhism and other religions, and even real events, settings, and people experienced by others (including the earlier-mentioned waterfall incident) that *The Teachings of Don Juan* and its successors acquired—at least for a brief time—the aura of ethnographic authenticity, even for many anthropologists. But Castaneda's writings also had a positive effect: fiction or not, they helped open the eyes and minds of ethnologists to other ways of "seeing" the world and to "other realities" than their own.

REFERENCES

Benítez, Fernando.
    1968–1980.
        Los Indios de México. 5 vols. Vol. 1, *Los Huicholes*. México, D. F.: Biblioteca Era.

Caffey, David L.
    1988. *Yellow Sun, Bright Sky: The Indian Stories of Oliver La Farge*. Albuquerque: University of New Mexico Press.

De Mille, Richard.
    1976. *Castaneda's Journey: The Power and the Allegory*. Santa Barbara: Capra Press.

1990. *The Don Juan Papers: Further Castaneda Controversies.* Belmont, Calif.: Wadsworth. (Expanded reprint of the 1980 Ross-Erickson edition.)

Diguet, Léon.
1899. "La Sierra de Nayarit et ses indigínes, contribution la l'étude ethno-graphique des races primitives du Mexique." *Nouv. Arch. Missions sci. litt.* 9.

1911. "Idiome Huichol, contribution de l'étude des langues mexicaines." *Journal des Américanistes,* n.s., 8, pp. 23–54.

Eger, Susan (Susana Valadéz) in collaboration with Peter R. Collings.
1978. "Huichol Women's Art." In *Art of the Huichol Indians,* Kathleen Berrin, ed., pp. 35–53. New York: Harry N. Abrams.

Eliade, Mircea.
1964. *Shamanism: Archaic Techniques of Ecstasy.* New York: Pantheon Books.

Furst, Peter T.
1967. "Huichol Conceptions of the Soul." *Folklore Americas* 22, No. 2, pp. 39–106. Center for the Study of Folklore and Mythology, University of California at Los Angeles.

1969. "The False Peyote: A Huichol Tradition." *Genre,* Nos. 1–3, pp. 31–39. California State University at Long Beach.

1972. "To Find Our Life: Peyote Among the Huichol Indians of Mexico." In *Flesh of the Gods: The Ritual Use of Hallucinogens,* Peter T. Furst, ed., pp. 136–185. New York: Praeger. (Reprinted in 1990, with a new introduction, by Waveland Press, Prospect Heights, Ill.)

1973. "The Roots and Continuities of Shamanism." *Artscanada,* Nos. 184–187, pp. 33–60.

1976. *Hallucinogens and Culture.* San Francisco: Chandler and Sharp.

———.

1978. "The Art of 'Being Huichol.'" In *Art of the Huichol Indians,* Kathleen Berrin, ed., pp. 18–34. New York: Harry N. Abrams.

———.

1989. "The Life and Death of the Crazy Kiéri: Natural and Cultural History of a Huichol Myth." *Journal of Latin American Lore* 15, No. 2, pp. 155–179.

Furst, Peter T., and Stuart D. Scott.

1975. "La Escalera del Padre Sol: Un Par lelo Etnográfico-Archaeológico en México Occidental." *Boletín del Instituto Nacional de Antropología y Historia de México,* No. 12, pp. 13–20.

Gingerich, Willard.

1988. "Chipauacanemiliztli, 'The Purified Life.'" In *Smoke and Mist: Mesoamerican Studies in Memory of Thelma D. Sullivan,* Vol. 2, J. Kathryn Josserand and Karin Dakin, eds., pp. 517–544. Oxford: BAR International Series 402 (ii).

Knab, Tim.

1977. "Notes Concerning Use of *Solandra* Among the Huichols." *Journal of Economic Botany* 31:80–86.

Lumholtz, Carl.

1902. *Unknown Mexico,* Vol. 2. New York: Charles Scribner's.

Mason, J. Alden, and George Agogino.

1972. *The Ceremonialism of the Tepecan.* Eastern New Mexico State University Contributions in Anthropology, Vol. 4, No. 1.

Myerhoff, Barbara G.

1966. "The Doctor as Culture Hero: The Shaman of Rincon." *Anthropological Quarterly* 39, No. 2, pp. 60–72.

———.

1974. *Peyote Hunt: The Sacred Journey of the Huichol Indians.* Ithaca: Cornell University Press.

———.

1976. "Shamanic Equilibrium: Balance and Mediation in Known and Unknown Worlds." In *American Folk Medicine,* Wayland D. Hand, ed., pp. 99–108. Berkeley: University of California Press.

Perrin, Michel.
   In press.
      "The *Urukame*, A Crystallization of the Soul: 'Tradition,' Death and Memory."
      In *People of the Peyote: Explorations in Huichol Religion, History, and
      Survival,* Stacy Schaefer and Peter T. Furst, eds. Albuquerque: University
      of New Mexico Press.

Preuss, Konrad Theodor.
   1907. "Ritte durch das Land der Huichol-Indianer der mexikanischen Sierra Madre."
      Globus 92, No. 10, pp. 155–161.

———.
   1908. "Die Religiösen Gesänge und Mythen einiger Stämme der mexikanischen
      Sierra Madre." *Archiv für Religions-schaft* 2, pp. 369–398.

———.
   1909. "Dialoglieder des Rigveda im Lichte der religiösen Gesänge mexikanischer
      Indianer." *Globus* 95, No. 3, pp. 41–46.

———.
   1932. "Au sujet du caractre des mythes et des chants huichols, que j'ai recueillis."
      Revista del Instituto de Etnología, tomo 2, pp. 445–457. Universidad
      de Tucuman.

Radin, Paul.
   1927. *Primitive Man as Philosopher.* New York and London: D. Appleton and Co.

Sahagún, Fray Bernadino de.
   1950–1963.
      The Florentine Codex. General History of the Things of New Spain. Transl. by
      Arthur J.O. Anderson and Charles E. Dibble. Santa Fe: School of American
      Research and University of Utah Press.

Schaefer, Stacy.
   1989. "The Loom and Time in the Huichol World." *Journal of Latin American
      Lore* 15, No. 2, pp. 179–194.

———.
   1990. "Becoming a Weaver: The Woman's Path in Huichol Culture." Ph.D.
      dissertation, Department of Anthropology, University of California
      at Los Angeles.

Schultes, Richard Evans, and Albert Hofmann.
  1979. *Plants of the Gods: Origins of Hallucinogenic Use.* New York:
         Alfred Van der Marck.

Valadéz, Susana Eger.
  1986a.
         "An Interview With Ulu Temay, Huichol Shaman." *Shaman's
         Drum* 6, pp. 18–23.

———.
  1986b.
         "Mirrors of the Gods: The Huichol Shaman's Path of Completion."
         Shaman's Drum 6, pp. 29–39.

———.
  In press.
         "Wolf Power and Inter-Species Communication in Huichol Shamanism."
         In *People of the Peyote: Essays in Huichol Religion, History, and Survival,*
         Stacy Schaefer and Peter T. Furst, eds. Albuquerque: University of
         New Mexico Press.

Wilbert, Johannes.
  1972. "Tobacco and Shamanistic Ecstasy Among the Warao Indians." In
         Flesh of the Gods: The Ritual Use of Hallucinogens, Peter T. Furst, ed.,
         pp. 55–83. New York: Praeger. (Reprinted in 1990, with a new introduction,
         by Waveland Press, Prospect Heights, Ill.)

———.
  1976. "To Become a Maker of Canoes: An Essay in Warao Enculturation."
         In *Enculturation in Latin America*, Johannes Wilbert, ed., pp. 303–358.
         Los Angeles: UCLA Latin American Center Publications.

Zingg, Robert M.
  1938. *The Huichols: Primitive Artists.* New York: G. E. Stechert.

OTHER WORKS

Casillas Romo, Armando.
  In press.
         "Traditional Huichol Medicine." In *People of the Peyote: Explorations
         in Huichol Religion, History, and Survival,* Stacy Schaefer and Peter T. Furst,
         eds. Albuquerque: University of New Mexico Press.

Furst, Peter T.
    1965. "West Mexican Tomb Sculpture as Evidence for Shamanism in Prehispanic Mesoamerica." *Antropológica,* No. 15, pp. 29–80.

Wilbert, Johannes.
    1987. *Tobacco and Shamanism in South America.* New Haven: Yale University Press.

PEYOTE RELIGION

OMER C. STEWART

An interesting development in the acculturation of the American Indian in the western United States during the past century and a half is the rise of peyote religion and its continued popularity. The peyote cactus, well-known for centuries in Mexico where it grows, was valued among the natives there as a ceremonial object, a medicine, and a stimulant; as useful to tell fortunes and to find lost objects and so forth. Peyote was used in many religious ceremonies during the occupation of Mexico by the Spaniards, who brought the authority of the Inquisition against its use. Nevertheless, by the nineteenth century some of these ceremonies had become set in tradition and practice.

The American Indians became aware of peyote when they obtained horses. During the nineteenth century the Plains Indians—the Kiowa, Comanche, Cheyenne, and Arapaho, to name a few—raided Mexico every year, rounding up horses, stealing from settlers, and learning everything they could. Undoubtedly, they ate peyote in Mexico and found it gave them a pleasant kind of intoxication. They heard that peyote had magical properties, could cure one of sickness, was useful in finding lost objects, and made one strong; and they observed and participated in some of the peyote ceremonies.

In about 1875, most of the so-called "wild Indians" of the Plains were forced to surrender their horses and to settle down and live on reservations. Most of these Indians were located on reservations in Oklahoma, formerly called Indian Territory. The Cheyenne, Arapaho, Kiowa, Wichita, Caddo, Osage, and many others—formerly free to roam all of the western United States—found themselves unable to move, confined in close proximity with unfamiliar tribes, completely dependent upon the white government for everything, and supervised by whites interested in destroying their customs, languages, and religions and in rapidly turning them into English-speaking Christians and farmers.

It was a tragic time for these Indians; many large tribes lost more than half of their members, and some tribes disappeared forever.

It was under these conditions that the peyote ceremony gained a foothold among the Indians of the western United States. The peyote ceremony adopted by the Indians of Oklahoma must have existed for a long time among Indians along the Rio Grande in what is now southern Texas, where peyote grows in abundance. I say a long time because this ceremony was so set in tradition that it has changed little since it was first described by ethnologists in 1890. The ceremony is an all-night ritual held in a brush enclosure or a tipi in which the members sit in a circle around a sacred fire and a half-moon-shaped altar on which is placed a Chief Peyote. They sing traditional songs, accompanied by a drum and rattle, smoke ceremonial cigarettes, pray, and eat peyote. A very specific ceremonial pattern is followed in these songs and prayers and the other events in the ritual, which lasts until dawn. After the meeting, everyone gathers again for visiting and a ritual breakfast.

The peyote cactus is essential for a peyote meeting; it is the sacrament. The theology of peyotism is the belief in the supernatural origin of the peyote plant and its ability to work miracles. The peyote plant is a small, spineless cactus with psychedelic properties. It grows in a limited area, principally in northern Mexico and southern Texas. It is light green and segmented, about one to two inches across, growing singly or in clusters close to the ground from a long taproot. It is harvested by cutting off the tops of the clusters, leaving the root to produce more "buttons," as the tops are usually called. The buttons are generally dried before being eaten, and they are extremely bitter to the taste, frequently producing vomiting. However, they also produce a warm and pleasant euphoria, an agreeable point of view, relaxation, colorful visual distortions, and a sense of timelessness that is conducive to the all-night ceremony. Peyote is not habit-forming, and in the controlled ambience of a peyote meeting, it is in no way harmful. Peyote is seldom eaten by Indians except at a peyote meeting.

The circumstances of the diffusion of peyotism from the Rio Grande to Oklahoma are somewhat speculative. We do know that the ceremony developed along the Rio Grande where the plant grows and that without horses, peyote was difficult to obtain; even with horses, it was not easy to get. The decade of the 1870s in Laredo, Texas—the center of peyote growth in Texas—was a period of violence, a time when no Indians were officially located in or even allowed to be in Texas. In southern and western

Texas, an active war was being waged by Texas Rangers and forces of the U.S. Army. Nevertheless, a few enterprising Indians did bring peyote to Oklahoma, and meetings were held on the Kiowa-Comanche Reservation.

In the 1880s the situation changed, and peyote from Laredo became easily available in Oklahoma. Not only was the ban on horses lifted, but, more important, railroads were completed that linked the peyote gardens of southern Texas with points in Texas near the Kiowa-Comanche Reservation. Peyoteros around Laredo cut, dried, and shipped barrels of peyote to the new market in Oklahoma, where peyote sold for five cents a button. Other events helped peyotism to spread rapidly. Whatever promoted intertribal association tended also to spread the idea of a new religion. The tribal war leaders in the prisoner-of-war camp in Florida—where many were sent for indoctrination about democracy, English language instruction, and Christianity—also spread information about peyote. Many who attended the prisoner-of-war camp returned home to become leaders of peyote ceremonies.

Another event that brought the tribes together was the Ghost Dance, which was popular in Oklahoma around 1890. The tribes that gathered because of the hopes and inspirations fueled by the Ghost Dance found even more hope and inspiration in the new religion of peyotism. Before the end of the century, almost all of the new arrivals in Oklahoma were acquainted with the ceremony, and many devoutly and regularly attended meetings. They included the Kiowa, Comanche, Kiowa-Apache, Wichita, Delaware, Cheyenne, Arapaho, Osage, Quapaw, Seneca, Ponca, Kaw, Sac and Fox, Iowa, Kickapoo, and Shawnee.

Peyotism spread into the natural course of daily life. Someone who had learned the ceremony was asked to conduct a meeting, probably for a reason such as an illness, and people came. Frequently, a person from another tribe or reservation attended and stayed to learn how to be a roadman, as the leader of a peyote meeting is called. When he felt he knew how to be a roadman and had learned how to get peyote for a meeting, he returned home to teach the methods to his people. Generally, the person who wanted to become a roadman was already distinguished as a medicine man. Often he was a tribal leader or chief who had attended one of the schools or the prisoner-of-war camp, who understood English and something about white culture and religion, or who was otherwise outstanding. Most were members of a Christian mission, and some were active participants. Few found conflict in participating in shamanistic

curing practices, ancient Indian ceremonials such as the Sun Dance, peyotism, and Christian Sunday schools.

As peyotism developed, some roadmen devoted themselves exclusively to it, becoming avowed missionaries. Missionary life offered
many rewards, including the feeling of being important and of doing
good and receiving economic benefits. Throughout the Plains culture,
payment was the rule for shamanistic services or instruction in ritual,
and it was assumed that some sort of payment would be given to a
roadman who gave a meeting or instructed another in the ceremony.
There was no set fee, and payment was always viewed as a gift. An
"article of faith," or idealism, in the peyote religion says that because
peyote is a divine plant, it should not be corrupted by commercialism
but should be distributed freely, as an act of religious charity or as a
sacred duty, to anyone who desires to use it as a sacred medicine.
Therefore, a price was not put upon it; it was freely given by the host
or leader at a meeting. However, it was appropriate, and even expected, for one to give a present of money, jewelry, ponies, blankets, and
the like, to the roadmen. A talented missionary could profit well. Yet, if
he became ostentatious about his wealth or seemed avaricious, he
might receive criticism.

In the 1880s, there were two peyote roadmen of great importance
whose influence on the peyote religion extends to the present day.
They were Comanche Chief Quanah Parker and Caddo-Delaware medicine man John Wilson. The most traditional form of the peyote ceremony is that followed and taught by Parker, which is often called the
Halfmoon Way or the Tipi Way. Wilson introduced a variation in the
shape of the moon altar, added some Christian references, and forbade
the use of tobacco. His ceremony is called the Big Moon Way or the
Cross Fire Way.

Peyotism spread from Oklahoma to other western Indians, those of
Kansas, Nebraska, Iowa, Wisconsin, Minnesota, North and South Dakota,
Montana, Idaho, Wyoming, Colorado, Utah, New Mexico, and, later,
Nevada, California, Washington, and Arizona. It never attracted a majority of Indians, but nevertheless it was significant both to its adherents and
to those who saw in it a heathen practice that must be eliminated. Many
tribes were quick to accept it, but others rejected it altogether. The varied and broken histories of tribes, the varieties of languages and customs, the efforts of Christian missionaries and government authorities to
suppress it, as well as the abilities of peyote missionaries all influenced

its acceptance. It never gained more than 90 percent acceptance on any one reservation at any time, and the number was more likely to be between 35 and 50 percent.

Its greatest appeal was among the young, newly educated Indians who found in it a form of Indian Christianity and often became its leaders. They felt comfortable with the ceremony, in which they could celebrate the Christian ideas they had recently learned at school in a setting that was familiar and indigenous. It was a curing ceremony, and the newcomers to reservation life needed many cures. The serious but controlled ambience of the ceremony, together with the euphoria produced by the plant, produced many miracles. When we consider the physical, psychological, and social problems of these early peyotists, when entire tribes were dying from depression as well as from disease, we can sympathize with a ceremony and a sacrament that gave emotional strength and were followed by a good breakfast.

When peyote use became apparent to missionaries and Indian agents, they immediately sought to suppress it. To them, as to the Catholic fathers in Mexico two hundred years earlier, the plant and the ceremony seemed the very essence of heathenish Indian practices, a veritable "root" of all evil. At first the antipeyotists of Oklahoma used the 1897 Prohibition Law, adding, without authority, the prohibition of peyote. Uneasy because the 1897 law did not cover peyote, in 1899 the antipeyotists succeeded in getting a territorial law passed that prohibited the use of "mescale beans." An attempt to amend this law to refer to peyote was roundly defeated in 1907 by the state of Oklahoma because of the eloquence and strategy of its Indian opposition. But peyotism seemed so strange, frightening, and downright sinful to the antipeyotists that they continued to forbid its practice and to harass its adherents under the old 1897 law or simply by an order from the Indian agents. There were arrests, confiscation of property, fines, jail terms, and verbal abuse on every reservation that dared to experiment with the new religion.

Those against peyote argued that it made the Indians drunk, lazy, and sick; that it sometimes killed them; that peyotists were those Indians who were shiftless, good-for-nothing, and impossible to educate. However, the facts belie this. These Indians were often tribal leaders, diligent workers, and eager to learn, and, most of all, they were never drunk. Regardless of whether something about peyote destroys the desire for alcohol, the idea that peyotists do not drink is one of their fundamental beliefs. Wilson would never allow anyone who had

◣

been drinking to attend his meetings, saying he should come back when he was sober.

Eventually, after the opposition to peyote had largely failed on the local level, the leaders of the opposition brought the matter to national attention. In 1918 Congress held extensive hearings on a bill that sought to prohibit "traffic in peyote, including its sale to Indians, introduction into the Country, importation and transportation," providing for penalties of "imprisonment for more than sixty days and less than one year, or by a fine of not less than $100 nor more than $500, or both." The bill was passed in the House of Representatives but was rejected in the Senate when the Oklahoma senator, responding to his Indian constituency, persuaded his Senate colleagues to vote against it. Although a similar law was introduced every year for a number of years, it never had a full hearing until 1937, when again it was rejected.

The Indians who defended peyotism in the hearings had received a vivid education in U.S. government. They heard the case against peyote argued by their powerful white adversaries, and they defended it—with the help of white scholars from the Smithsonian Institution—before the high court of the U.S. House of Representatives. It was a tough fight, and they won a close victory. But they knew the fight was not over. They realized that in order to prevail again, they must learn to conform to the nation's other religious institutions. They said that their religious ceremony was similar to the Presbyterian, Mormon, Catholic, or any other church ceremony. But in the eyes of the world it was different because it was not organized. It needed a name and needed to be known by that name; it needed a set of rules, officers, stated responsibilities; it needed to be "incorporated." And so, in 1918 the Native American Church of Oklahoma was born and was incorporated.

The antipeyotists answered by enacting state laws against peyote. Utah, Colorado, Nevada, Kansas, Arizona, Montana, North and South Dakota, New Mexico, and Wyoming soon had such laws. But the state laws were largely futile, because states and their courts had little jurisdiction over Indian reservations. State laws probably discouraged the halfhearted but at the same time challenged the devout, and peyotism continued to flourish. The peyotists responded to the proliferation of state laws by incorporating more churches. This was not legally necessary, but they thought it might help. As they became more sophisticated in their organization, their purposes of incorporation sometimes included more than the right to hold a peyote ceremony. The incorporation of

▼

the Native American Church of Charles Mix County, South Dakota, stated: "The purpose . . . is to foster and promote Christian beliefs among the Sioux Indians . . . and to teach them the scriptures, morality, charity, right living, to cultivate the spirit of self-respect, brotherly love and union among all American Indians." The right to conduct funerals and maintain cemeteries was covered under the provision to "buy, sell, own and care for property for religious purposes." Roadmen were also granted permission to preach the gospel, baptize, solemnize marriages, and administer the Holy Sacrament of the church, which, of course, was peyote.

As peyotism spread and annual meetings of different groups took place, the Native American Church of the United States was incorporated, followed by the Native American Church of North America when some groups in Canada became established. Peyotism also spread to the far west—to Washington, Oregon, Nevada, and California—and south to Arizona and New Mexico. And new problems arose. This time Indians were the enemy, the antipeyotists. The elected Indian governors of Taos disapproved of peyote. Probably goaded by some white residents, they forbade peyote on the reservation, jailed some peyotists, and confiscated property as payment of fines. This time, the U.S. government came to the aid of the peyotists. With the election of Franklin D. Roosevelt in 1932 and the appointment of Superintendent John Collier, a new philosophy prevailed at the Bureau of Indian Affairs. Until that time, the purpose of the bureau had been to encourage Indians to forego everything Indian as soon as possible and to strive to be like white people. Collier felt the very presence of Indian culture was a great asset to U.S. society:

> He said that the government had the duty to bring education and modern scientific knowledge within the reach of every Indian. And, at the same time, the government should reawaken the soul of the Indian; not only pride in being an Indian, but hope for the future as an Indian. It had the obligation to preserve the Indians' love and ardor toward the rich values of Indian life as expressed in their arts, rituals, and cooperative institutions. (Philip 1977:118)

Collier saw the issue at Taos clearly as a matter of religious freedom and insisted that the peyotists be allowed to practice their religion.

Within a few years the same issue arose on the Navajo Reservation. This time, however, Collier waited for the Navajo Tribal Council, which had outlawed peyote on that reservation, to come around to the principle of religious freedom on its own. It took a long time and some court battles before the Navajo Nation accepted the U.S. Bill of Rights, including the right of religious freedom, but they finally did so in 1967.

Today, peyotists are free to practice their religion in all parts of the United States, and peyote ceremonies are held at times in almost all of the western states. The basic ceremony remains the same: it is still an all-night ceremony, usually held on a Saturday night; it still involves a circle around the sacred fire and sand altar, the four officials (roadman, fireman, cedarman, and drummer), the singing, drumming, praying, in turn, following a clockwise direction, the eating of peyote, the sacred number four, the gourd rattles, the feather fans, and, finally, the breakfast and social gathering following the meeting. The meeting remains dedicated to curing, sobriety, and Christian ideals. There are still two basic patterns, the Parker Halfmoon or Tipi Way and the Wilson Big Moon or Cross Fire Way. Peyote members, although well aware of the two types of ritual and sophisticated in the observance of the distinction, participate in both. They also participate in other rituals, such as the Sun Dance, Christian services, and curing ceremonies.

The big problem for peyotists today is the scarcity of peyote. Occasional shortages and increased demand have resulted in substantial price increases. In 1955 the price paid for one thousand peyote buttons was $9.50 to $15.00. Today the price is $100.00 for a thousand buttons. Increased prices have resulted in lower levels of consumption at meetings, and many tribes now use only one-half to one-third the amount they used a few years ago. The future of the peyote plant, at least in the United States, seems to be that of an endangered species.

REFERENCES

Philip, Kenneth R.
  1977.   *John Collier's Crusade for Indian Reform, 1920–1954.* Tucson: University of
          Arizona Press.

Stewart, Omer C.
  1987.   *Peyote Religion: A History.* Norman: University of Oklahoma Press.

FROM SHAMAN TO MEDICINE MAN: TRANSFORMATION OF SHAMANIC ROLES AND STYLES IN THE UPPER GREAT LAKES REGION

JAMES A. CLIFTON

The date—March 1964. The place—Prairie Potawatomi Reservation in eastern Kansas. For hours I had been working with Young Dawn Man at the most tedious of all ethnographic tasks: he indulgently dictating, I doggedly transcribing the long series of Dream Dance ritual songs he had in his head. We took a coffee break. I was massaging my numb writing hand when from Dawn Man issued an unexpected declaration.

"It's not true what people say about them communists," he intoned flatly, straight of face. Startled by this change of subject, I was just wondering should I ask, "What's not true?" when, seeing he had grabbed my attention, he continued.

" No, that's not true. And it's not true either what people say about them Texas oil millionaires," Dawn Man sermonized.

I had too little time to recall—*Of what had both bolsheviks and capitalists recently been wrongfully accused?*—before a dramatic answer was delivered.

"No, that's not true," declaimed Dawn Man, no expression in voice or eyes. "We *Neshnabek* fixed it up. At the Fall Drum doings we did it. We all prayed for the Thunders to put the idea in Oswald's head, so he would go and kill President Kennedy. We did it so's to show how we feel about all the bad things the *Kitchimokoman* did to us."

Done with this discourse, to signal end of episode Dawn Man added, "Drink your coffee. I want to tell you about the Brave Dance songs." Knowing him, I understood implicitly—no follow-up queries allowed.

Dawn Man's "confession" was not what it seemed, I knew. When he interjected information in this manner, entirely out of context, he intended deep connotative communication and a test of my ability to understand. It helped that I knew he was lying, that he knew I knew this, and that I understood he appreciated that I recognized he would

▼

know I knew. I am not passing judgment. Dawn Man was a man to lay out some parts of a puzzle and let me piece them together if I could. I had participated in and observed the whole Fall Dream Dance ritual round and had witnessed no such prayer, collective or solo. Had I missed some sotto voce communication to the spirit even by a single individual, others would have noted and commented on it later, strongly and negatively so. The first part of the test was easy: praying to any spirit for power to harm anyone in Dream Dance rituals just was not done. Dawn Man's refrain was badly out of tune.

What, then, was he communicating? He was delivering an object lesson about the cognitive and affective style of a malevolent Potawatomi shaman, the form of thought behind the terror tactics of sorcerers Ruth Landes had observed three decades earlier (1963; see also, Landes 1970). He was simulating how, in earlier years, spiteful Potawatomi shamans, after a riveting tragedy, would boast publicly of their power to bid the gods do horrendous deeds for them. For months I had been muddling around trying to locate such a practitioner. I had succeeded in running to ground maybe the last such surviving sorcerer, to the Potawatomi an enemy of the people. The results of this encounter were embarrassing to me, which Dawn Man knew about (Clifton 1992). In that incident I experienced the sorcerer in action. Being the target of an adept whose forte was nasty deeds, not words, I had little opportunity to learn about his thought world. Dawn Man, in strong contrast, was a man of many words, much wisdom, and notably kind deeds. He was not confessing Potawatomi complicity in the Dallas tragedy. He was rounding out my knowledge of the dark underside of the Potawatomi ethos.

Dawn Man's allegation came at one end point in the Potawatomis' three-century-long history of dealing with neighboring native peoples and those of European origins. In 1964, approaching sixty years, his life spanned most of the twentieth century. A précis of his career as an eclectic ritualist will serve to highlight important features of that community's religious history, introduce similarities in the histories of related Central Algonquian peoples, and define the terms and underscore the themes of my discussion.

An abandoned orphan with few extended kin to aid him, as a youth Dawn Man had to go it alone in finding a significant part for himself. Adopting an elderly religious functionary as father, a man who in the 1850s hunted buffalo and ripped scalps from Cheyenne and Lakota

▼

in the west, he entered manhood in the classic Algonquian fashion, by way of a vision quest. At that point he obtained supernatural dispensation for acquiring an important ritual position and took as his family name the title of his adopted father's key religious role—*Wabino*, or "Dawn Man." The Wabino was one of the three shamanic roles the Potawatomi and neighboring western Great Lakes Algonquians commonly recognized, this one functioning ordinarily as supernatural adviser, clairvoyant, medium, and tent shaker. The other two conventional shamanic roles included the specialized diviner, or *Chasgyd*, and the generic healer-therapist. Among the Potawatomi and related societies, separate individuals might perform one or the other of these roles, or they might be combined in one ritually multifaceted public identity.

However, his adopted father advised him against settling on such a part-time, individualistic religious avocation. This was losing sense and value in the reservation community of the early twentieth century, he was counseled—a conclusion verified by his own experience. Also, in my judgment, Dawn Man was not temperamentally disposed to such a part: he lacked the overweening egocentric narcissism and grandiosity typically associated with such practitioners (LaBarre 1970). Dawn Man, in contrast, was inclined toward a less ostentatious community-service religious place for himself, one situated in a more complex, promising, viable ritual institution.

A century or so earlier he might have sought significant position in Potawatomi patriclan-patrilineage ritualism, but during his youth the clan system ceased effective functioning. Although too young and inexperienced to have participated personally, he knew firsthand of the arrangements made by the few surviving, knowledgeable clan elders for the abandonment of clan rituals and safe burial of their remaining *pitchkosan*, or clan bundles (Landes 1963; Clifton 1977).

In his early years there were still some *Midewiwin* priests operating on the Kansas Potawatomi Reservation, who often "rode the rods" to attend *Mide* ceremonies among the Chippewa in Minnesota. However, the flamboyant performances conducted by Mide priests were not personally appealing to him, and he could not see this institution as having much of a future in or for his community. Indeed, when I knew him, the Potawatomis' Mide priests had declined to just three: an elderly Minnesota Chippewa and his two adult sons by a Potawatomi woman, who were by then cut off from regular contact with others like themselves in Minnesota because the railroad freight lines they were using for transportation had shut down. Of larger consequence for Dawn Man's turning away from the Midewiwin, however, was the enormous expense of initiation and training into its priesthood. An impoverished, orphaned youth, he lacked the money to pay the costs of instruction even had he been attracted by the Midewiwin.

By his teen years, the Native American Church, or Peyote religion, was well established in his community (Bee 1964, 1965), but these highly specialized rites held little appeal for Dawn Man. Regarding the consumption of alcohol, he was a pure Southern Baptist teetotaler. Moreover, his life had never been marked by the anomic identity confusion whose symptoms are still so well managed by the powerful psychotherapeutic rites of that religious institution, the Peyote religion. Also available to him for consideration and involvement was an extraordinary variety of other religious practices of various origins and variable antiquity. Among these were odds and ends of Potawatomi and other Indian institutions, such as the Underwater Panther bundle ceremony, a Mescal ceremony, the Shawnee rite, and, among the nearby Kickapoo, the Kenekuk religion (Howard 1960, 1962, 1965; Herring 1988). Likewise accessible and open for his consideration were various Christian denominations, among those ready at hand, a Catholic and a Methodist mission.

Through his lifetime Dawn Man dabbled alternatively or in series with all available forms of religion, and he continued to do so until his death. A bit of Mide, a fragment of *dodem* (clan) ritualism, a pinch of salt thrown over his shoulder, an occasional Catholic mass, a re-enactment of the Shawnee Prophet's rite, a Methodist love feast, a visit to a Peyote meeting, regular perusal of *Astounding Science Fiction*—all were grist for his metaphysical mill. I will swear, had nearby Topeka housed a Buddhist temple, Dawn Man would have spent some time there listening wide-eared to the Bonze, sniffing the incense, mind open, looking for something of value to him and his community. He was a ritual omnivore, but he was also a finicky gourmet questing for the most nutritious of transcendental delicacies. Of greater importance, his was an intellect of considerable synthesizing power, and he applied much of his talent to putting the religious pieces together in carving out a place of substance and meaning for himself, simultaneously working to serve the economically and politically hard-pressed Prairie Band traditionalists.

A prophet this Dawn Man, we might infer? Not so. To so label him would be entirely mistaken. Certainly, he had a large capacity for imposing meaning on and finding moral direction in ambiguity and confusion, but in this capacity he was little different from traditional Algonquian and other shamans, although I estimate his ability to integrate and harmonize was greater than most (Shweder 1979; LaBarre 1970; Wallace 1966; Grim 1983; Eliade 1964; Geertz 1966). Was he, then, a shaman, or at least shamanlike? Again, this would be an illusion. Throughout his career Dawn Man sought *official* position, appointment, and recognition. His was not an ecstatic inspiration direct from the *Manidoweg,* or Spirit Powers. He claimed no divine gift. He did not play with altered states of consciousness, possession trance, or even altered states of conscience (Von Furer-Haimendorf 1970). His was a reality-oriented, ego-directed, firmly organized, fully conscious, cool-thinking manner of being and performance.

But again, why not a prophet? Dawn Man's life did not contain a record of identity-dissolving failure, symbolic death, and rebirth. He rejected no traditions, and he proclaimed no strong new visions of a radically revised moral order. He did not exude charisma, and he and his colleagues would have flatly rejected any such claim to spiritual or social magnetism and superascendancy (Barnes 1978). If anything, there was more than a touch of scholarly mystic to Dawn Man. He fully recognized that what he knew, practiced, and taught reflected the contributions of others, and he saw none of them as absolute in meaning. However, Dawn Man's research was that of a believing pragmatist, not a disenchanted footnoter. He constantly sought to achieve particular ends by whatever supernatural means seemed to work. To expand on Claude Levi-Strauss's classic term (1962), he was a *bricouler,* a jack-of-many-ritual-trades, but one with a strong organizational center of supernatural balance.

In early adulthood Dawn Man fixed on a religious institution fitting his temperament, his talents, his concerns, and his understanding of the ritual needs of the Kansas Potawatomi. This was the Dream Dance, sometimes called the Drum religion, new to the generation preceding his when its fervent advocates arrived from northern Wisconsin preaching this new way. By the mid-twentieth century, the Prairie Band Dream Dance religion had become the dominant religious institution in this community, and Dawn Man had helped make it so. In the early 1960s it consisted of six ritual sodalities, each organized around one great drum personified as *Mishomonon,* our Grandfather, the old kin term used to refer to the Maker-Of-All-Things (Wishke, their culture hero). Whatever its zealous utopian origins in the 1870s, by the middle of this century the overriding ritual aims of the Dream Dance were centripetal and preservationist, countering the enormous centrifugal forces constantly threatening to dismember the community, to cope with what these Potawatomi called "confusion," to reinforce, cultivate, and perpetuate Potawatomi social and political roles, language, and ethos.

A measure of Dawn Man's success in establishing himself as a religious leader is this. The toughest problem Dream Dance members faced was to staff the some 282 ritual roles in the six sodalities with experienced, qualified personnel. Their quandary was too many "offices," as they called them, and too few able and available officers. Dawn Man, the jack-of-all-ritual-trades, held six key offices, acting out a role in each of the sodalities, serving also as the first choice for master of ceremonies. Neither shaman nor prophet, Dawn Man had become—in the technical language of anthropology—a priest (LaBarre 1970; Von Furer-Haimendorf 1970). Like any devoted priest, he was a devoted spiritual and institutional conservationist.

He was not, however, a "medicine man." To clarify this denial, traditional Prairie Band ritualists deeply resented being called medicine men or medicine women by anyone—whether well-meaning, if not clear-thinking, anthropologists, or others unwittingly relying on this usage, of early nineteenth-century European-American origin. For Dawn Man and his colleagues, to be labeled a medicine man was not only insulting, it was dangerous, because for them the strong connotation was that of sorcery, and such practices they sought to stamp out. So much for the Potawatomi side of the emic or folk-thinking coin. As regards *Our* traditional constructions about *Them* instead of *Theirs* about *Themselves*, without too much anticipating the denouement, let me now merely indicate that as well as an American neologism, the role of primitive medicine man was an outsider's invention, too.

This sketch of Dawn Man's career in this century is useful as a kind of biographical microscope to focus attention on key features and themes in the history of religious roles and styles of the Algonquians of the western Great Lakes over the course of the past three centuries. If our broader aim is to understand the fate of Siberian-style shamanism in the Americas, I think it useful to attend closely to these matters.

In the beginning, long before the arrival of *Coureurs de Bois* and Jesuits in the 1640s, there was much diversity of religiosity among the Algonquian societies of the region, resulting from a long prehistory of adaptation and cultural change and reflecting the large social, political, and economic differences among them. Broadly speaking, as of the early 1600s, we can distinguish two general varieties of native societies in the area. To the north predominated the more nomadic, politically less centralized, socially less stratified, small bands of foragers—lacustrine and riverine communities whose major mode of transportation was the bark-sheathed canoe. These peoples were ancestral to those later identified as Chippewa and Menomini. In the south were societies of a larger scale, the more sedentary, horticultural, multivillage tribes and chiefdoms, ancestors of those later known by such names as Ilini, Miami, Shawnee, Sauk, and Fox. These were quickly characterized as "Great Pedestrians" by the first French to visit them, but they also used dugout vessels for water transportation. Intermediate were peoples like the Potawatomi and Ottawa, who occupied lands with microclimates where corn farming was productive but who continued relying on bark canoes.

Although all Algonquian peoples were greatly affected by the fur trade, by the Iroquois and other frontier wars, and by dealings with colonial outposts and agents, these broad political-ecological distinctions continued to be significant well into the era of American and Canadian sovereignty and settlement. By the time of the American Revolution, for instance, all horticultural peoples in the south had become horse nomadic, whereas none of the northernmost band-level foragers had done so (Clifton 1986). Similarly, half a century later it was the more sedentary southern horticulturists occupying lands directly in the path of American agricultural expansion who were displaced and resettled southwest of the Missouri River in the newly established Indian Territory. With a few exceptions, in the north the hunting-fishing-gathering bands escaped or avoided this expulsion entirely (Clifton 1987).

At the time of first French contact, nowhere among these Algonquians was the shaman the only or even the dominant focus of religiosity. To follow Anthony F.C. Wallace's useful outline of religious roles and ritual institutions and aims (1966), the peoples of this region exhibited great diversity well before the ramifications of 1492 fell upon them. There were shamans and priests and mystics and prophets of new ways, certainly. There were entirely individual ritual activities (personal magic, let us say); times when a part-time specialist ran the religious show; collective cults serving households or extended kin groups such as lineages, clans, phratries, and moieties or whole societies; rites that were intersocietal in nature. The only type of religious institution seemingly absent before the arrival of the French was a hierarchical, bureaucratized ecclesia, and this gap was probably filled within a generation or two—by innovative native religious figures, not Christian missionaries.

Such diversity persisted, becoming even more pronounced after the arrival of French, English, and Americans. An overview of the religious history of the region must start with this understanding. Dawn Man was but one of many tens of thousands of Algonquians who experienced religious role conflict, tension and opportunity, ritual miscellanea, innovative development, and the recurrent need to adapt supernatural style and ideology to changing social, economic, and political imperatives throughout their lifetimes.

However we may conceive the process, whatever feature of social and cultural dynamics we wish to remark upon, there were numerous examples among the religious life of Algonquians of the western Great Lakes after the 1640s. There was much simple diffusion—for instance, the acceptance, reinterpretation, and incorporation of elements of Christian symbolism. Soon after 1640 an observer would be likely to find cross-shaped icons amid otherwise native ritual paraphernalia or memorized prayers used to serve local purposes: crosses employed in clan and Midewiwin contexts, for example, or men genuflecting before setting out for war. Early records are full of reports of Algonquian ritual actors closely observing a Jesuit curing by bloodletting or a trader dividing distance by leagues per day to estimate travel time, thereby enlarging their therapeutic or divinatory inventories. This process of intercultural communication of cultural elements remains at work even today, as with the widely accepted conviction that Indians recognized and worshipped a female deity symbolic of the earth and its bounty, the alleged "Mother Earth" goddess, a legend whose origins are clearly modern American (Gill 1987).

On a more transformational level, in the early years there were some proper conversions to Christianity, but these were mainly among small children, a few women, and the aged and infirm. We must be cautious here. The religious conversion experience, we know, is rarely of the sudden, all-or-none "Paul on the Trail to Damascus" variety. Generally, conversion is a hesitant, tentative, piecemeal, experimental, psychosocial experience, with much backsliding and selectivity. We must also use care in accepting early reports from Catholic or Protestant missionaries about the numbers of "Indian" converts or mission school scholars they had suddenly acquired. For two centuries or so, these converts were mostly "Indians-by-definition," the progeny of French or British males by native women or children pushed toward Christianity by non-Algonquian Catholic or Protestant fathers.

Nonetheless, there were many full-scale conversion experiences among authentic Algonquians later, after much disruptive social and political change. We have numerous reports of Algonquians arriving on the doorsteps of priests and parsons, fervently proclaiming their wish for religious changeover, sometimes even of shamans delivering up their pitchkosan, symbolically discarding their old supernatural powers and ways. And we also have the correspondence and personal journals of some who experienced such religious transformation, unmistakably marking the depth, scope, and finality of their conversion. Today, for some this evidence is hard to accept, but we must do so. To deny a nineteenth-century Ottawa or Mesquakie the experience of conversion to Christianity or any other faith would be to refuse them the basic human right of disillusionment with decaying worldviews.

Christian denominations were by no means the only new, alternative forms of religious expression available to these Algonquians. Indeed, their own capacity for ritual innovation was strong enough to reject or blunt the appeals of Catholic and Protestant evangelists for many years. They were entirely capable of developing their own champions of new myths and rites. Thus, for many decades following first French contact, such dissatisfaction with existing ritual roles and institutions as developed did not necessarily drive a bewildered Ottawa trapper or a perplexed Mesquakie corn farmer into the arms of alien proselytizers.

In the two centuries following 1640, there were certainly more unremarked, would-be, or failed prophets than those who left historical or enduring cultural tracks. Just as certainly, there were many lesser ritual innovations tried and rejected or sharply modified. We know best only those few major revisions of old religious forms that were so spectacular, so broadly accepted, or so persistent that our ethnohistorical chronicles and ethnographic observations are filled with information, interpretations, and speculations about them. Four of these will underline an important point about the fate of ancient shamanic and later ritual traditions among the Algonquians of the western Great Lakes; older ritual roles and styles there changed rapidly into new ones as the physical and political-economic environments of these peoples were transformed.

In chronological sequence, these four new ritual institutions are the Midewiwin, then the Shawnee Prophet's visionary rebellion, the Kenekuk religion, and lastly the Dream Dance cult. Together, these have remarkably little in common, except they were post-1640 and Algonquian in origin and they all represented special efforts to apply new forms of mythic and ritual powers to the extraordinary stresses of rapid social change. Simply calling them nativistic or revitalization movements would only obscure the distinctive features of each.

About the Midewiwin there is still some dissent as to its antiquity, whether it is prehistoric or early historic in origin (Brown and Brightman 1988; Brown and Peers 1988). Nonetheless, I think Harold Hickerson (1962a, 1962b, 1963, 1988), supplemented by the work of Selwyn Dewney (1975), got it pretty well right, not to say their interpretations are beyond refinement. I will try to do so in a few details.

Hickerson's key conclusion is that the Midewiwin originated among the Chippewa at their center on the south shore of Lake Superior, Madeline Island in Chequamegon Bay, replacing the older Feast of the Dead. The date was about 1680, following around forty years of involvement in the fur trade and the emergence of larger, multiclan communities. Hickerson stressed one major function addressed by this emergent religious institution: the need to apply fresh supernatural solutions to new problems of social control—increased dissent and divisiveness within these communities. I believe Hickerson and others have overly emphasized the Chippewa version of the Midewiwin and its use for purposes of managing internal political affairs and that they have overlooked other salient features of this new ritual institution.

Although largely Chippewa in original composition, the Midewiwin quickly became a missionary-spread cult that was soon adopted by neighboring communities, mainly Algonquians. Fully developed, it was organized as a hierarchical part-time priesthood, with officers ranked in several degrees of orthodox knowledge and power, whose practitioners applied their ritual thinking and skills to various pressing problems. In addition to matters of social control, the management of the ravages of newly introduced epidemic disease was one example. Absent firsthand, contemporary observations of its emergence and development, we must apply some ethnohistorical imagination. What I think we can infer runs like this. In the 1660s and 1670s, Chippewa and other Algonquian shamans found they could not cope individually and severally with the new problems facing their kinfolk and communities, so they combined forces, pooling their individual talents and skills to fashion an inegalitarian, ritual collective.

This was the Algonquian-in-origin ecclesiastical cult I mentioned early in this chapter. We must not fail to note that the influence of the Mide priests reached beyond their home communities, so that it had intersocietal consequences as well. In one interesting way, the Midewiwin differs sharply from the other new religious movements that emerged among these Algonquians: there is no good evidence that its organization or teachings sprang from the visions of a single prophet. For this and other reasons, rather than seeing the Midewiwin as a nativistic or revitalization movement, I suggest it is more useful to interpret its appearance as a powerful effort at ritual reform, one mobilized by those most concerned and involved—a group of established shamans. However, it is also clear that the Midewiwin had a sharp up and a precipitous down trajectory. Its heyday was the eighteenth and early nineteenth centuries. By the opening decades of the twentieth century, it was everywhere in rapid decline. By then, Mide priests were competing with leaders and adherents of other new religious institutions, who gradually displaced and replaced them.

One factor in the twentieth-century decline of the Midewiwin is that as the numbers of its priests became fewer, novices found it increasingly difficult to obtain full, comprehensive instruction into its upper ranks. Moreover, one problem in assessing the nature of Great Lakes Algonquian religion in our century is that as the Mide practitioners became scarcer and isolated from one another, it became difficult to distinguish a solo Mide actor from a older shaman. I suggest what we have here is a process of ritual devolution. Indeed, as with a modern Minnesota Chippewa ritualist, Dan Raincloud (Black-Rogers 1989), the hard-pressed, partly trained solitary ritualist would be forced to carry an enormous supernatural burden on his shoulders, comprising elements of various older rituals and roles, as he or she fought to sustain some form of identifiable, meaningful "Indian way."

No top political leader in North America or Europe ever came to know any Mide priest as a personality. Several British prime ministers, American presidents, and lieutenant governors of Upper Canada had to know about him so as to cope with the extraordinary historical presence of Tenskwatawa—the Shawnee prophet—and his elder brother, Tecumseh. This is all the more interesting because Tenskwatawa's appearance and disappearance as a mover and shaker on the Great Lakes–Ohio Valley frontier covered a scant eight years, from about 1806 through 1814, and because his brief visionary venture left behind him exceedingly little. His lasting reverberations included, mainly, a modest rise in the influence of younger men as against elder chiefs in the political councils of Algonquian and allied societies in the region and an inconsequential ritual, the Shawano rite, occasionally performed by some of these communities in later years. To these two we should also add the perennial infatuation biographers addicted to the Great Hero school of historiography have expressed toward Tenskwatawa and Tecumseh's entwined fraternal careers (Edmunds 1983; Sugden 1985).

Tenskwatawa's attempts at religious rehabilitation, and his and his brother Tecumseh's rebellion, read like a scholar's idealized definitions of the prophet and the cultural revitalization movement. An abysmal failure as a Shawnee male, Tenskwatawa experienced a symbolic death and rebirth, arose to proclaim supernatural empowerment and personal possession of the one and only true word, demanded all turn away from their old religious and political leaders to follow only him and his way. There was a wide streak of absurd authoritarian arrogance in this man, in stark contrast to the sensitively calculating political, diplomatic, and military leadership of his counterpart, Tecumseh. Together they fashioned what Thomas Jefferson called their "budget of reform," the specifics of which addressed the nearly overwhelming problems facing the native societies of the region. Essentially, the heart of their efforts at revitalization were nativistic, backward-looking. The aim, with both supernatural and British military assistance—neither of which proved at all reliable—was to reverse the drift toward the sloughs of dependency that afflicted native societies of the area.

The imperative need of the native societies concerned with their increasing subordination was workable alliances and coalitions, a degree of political coordination pursued capably by Tecumseh. Meanwhile, the Shawnee Prophet proved himself adept mainly at raising tempers, generating high emotion, inflating expectations, and making enemies. He was, to the misfortune of many who followed his lead, never able to deliver the supernatural goods. Those attracted by his message were a minority—mainly young men from several tribes—notwithstanding the wide travels of disciples sent forth to proselytize and indoctrinate. But he was simultaneously self-destructive. His proclivity for putting out contracts on elder political leaders who rebuffed him did not endear him to many. In addition, established religious figures in many societies saw him as a grave threat to their status quo. They saw no future for themselves in subordinating their beliefs to the infallibility of a theological satrap. In the end, Tenskwatawa's ambitions helped precipitate a premature frontier war, which merged with the War of 1812, resulting in crushing defeats and suppression. After 1814, and a sojourn as exile in Canada, Tenskwatawa's later years were proof of the adage that there is nothing grimmer than the life of a failed prophet who once briefly tasted celebrity.

Kenekuk, a Kickapoo prophet, worked to cope with the aftermath of Tenskwatawa's rise and fall. His setting was among the Kickapoo bands of central Illinois and Indiana, and his message appealed to many neighboring Potawatomi as well (Herring 1988). Like his predecessor, Kenekuk was an explicit prophet, one with power and messages from the gods, but a visionary of far more modest and attainable aims. The problems he and his followers faced were like those of earlier decades, but during the 1820s armed resistance based on Algonquian and British military alliances was out of the question. He and his disciples had to cope in other ways with a rush of immigrants into his people's territory, with land loss, and with increasing pressure to relocate in the West—stresses they managed effectively, seeking the best choices in fields filled with odious alternatives.

On the positive side of Kenekuk's visions of a new way were his creation and institutionalization of a novel communal religious institution. This Kickapoo "church" centered on worship by believers and preaching of a new Amishlike moral order—one stressing internal and external peace, sobriety, industrious farming, and modest expectations. The process of institutionalization—overcoming what Barnes calls the "crisis of continuity" (1978)—was effected through the quality of his teachings, recounted and embellished by an organization of followers who were vestrymen, not crusaders. Solidifying and perpetuating the Kenekuk religion was certainly helped by directing the appeal inwardly to a relatively few, whose numbers were enlarged by others coming voluntarily, not broadcasting it far and wide indiscriminately.

The success of Kenekuk's words and deeds can be measured by subsequent developments. Today, a century and a half later, in northeast Kansas the Kenekuk religion is still viable on the Kickapoo Reservation. Moreover, Kenekuk's posterity in Kansas have recently shown themselves capable of coping with the latest deluge of utopian enthusiasts preaching a radically changed new moral order to them—the antipoverty warriors, marginal, long-unseen, absentee Kickapoo who arrived riding the crest of the war on poverty during the 1960s and

1970s; and, later, applied anthropologists seeking to "collaborate" in their modernization.

Last among this overview of emergent religious institutions in the western Great Lakes is the Dream Dance, or Drum Religion, which originated in the mid-1870s (Clifton 1969, 1977). The place again is far-northern Wisconsin, and those most involved in this revitalization movement were some Wisconsin Chippewa and a small group of refugee Potawatomi. The latter were landless Potawatomi who had evaded relocation to the West forty years earlier. The Chippewa bands, in contrast, owned rights to reservations guaranteed by treaty twenty years before, but many were unwilling to settle and to stay on these small tracts. The pine forests were being clear-cut, American and immigrant European settlers were arriving in droves, and state law was being imposed—all stresses falling on these still foraging bands, who were known as "strolling" Indians.

In 1876, or thereabouts, there appeared not a prophet but a prophetess. Unfortunately, far too little is known about her. Although historical records are exceedingly few and not terribly informative concerning this woman, her place in the origin myth of the Dream Dance religion is a large one. Called Wananikwe, she was apparently a stranger, a Mdewakanton Dakota woman. The myth recounts a classic prophetic experience—flight from grave danger, four days beneath the waters of a great lake, surfacing to see before her eyes two Christ figures, one good, one evil. Choosing the good Christ, she was delivered the exemplar great drum, associated ritual paraphernalia, a long catalog of ritual music and dances, a list of the many roles, other directions, and a message to give to others like herself.

The directions, followed for some years by the first cadres of converts, were to carry the message forth to other oppressed native communities in a great circle—one reaching southwest into Iowa, Kansas, and Indian Territory, then north through Nebraska and the Dakotas, lastly east through Minnesota—starting and terminating in northern Wisconsin. Here we have some ancient shamanic symbolism, a magical hunter's encirclement. Their prey was "the white man." At first, Wananikwe's great promise was that faithful performance of the new rituals would cause the enemies to fall paralyzed, so believers could dispatch them easily. Incapable of effective political-military resistance, these Chippewa and Potawatomi were relying on purely supernatural power to aid them, a measure of their desperate helplessness.

The great circle was never completed, and for this and other reasons, the magical promise was never fulfilled. Great drums coming down the ritual pipeline piled up on the Prairie Band Reservation in Kansas, which ultimately played host to eight of them, an expensive business because the Chippewa were not giving them away. The Kansas Potawatomi managed to dump two drums on unreceptive but unwary Osage and other Oklahoma Indians but then abandoned efforts to keep the ritual conduit flowing. Along the way, the promised deliverance not forthcoming, instead of abandoning their new faith, converts among the Mesquakie, Kickapoo, and Prairie Band—like true believers anywhere—simply revised the mythic message and ritual goal. The new promise was that if practiced assiduously, the Dream Dance religion would help them sustain their identities, language, and ethos.

This it accomplished very well for some decades, indeed. I am brought nearly now full circle, because my opening sketch of Dawn Man's career illustrates that point. The later history of the Dream Dance religion in Wisconsin, Michigan's Upper Peninsula, and eastern Minnesota (Parades 1980) is such as to renew an anthropologist's faith in one of our own old mythic standbys—the antique-age area hypothesis. During the 1950s, to observe experienced, trained Dream Dance believers assembled and worshipping in concert, an anthropologist would have had to go to the farthest point of this new cult's spread—into Kansas. By then, in Wisconsin where the Dream Dance had originated, the rites were so little observed and had fallen into such disrepair that concerned Menomini elders employed an anthropologist to write down a sort of ritual script of the religion for them so its tenets might be preserved for posterity. This scribe managed to confound matters by calling it their Pow Wow, confusing a decaying new religion with that entirely secular variety of commercialized, contemporary Mac-Indianism (Slotkin 1957).

It is at powwows and similar mass-market celebrations that we can, today, often find individuals identified and performing as medicine men, although some in North America and Europe much prefer smaller, ethnically mixed audiences organized as seances-for-hire (Kehoe 1990). But do these actors represent authentic continuities with ancient North American and Siberian shamanism? I conclude not so. A look at the history of the medicine man in North America will help make my last point.

Of frontier American coinage, the phrase came into common use only early in the nineteenth century, replacing the older French usage "conjurer." For some years "medicine" alone, without the person qualifier, was used to denote indiscriminately whatever sort of native religious actor an explorer, trader, missionary, or government agent was dealing with. Only later was it expanded to medicine man. The phrase came into wider, standardized usage, I regret having to say, through the writings of early anthropologists such as J. Lubbock and E. B. Tylor.

This neologism became part of the special vocabulary at first used solely when speaking of Indians, or, broadly, other "primitive" peoples, but was later extended and employed figuratively in other contexts, as were warpath, squaw, tom-tom, powwow, and the like. Meanwhile, in American popular culture a revised image of "the Indian" was being invented. Enhancing this image was the notion that the Indian ritualist possessed powerful esoteric knowledge of many nostrums and specifics for the numerous untreatable chronic and acute diseases afflicting Americans in this era. In fact, this conviction remains alive and widespread nowadays. I have seen late-model cars arrive at Menomini and Chippewa households in the 1970s, to disgorge well-dressed occupants who desperately plead for directions to the "medicine woman" known to have the Indian cure for Grandma's arthritis or Daughter's leukemia.

In the late nineteenth century, with so much demand for cures of all kinds, so little potency available from American physicians, and the powerful conviction that the Indian knew of secret treatments, it was no accident that many stepped forth to assume public identities as Indian doctors—the medicine man. Thus, into the early part of this century, we find medicine men hawking their potions and lotions on street-corner markets in cities or featured performers with traveling medicine shows in rural areas (Green 1988:601). What the real ethnic antecedents of such health care delivery personnel were is often impossible to determine. Few peered behind the standard-issue Indian suits, face paint, and feathers to ask such questions.

As improvements in scientific medicine unfolded in our era, the popularity of treatments for physical ailments from Indian medicine men waned. But medicine men and women (in the most modern orthodoxy, medicine persons) have flourished nonetheless, continuing to serve the complaints of a great many in both North America and Europe (Feest 1990). Only the nature of the affliction treated changed. Today medicine men are consulted overwhelmingly for disorders of the mind, soul, or spirit, and their treatments commonly consist of seances and similar encounter sessions. In our time, the increasingly popular medicine man blends almost imperceptibly into various other forms of pop religiosity and weekend cures for identity confusion, such as the Crystal Power and New Age cults (Kehoe 1990).

Anthropologists not yet cut loose from the baggage of nineteenth-century primitivism continue to speak of native religious figures in the terms favored by Lubbock and Tylor. I greatly doubt David E. Jones intended ill by calling the Comanche healer Sanipia a Medicine Woman, but in full justice to her specific demonstrated skills and effectiveness I recommend identifying her with a more accurate title, that of psychotherapist.

Medicine men, so-called, are found at work in various other curious contexts. When the public relations director of the Great Lakes Fish and Game Commission (after sending out press releases) showed up in a Wisconsin cemetery dragging an aged medicine man behind him, to have the old fellow cast tobacco on the graves of the state governor's grandparents, the ever gullible, always eager mass media swallowed the bait hook, line, and fishing boat. Nonetheless, we can doubt this as honest expression of authentic, ancient ritual tradition and recognize media stunts and political theatre for what they are. Similar questions might be asked—such as, what is really going on?—when an anthropologist badgers a state corrections system for permission to import medicine men into penal institutions to serve the identity needs of some inmates or to transport inmates to extramural communal rituals (Grobsmith 1989). American anthropologists are increasingly noted for the variety of service roles they assume. But the role of missionary advocate for a religion?

At best, the phrase *medicine man* is an American invention, as is the associated role. In common American folk usage, it is a hopelessly ethnocentric, entirely ambiguous, ordinarily patronizing label, part of the old special vocabulary of primitivism (Kuper 1988). It represents one of those grotesquely simplified *We/They* terms of disjunction. *We* have priests, mystics, psychotherapists, surgeons, naturopaths, philosophers, faith healers, chemical-abuse counselors, sauna owners, dowsers, stand-up comics, futurologists, and so on. *They* have only Medicine Persons. To be sure, occasionally an anthropologist has tried to hang a fresh technical meaning onto medicine man, as Harold Driver (1961) did by suggesting it be used interstitially when the ritual roles of a particular society were not categorically those of priest or shaman. More commonly, scholars of all persuasions do try to use *medicine man* in tones expressing toleration, but the depreciating *We/They* dichotomy still stands, as does the ambiguity. In American street idiom and practice, the medicine man can represent no continuity with ancient traditions. It is a fully modern invention whose shallow roots are West European, not North American or Siberian, in origin. And as to proper shamans in the technical sense scholars use? In the western Great Lakes area today, none remain. They have long since been replaced by a wide variety of ritual and other specialists, many representing freshly minted traditions.

REFERENCES

Barnes, Douglas F.
    1978.   Charisma and Religious Leadership: An Historical Analysis. *Journal for the Scientific Study of Religion* 17: 1–18.

Bee, Robert L.
    1964.   Potawatomi Peyotism: The Influence of Traditional Patterns. *Southwestern Journal of Anthropology* 22: 194–205.

———.
    1965.   Peyotism in North American Indian Groups. *Transactions of the Kansas Academy of Science* 68: 13–61.

Black-Rogers, Mary.
    1989.   Dan Raincloud: "Keeping Our Indian Way." In Clifton, 1993. *Being and Becoming Indian,* pp. 226–248.

Brown, Jennifer S.H., and Robert Brightman.
    1988.   *The Orders of the Dreamed: George Nelson on Cree and Northern Ojibwa Religion and Myth, 1823.* Winnipeg and St. Paul: University of Manitoba Press and Minnesota Historical Society Press.

Brown, Jennifer S.H., and Laura L. Peers.
    1988.   The Chippewa and Their Neighbors: A Critical Review. In Hickerson, 1988. *The Chippewa and Their Neighbors,* pp. 135–146.

Clifton, James A.
    1969.   Sociocultural Dynamics of the Prairie Potawatomi Drum Cult. *Plains Anthropologist* 44: 85–93.

———.
    1977.   *The Prairie People: Continuity and Change in Potawatomi Indian Culture.* Lawrence: Regents Press of Kansas.

———.

1986.   From Bark Canoes to Pony Herds: The Great Lakes Transportation Revolution, 1750–1775. *Henry Ford Museum and Greenfield Village Herald* 15: 12–18.

———.

1987.   Wisconsin Death March: Explaining the Extremes in Old Northwest Indian Removal. *Transactions of the Wisconsin Academy of Sciences, Arts, and Letters* 75: 1–39.

———.

1990.   *The Invented Indian: Cultural Fictions and Government Policies.* New Brunswick, N.J.: Transaction Publishers.

———.

1992.   "Don't Mess With Eagle Power." In Philip DeVita, ed., *The Naked Anthropologist: Tales From Around the World.* Belmont, Calif.: Wadsworth, pp. 35–46.

———.

1993.   *Being and Becoming Indian: Biographical Studies of North American Frontiers.* New Edition. Prospect Heights, Ill.: Waveland.

Dewney, Selwyn.
1975.   *The Sacred Scrolls of the Southern Ojibway.* Toronto: University of Toronto Press.

Driver, Harold E.
1961.   *Indians of North America.* Chicago: University of Chicago Press.

Edmunds, R. David.
1983.   *The Shawnee Prophet.* Lincoln: University of Nebraska Press.

Eliade, Mircea.
1972.   *Shamanism: Archaic Techniques of Ecstasy.* Princeton: Princeton University Press.

Feest, Christian F.
1990.   Europe's Indians. In Clifton, 1990. *The Invented Indian*, pp. 313–332.

Geertz, Clifford.
    1966.   Religion as a Cultural System. In M. Banton, ed., *Anthropological Approaches to the Study of Religion.* London: Tavistock, pp. 1–46.

Gill, Sam.
    1987.   *Mother Earth: An American Story.* Chicago: University of Chicago Press.

Green, Rayna.
    1988.   The Indian in Popular American Culture. In Wilcomb E. Washburn, ed., *History of White-Indian Relations. Handbook of North American Indians,* Vol. 4. Washington, D.C.: Smithsonian Institution pp. 587–606.

Grim, John A.
    1983.   *The Shaman: Patterns of Siberian and Ojibway Healing.* Norman: University of Oklahoma Press.

Grobsmith, Elizabeth S.
    1989.   Inmates and Anthropologists: The Impact of Advocacy on the Expression of Native American Culture in Prison. Paper presented at the Annual Meeting of the Society for Applied Anthropology, Santa Fe, New Mexico.

Harner, Michael.
    1982.   *The Way of the Shaman.* New York: Bantam.

Herring, Joseph B.
    1988.   *Kenekuk: The Kickapoo Prophet.* Lawrence: University Press of Kansas.

Hickerson, Harold.
    1962a.   The Southwestern Chippewa: An Ethnohistorical Study. *American Anthropologist* 64, No. 3, Part 2, Memoir 92.

_____.
    1962b.   Notes on the Post-Contact Origin of the Midewiwin. *Ethnohistory* 9: 404–423.

_____.
    1963.   The Sociohistorical Significance of Two Chippewa Ceremonials. *American Anthropologist* 65: 67–85.

_____.
    1988.   *The Chippewa and Their Neighbors: A Study in Ethnohistory.* Prospect Heights, Ill.: Waveland (revised and expanded edition of 1970 Holt, Rinehart and Winston original).

Howard, James H.
    1960.   When They Worship the Underwater Panther: A Prairie Potawatomi
          Bundle Ceremony. *Southwestern Journal of Anthropology* 16: 217–224.

———.

    1962.   Potawatomi Mescalism and Its Relationship to the Diffusion of the
          Peyote Cult. *Plains Anthropologist* 7: 125–135.

———.

    1965.   The Kenakuk Religion: An Early 19th Century Revitalization Movement 140
          Years Later. *Museum News* 26: 11–12. University of South Dakota Museum.

Kehoe, Alice B.
    1990.   Primal Gaia: Primitivists and Plastic Medicine Men. In Clifton, *The
          Invented Indian,* pp. 193–210.

Kuper, Adam.
    1988.   *The Invention of Primitive Society: Transformations of an Illusion.*
          New York: Routledge.

LaBarre, Weston.
    1970.   *The Ghost Dance: Origins of Religion.* New York: Dell.

Landes, Ruth.
    1963.   Potawatomi Medicine. *Transactions of the Kansas Academy of
          Science* 66: 553–599.

———.

    1970.   *The Prairie Potawatomi: Tradition and Ritual in the Twentieth Century.*
          Madison: University of Wisconsin Press.

Levi-Strauss, Claude.
    1962.   *The Savage Mind,* J. Anthony Parades, ed. Chicago: University of
          Chicago Press.

Shweder, Richard A.
    1979.   Aspects of Cognition in Zinacanteco Shamans: Experimental Results.
          In William A. Lessa and Evon Z. Vogt, eds., *Reader in Comparative
          Religion: An Anthropological Approach.* New York: Harper and Row,
          pp. 327–331.

Slotkin, James S.
    1957.   *The Menominee Pow-Wow: A Study in Cultural Decay.* Milwaukee:
              Milwaukee Public Museum Publications in Anthropology, No. 4.

Sugden, John.
    1985.   *Tecumseh's Last Stand.* Norman: University of Oklahoma Press.

Von Furer-Haimendorf, C.
    1970.   Priests. In Richard Cavendish, ed., *Man, Myth, and Magic,* Vol. 16.
              BPCC/Phoebus Publishing, pp. 2,248–2,255.

Wallace, Anthony F.C.
    1966.   *Religion: An Anthropological View.* New York: Random House.

OTHER WORKS

Harner, Michael.
    1973.   *Hallucinogens and Shamanism.* New York: Oxford University Press.

Kuper, Adam.
    1970.   *The Ghost Dance: Origins of Religion.* New York: Dell.

Levi-Strauss, Claude.
    1980.   *Anishinabe: 6 Studies of Modern Chippewa.* Tallahassee: University
              Presses of Florida.

Ritzenthaler, Robert E., and Pat Ritzenthaler.
    1983.   *The Woodland Indians of the Western Great Lakes.* Milwaukee:
              Milwaukee Public Museum.

Schutz, Noel W., Jr.
    1975.   *The Study of Shawnee Myth in an Ethnographic and Ethnohistorical
              Perspective.* Ph.D. dissertation, Anthropology, Indiana University.

Slotkin, James S.
    1985.   *Tecumseh's Last Stand.* Norman: University of Oklahoma Press.

Turner, Victor.
    1972.   Religious Specialists. In David L. Shils, ed., *International
              Encyclopedia of the Social Sciences,* Vol. 13. New York: Crowell
              Collier and Macmillan, pp. 437–444.

Vecsey, Christopher.
  1983. *Traditional Ojibwa Religion and Its Historical Changes.* Philadelphia:
          American Philosophical Society.

Wallace, Anthony F.C.
  1956. Revitalization Movements. *American Anthropologist* 58: 264–281.

SHAMANISM IN THE
COLUMBIA-FRASER PLATEAU REGION

ROBERT J. THEODORATUS

The aboriginal cultures of the Columbia-Fraser Plateau are the least known among those of North America. The plateau (cultural-geographical) region centers in the interior drainage basins of the Columbia and Fraser Rivers, as seen in Figure 8.1. The Cascade Mountains form the western boundary, the Rocky Mountains in part the eastern boundary, the northern margins of the Great Basin the southern boundary, and the boreal forests of the headwaters of the Fraser River the northern boundary. Mountain spurs, tributary valleys, and uplands further divide this semiarid region into a series of local subregions. Linguistically, the Salishan and Sahaptin languages predominated except in the northern fringes, where some Athapascan-speaking groups were found. The subsistence base was hunting and gathering. Near the rivers, fishing, especially for salmon in the late summer and autumn, was common. Small, independent bands with winter "villages" were the norm. These egalitarian peoples had no chiefs, only headmen and at times shamans as situational leaders. Some of the better-known groups are the Nez Percé, Spokane, Yakima, Okanagon, Sanpoil, Klamath, Thompson, and Kalispel.

Ethnographic research in this culture area has been minimal and sporadic, although some of the earlier work has been very influential in developing anthropological thought. In the late nineteenth century, James Teit, under the supervision of Franz Boas, collected data on the Thompson, Lillooet, Shuswap, Okanagon, Coeur d'Alene, and others. His somewhat sketchy data on shamanism were utilized by Ruth Benedict as a type example in her early study of the vision quest in North America (Benedict 1923). In the 1920s Leslie Spier (1930) worked among the Klamath, and Verne Ray (1932) worked among the Sanpoil/Nespelem—both ethnographies are outstanding. In the 1930s Leslie Spier (1936), Verne Ray (1939, 1942), Walter Cline, Alan Smith (1938) and Diamond Jenness did further work. Since 1940, with the

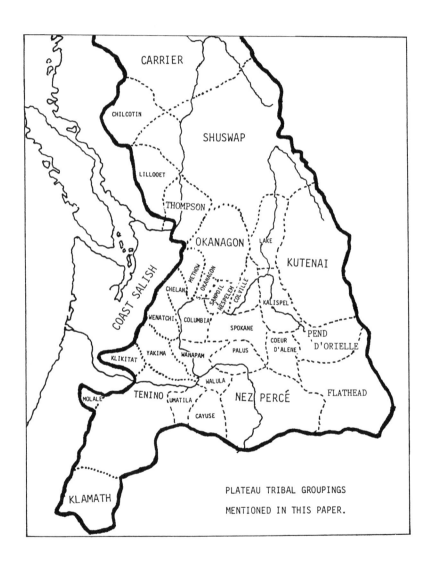

FIGURE 8.1
Tribal groups of the Columbia-Fraser Plateau.

exception of Theodore Stern, David French, and Deward Walker (1970), little significant research has been done in the plateau. In this chapter, I utilize my own data on the Methow and Southern Okanagon and the earlier ethnographies.[1]

I examine what I consider the core elements of plateau shamanism in northcentral Washington state. Comparative examples from other plateau groups are also noted. These core elements consist of the guardian spirit or vision quest, the winter evening narrations of the sacred stories (we call them myths), the winter dance, shamanistic curing, and shamanistic power contests. As we will see, being a shaman was not a matter of being different but was one of degree. A shaman sought spirit powers and used those powers to seek social recognition, as did everyone else in the group. The difference was that he or she had more powers, was more successful in curing, and directed rituals more frequently than did others.

SUPERNATURALS

For every animal species and some natural forces, such as the south wind, there was a corresponding supernatural being, usually referred to in the literature as a "spirit." Although each normally appeared in human form, it could change into its animal (or whatever) shape at will. In the Myth Age, before people appeared, these beings had great and often destructive powers, which Coyote, the trickster-transformer, was sent to reduce to less dangerous levels so people "who were coming soon" would be able to survive in this world. Through a series of adventures and misadventures—some highly erotic—Coyote, with the help of his own powers and those of others, accomplished this task. Each Myth Age supernatural then became the ancestor of its animal-name species or natural phenomenon. Each also became a supernatural desirous of establishing helpful relationships with individual humans to whom it gave specific powers, help, and skills.

The actual power or strength of any supernatural could vary vis-à-vis any human recipient. To many, Grizzly Bear, Mountain Goat, Cougar, and Black Bear were very powerful because they gave strength, stamina, courage, and aggressive shamanistic powers; to others, these were very weak powers. Some of my informants claimed that Chickadee, Hummingbird, Yellow Jacket, and even Fly were the most powerful supernaturals. Most agreed that Owl and Blue Jay were strong powers because they gave the ability to see at night and clairvoyant power. Rattlesnake and Black Widow Spider were obviously useful in treating the bites of those creatures. Daddy-Longlegs Spider tended to be somewhat silly and useless.

THE VISION QUEST

Before being sent out on a guardian spirit vision quest, every child had been fully socialized into knowing what to seek and how to conduct himself or herself in the search for a visionary experience. Much of the mental conditioning was derived from the annual winter narrations and dramatizations of the sacred myths by the elderly of each village. In these stories the Myth Age beings exhibited and related their powers and also related how people would seek and use spiritual power when they came onto the land. In one sense these were annual schooling sessions in religion that also contained much necessary knowledge relating to the practicalities of everyday life. Every child knew the potential powers, songs, and dances of each supernatural.

The vision quest normally occurred in the summer or early autumn, and those seeking supernatural power were usually between age eight and puberty. Once puberty had been reached, one's vision quests ended. There were no specific "sacred places"; the site usually chosen for the all-night vigil was secluded, isolated, and quiet, where it was hoped no human or other distractions would interfere with the quest. Secluded mountainsides, forested areas, lakesides or streamsides, and small valleys around creeks were preferred. Silence broken only by the wind and night cries of nocturnal creatures was essential. Each child was told specifically where to go and spend the night, what to do, how to watch and listen, and, above all, to be alert and not to fall asleep. Commonly, repetitive tasks were assigned to make sure the child had no opportunity to sleep; a usual task was to pile up stones in a wall-like line. Many of these can still be found along isolated mountainsides in the plateau. No food or water was allowed. Also, some object, such as a tool, a piece of deer antler, or something similar, would be given to the child, who was told exactly where to leave it. The following day an older relative would retrieve that item—just to make sure. This vigil would be repeated for several nights in a row, or until the child was successful. We do know that not every child was enthusiastic about this venture, and some had to be physically coerced into undertaking it.

Along the eastern and northern borders of the plateau, some variations of the vision quest were found. Among the Kutenei and others bordering on the plains, parents instructed their children to seek specific supernaturals, and the site where the vision occurred thereafter became a sacred place to that person. For the Nez Percé, ritual and physical purification were additional prerequisites (Spinden 1908:247–248; Walker 1970:270–271). Among the Lower Carrier, only a few individuals sought a vision, and the boy's or girl's father selected the spirit to be sought. Only the oldest child in a family was allowed to personally select his or her own spirit. Here the person who sought lay power went out in the daytime; seekers of shamanistic powers sought them at night, usually in a sweat house with an accompanying shaman as a proctor. Vigils at cremation places also occurred in order to be near those forces of life and death as well as the ghosts of deceased shamans (Ray 1939:70–72).

Not all vision seekers were successful. Several of the Methow and Southern Okanagon I worked with stated that they had been unsuccessful in their quests. Ray estimated that among the Sanpoil, 70 to 80 percent of the boys were successful, whereas only 20 to 30 percent of the girls were. As we will see, there were alternative means of acquiring a "power" (Ray 1932:68–69).

In a vision experience the supernatural always first appeared as a human who announced that it wished to help that young person when he or she became an adult by giving him or her good health and specific skills such as hunting, curing, stamina, and similar skills. It would then sing its power song and on occasion give a dance step. A Wenatchi woman who was married to an Upper Skagit emphatically informed me that each Wenatchi power song was very different, whereas those of her husband's people all sounded the same. The spirit would then identify itself and vanish. Often the species form of the spirit (owl, coyote, badger, rattlesnake, mouse, and the like) would then be seen moving away. When part of the quest activities included diving into a lake and remaining underwater as long as possible, Ray noted that the seekers found themselves in a large underwater house filled with spiritual beings. His claim that this was a coastal Salish influence is possible, given the many marriages that took place between Interior Salish and Upper Skagit individuals (Ray 1932:183). When the child returned at dawn, the parents and elders knew, given the emotional reactions, whether he or she had been successful.

When successful, the child was often sent out on additional or subsequent spirit quests in the hope that many supernatural helpers would later give that person greater power and, it was hoped, help him or her to become a shaman. Occasionally, an adult might have up to six or seven guardian spirits. However, once the guardian spirit had been obtained, the child was expected to forget or repress this until he or she was at least twenty-five years of age, or fully into adult life.

There were alternative or supplementary means whereby a supernatural helper could be acquired either by unsuccessful seekers or those after additional powers. The most common was when an elderly relative, whose physical health was declining or who was becoming senile, would send his or her powers to a younger, postpubescent relative—especially one who had repeatedly failed to acquire a power. The Southern Okanagon referred to this spirit as a *papaiot*. Cline's informants in the early 1930s stated that in prewhite times, these could come at any age and regardless of one's wishes. They could also bring difficulty and danger to the recipient. If an adult already had a guardian spirit, he or she should send it out to capture and tame the papaiot. However, if one's guardian spirit was not strong enough, the papaiot might steal his or her guardian spirit and cause the person to become ill (Cline et al. 1938:153). By the time I worked in the same area, the papaiot no longer posed this danger. A second means of gaining power was by theft—an activity usually associated with powerful shamans bent on acquiring further power and causing fear among others. This would also fall into the category of sorcery. A third means was by accident during children's imitative play activities. In these activities children sometimes imitated shamanistic curing or winter dancing even though their parents warned them not to do this. I have some examples of children as young as four years of age who had violent supernatural experiences in this context. Usually, when this occurred the parents summoned a shaman to help the child control the spirit by having it leave until the child was an adult.

WINTER: STORYTELLING AND THE WINTER DANCE

Winter was a time of relative economic inactivity; individual families returned to their semisubterranean winter houses, which were located in sheltered locations near rivers and creeks. By December people shifted more to the religious aspects of life, such as the narrations of the sacred stories and the forthcoming winter dances. Those elderly men and women renowned for both their knowledge and their artistic storytelling skills narrated and dramatized stories of the great events of the Myth Age. Every other evening all of the children and many adults gathered around the fireside for several hours in the home of an elderly couple. Through these dramatizations the Myth Age past became alive in the minds of those present, young and old. In these myths, which were taboo to tell in the summer, Old Man Coyote, the trickster-transformer, destroyed the fish weir on the Columbia River near the Dalles and led the salmon to upriver streams for all of the peoples. Through his powers (he had his own four spirit powers) and the powers of others, beings were transformed into all of the creatures of the plateau world, heroes died and were magically brought back to life, mysterious powers entered the landscape, and the rituals of shamanistic curing and power were described in detail, as were the methods to be used by people in acquiring and controlling their spiritual powers. In this context, young people could dream and older people could reflect on the spiritual.

Given this religious context, the relative physical inactivity, and perhaps the somewhat dull winter weather of that region, the thoughts of many adults shifted, consciously and unconsciously, to their own often unmanifested relationships to the spirit world. Individuals who had not reaffirmed their relationships to their guardian spirits encountered during a childhood vision quest began to feel morose and depressed and to come down with what was labeled *spirit sickness*. This was usually interpreted as being caused by a spirit who was returning and who was insistent upon activating a latent bond. This would then enable the person to begin to use his or her promised powers for hunting, curing, fishing, gaining wealth, and similar pursuits. A shaman would usually be consulted for verification. The shaman would say, "Your power has come and wants you to give a dance" (Cline et al. 1938:145).

The series of winter dances, which began around the winter solstice, lasted for up to two months. They occurred among all of the Interior Salish-speaking and Sahaptin-speaking groups in Washington and northern Idaho but were absent in the interior of British Columbia. A dance could be sponsored by a shaman, an initiate, or anyone whose guardian spirit had commanded him or her to sponsor a dance. Each dance normally lasted from two to three days, and, in any general locality, there could be a sequence of dances during the winter. Occasionally, an individual shaman would sponsor two in a given winter. An announcement was simply spread by word of mouth; no messengers were used.

A dance was usually held at a shaman's house. Before the ritual began the shaman and a boy would go into the woods to select and cut down a small fir tree about eight feet high. The shaman told the youth which side of the tree to stand on as the youth felled it under the shaman's direction. This was to protect the young man from harm. The boy carried the tree to the house, where the shaman removed all of the branches except those at the very top and peeled the bark from the lower part. Sometimes a spiral of bark or circular bands of bark were left on the tree. It was then placed in the center of the dancing area of the house and was utilized as a pathway for supernaturals arriving at and departing from the winter dance. Sometimes "power emblems," or deer hoof rattles, of the shaman and older dancers were suspended from the remaining upper branches. In the twentieth century this tree was replaced by "power symbols," or hand staffs, carried by each individual dancer (Cline et al. 1938:147).

The shaman would begin the dance by sweeping the room in order to remove ghosts or other supernatural dangers. Many would dance—older persons as well as the person or persons suffering from spirit sickness (Ray 1932:191). In addition to a doorkeeper, whose duty was to prevent people from entering and leaving during dances, one or more persons having Owl power would perch on the roof and act as the eyes of the shaman in watching for approaching spirit powers. Among the Sanpoil and Salishan groups to the east, Owls were replaced by men having Blue Jay spirit powers. During a dance they would paint their faces black, remove most of their clothing, and perch on the rafters as they watched and informed those below of approaching spirits. At the end of each evening they had to be forcefully held over smudge fires in order to be returned to normalcy (Ray 1939:115–116).

In addition to reuniting oneself with one's power, the winter dance provided a means of publicly and ritually announcing the identity of a person's power. The shaman sang and danced toward the pole (tree) and grasped and shook it in order to summon his own powers. He would then begin to call on the "novice's" power to approach the dance house. In a trancelike state the shaman—through his speaker, who repeated the shaman's soft-spoken utterances in a loud voice— would draw the hesitant spirit closer and closer, with each move also announced by the Owls or Blue Jays on the roof. Finally, the novice's spirit would enter the room and enter the novice's body. The shaman would sing and temporarily remove the possessing spirit in order to see if the novice's body could handle this new power. Among the Sanpoil the shaman would then rub and blow the spirit into the novice's body, after which the novice would go to the fir tree, grasp it, and sing his power song. Others would then join in the singing and dancing for about half an hour (Ray 1932:192–193). In addition, curings by the shaman took place at this time. At the end of two or three evenings the dance came to an end, and gifts would be distributed by the novice and the shaman or host.

Occasionally, other spirits would be attracted to a winter dance. If the shaman detected one he would try to capture it and add it to his own group of spirit helpers or send it away after appropriating some of its powers. Also, we have some accounts of "evil" shamans trying to steal a novice's power, an act that could result in the novice's death.

In eastern Washington and southward, among the peoples on the Oregon side of the Columbia River, the last dance of the winter was often referred to as the Chinook Dance. Its purpose was to help bring in the moist warming Chinook winds from the coast and thus bring an end to the winter weather. The active leader of this dance was a person who had "weather power." Others with different powers would also sing and dance in turn. Sometimes certain power songs were not fully appreciated. One Methow danced for his Grasshopper power and sang, "You can see when I step. You will get lots of fish bait next year." That summer they had so many grasshoppers that people asked him never to sing that power again.

SHAMANISTIC CURING

Curing was the most important activity of the plateau shaman. In this century Native Americans have usually referred to shamans as "Indian doctors"—that is, they treat Indian or spirit-caused illnesses, as opposed to "White Man doctors," who treat illnesses associated with white people and Euro-American medical traditions. Again we must remember that a shaman was usually an older, but not necessarily aged, person who had acquired many spirit helpers—spirit helpers who were or had given the shaman greater curing and other powers within the spirit world—and finally, the shaman was also a person who over time had achieved a reputation for success in curing illnesses and controlling supernaturals who caused difficulties for people. Younger adults normally did not practice curing or shamanizing for several practical reasons. Even after activating the bond with one's guardian spirit during a winter dance, the relationship was not fully secure, because it took several years to strengthen and fully develop these gifts. Also, curing tended to be socially regarded as a role for slightly older people. Finally, there was a real danger of arousing the competitive jealousy of an established shaman who had many powerful spirit helpers. Such a person could and did utilize his or her powers to steal or destroy a competing younger person's power(s) and soul. Usually, a shaman was only rewarded or paid if successful.

There were several standard explanations for illness. Object intrusion was the most common, with the belief that evil shamans or others magically directed certain objects toward and into the bodies of their victims. Typical objects were small pieces of stone, a hair, a bit of bone, a rattlesnake fang, or even bits of cottonwood fluff. The latter occurred among the Southern Okanagon, who believed the Northern Okanagon magically activated bits of cottonwood fluff and sent them down the valley with the prevailing early summer winds. Other causes were intrusive spirits (usually a guardian spirit), the loss or theft of one's guardian spirit by an evil shaman, the return of one's guardian spirit (cured at the winter dance), and soul loss. Object intrusion, guardian spirit loss or theft, and soul loss were fatal if they could not be treated by a shaman. Intrusive objects were removed by a shaman, who sucked them out. However, there were many local variations of the sucking procedure. Usually, the shaman would call upon his or her powers for help and begin to massage the victim's body in search of the object. Once located, as the shaman sang his or her power song, the shaman maneuvered the object to an arm, leg, or the forehead and then sucked it out. In the Canadian groups a sucking tube was used, whereas in the U.S. plateau the shaman's lips were either on or directly above the skin of the ill person. For the latter, Ray described examples of the shaman in a trance state held back with ropes by assistants. Once the object was removed it would be spat into a container of water and discarded later or, if sent by an evil shaman, blown back so as to strike the sender (Ray 1932:206–207).

The treatment of soul loss often involved extreme difficulties for the shaman, who had to utilize all of his or her powers to determine the cause of the loss and who was causing the condition, as well as to find the missing soul. While in a trance the shaman might journey to the land of the dead if the person's soul had wandered back with lonely, nocturnally wandering ghosts. Or if stolen by a jealous or evil shaman, the shaman would have to identify that person and find where the stolen soul had been hidden. Once these fact-finding journeys of the shaman's spiritual helpers or soul were complete, a scene ensued that had all of the physical and verbal drama and impersonations of the struggle between the treating shaman and his or her spiritual helpers as opposed to those of the opposing distant shaman. If successful, the soul or spirit was reunited with its rightful owner. The losing shaman could suffer death. The ritual, though less dramatic, was similar in the case of object intrusion.

In the northern, southern, and eastern regions of the plateau, some variant curing beliefs and practices occurred. Among the Klamath of southcentral Oregon, shamans having the following guardian spirits cured object intrusion: Fishhawk, Golden Eagle, Buzzard, Crow, Weasel, Magpie, Fisher, and Frog (Spier 1930:122–123). A Nez Percé shaman's helpers, such as Sun, Cloud, Eagle, and Fishhawk, lived in the sky (Spinden 1908:256). Thompson shamans painted their hair, hands, and chests red and wore a conical woven mask over their heads as they and their souls were sent into the Otherworld in search of a lost soul or as they sucked out an intrusive object from the victim's body. Among the Lillooet an object would be sucked out, placed in a container of urine to kill it, and then put into clean water. Or the shamans held it in their hands and asked the onlookers if they wanted it killed; if so, the shamans would throw it into the fire (Teit 1900:262–263; 1906:287–288; 1930:195–196).

Whenever a shaman was performing—whether curing, locating a lost or stolen soul, directing a winter dance, locating game, or conducting some other activity—there was the ever-present possibility that he or she might come into conflict with another shaman who was causing the crisis. As already noted, this would ignite a violent spiritual battle, often resulting in the destruction or theft of the powers or the soul of the loser. Often the winner would then appropriate those spirits or powers for his or her own use, thus increasing his or her power and others' fear of him or her. One such example was related by an elderly Southern Okanagon informant. Early in this century a Southern Okanagon became seriously ill. Several local shamans in succession were called in, but each, after seeing the causal force—a powerful

Yakima shaman who lived about 125 miles to the south—and in fear of his or her own life, refused to doctor the stricken person. Finally, a Nespelem shaman reputed to have great power was called in. He accepted the challenge, and the struggle between him and the Yakima shaman—who, in the form of a gigantic cougar, arched across the sky from 125 miles away—continued far into the night. In the end, the Nespelem shaman won and the "evil" Yakima shaman, who had been trying to steal the soul and spirit helper of the sick man, was destroyed by the superior powers of the Nespelem shaman. Sometimes two or three local shamans would combine forces to fight another shaman. Also, two shamans could battle each other when both were asleep—they simply sent their powers out when they were dreaming.

Shamans also had other duties or powers. These included helping men win at the stick game (a gambling game), aiding hunting parties in locating and killing big game, helping bring salmon into fish weirs, predicting the future, chasing away ghosts, officiating at funerals, selecting favorable campsites, curing barrenness in women, and advising war parties.

CONCLUSION

Among the aboriginal peoples of the plateau, being a recognized shaman and "shamanizing" were a matter of degree rather than absolute or clearly distinct roles and practices. Almost everyone in some way acquired at least one spirit power and made use of those abilities promised by that spiritual being. Shamans had more powers and individually achieved their status by being consistently successful in dealing with the supernatural.

The two most crucial activities through which individuals obtained their spirit powers and were enculturated into their importance were the vision quest and the sacred storytelling session during the winter months. The latter was especially essential as a body of knowledge through which individuals learned how to seek a spirit helper, what each spirit helper had to offer, and, once adults, how to reaffirm a bond to their guardian spirit.

NOTES

1. The data on the Methow and Southern Okanagon (Sinkaietk) are based upon information gathered from four informants in 1956. One, an eighty-year-old man, lived near Pateras, Washington, and the other three (one man who claimed to be near ninety, his wife, in her early seventies, and one woman in her sixties) lived near Malott, Washington. Some data were also obtained from a fifty-year-old Wenatchi woman who lived in Concrete, Washington. (*Note:* The ethnic group is spelled "Okanagon" and the river is spelled "Okanogan.")

REFERENCES

Benedict, Ruth Fulton.
 1923. The Concept of the Guardian Spirit in North America. *American Anthropological Association,* Memoir No. 29.

Cline, Walter, et al.
 1938. *The Sinkaietk or Southern Okanagon of Washington.* General Series in Anthropology, No. 6. Menasha, Wisc.: George Banta.

Ray, Verne F.
 1932. *The Sanpoil and Nespelem, Salishan Peoples of Northeastern Washington.* University of Washington Publications in Anthropology, Vol. 5. Seattle: University of Washington Press.

 ———.
 1939. *Cultural Relations in the Plateau of Northwestern America.* Los Angeles: Southwest Museum.

 ———.
 1942. *Culture Element Distributions: XXII. Plateau.* University of California Anthropological Records, Vol. 8:2, pp. 99–262. Berkeley: University of California Press.

Spier, Leslie.
 1930. *Klamath Ethnography.* University of California Publications in American Archaeology and Ethnology, Vol. 30. Berkeley: University of California Press.

 ———.
 1936. *Tribal Distribution in Washington.* General Series in Anthropology, No. 3. Menasha, Wisc.: George Banta.

Spinden, Herbert J.
　　1908.　*The Nez Percé Indians.* American Anthropology Association, Memoirs, Vol. 2. Lancaster: New Era Printing, pp. 165–274.

Teit, James.
　　1900.　*The Thompson Indians of British Columbia.* New York: American Museum of Natural History, Memoirs, Vol. 2, pp. 163–392.

———.
　　1906.　*The Lillooet Indians.* New York: American Museum of Natural History, Memoirs, Vol. 4, pp. 193–300.

———.
　　1930.　*The Salishan Tribes of the Western Plateaus* (ed. by Franz Boas). Washington, D.C.: Smithsonian Museum, Bureau of American Ethnology, Annual Report, Vol. 45, pp. 23–396.

Walker, Deward E., Jr.
　　1970.　Nez Percé. Sorcery. In Deward E. Walker, Jr. (ed.), *Systems of North American Witchcraft and Sorcery.* Moscow: Anthropological Monographs of the University of Idaho, No. 1, pp. 267–295.

OTHER WORKS

Jacobs, Melville.
　　1960.　*The People Are Coming Soon. An Analysis of Clackamas Chinook Myths and Tales.* Seattle: University of Washington Press.

Kroeber, Alfred L.
　　1939.　*Cultural and Natural Areas of Native North America.* University of California Publications in American Archaeology and Ethnology, Vol. 38. Berkeley: University of California Press.

Park, Willard Z.
　　1938.　*Shamanism in Western North America.* Northwestern University Studies in the Social Sciences, No. 2. Evanston, Ill.: Northwestern University Press.

Tcit, James.
　　1909.　*The Shuswap.* New York: American Institution of Natural History, Memoirs, Vol. 4, pp. 443–789.

Teit, James, Marian Gould, Livingston Farrand, and Herbert J. Spinden.
    1917.   *Folk-Tales of the Salishan and Sahaptin Tribes.* Lancaster:
           Memoirs of the American Folklore Society, Vol. 11.

Theodoratus, Robert J.
    1956a. Field notes on the Methow.

———.

    1956b. Field notes on the Southern Okanagon.

———.

    1956c. Field notes on the Wenatchee.

THE DARK EMPEROR: CENTRAL ASIAN
ORIGINS IN CHINESE SHAMANISM

Gary Seaman

The ultimate origin of the word *shaman* has been the subject of a surprisingly large number of learned discussions. Nineteenth-century Russian and German scholarship held that the Tungus word, and thus the European derivations from it, was ultimately to be found in some Indic language, related to the Pali term for an ascetic or the Sanskrit word for a Buddhist initiate. In the early twentieth century, however, Julius Nemeth (1913–1914) and Berthold Laufer (1917) developed the hypothesis that the word was natively Altaic, derived from a Turkic root. This meant that the word, and presumably also the "tradition" of shamanism, was of Central Asian origin. This opinion was widely entertained until the 1930s, when S. M. Shirokogoroff (1935; Mironov and Shirokogoroff 1924) concluded on the basis of extensive fieldwork that many aspects of shamanism among the tribal peoples of Northeast Asia developed, in fact, as the result of relatively recent contact with Sino-Buddhist institutions. Most modern scholars feel that the term itself, if not all aspects of the various local manifestations of shamanism, is derived from Indo-European origins: it passed through Chinese and Sino-Barbarian versions, was then adapted to the cultures of marginal hunters and herders who spoke Ural-Altaic languages, and finally met the Eastern European version of the expanding Western world system after the fifteenth century. It is well traveled from its early home on the slopes of the southern Himalayas, because the term probably passed to the Tungus and other peoples in Mongolia, Manchuria, and beyond through the medium of Chinese *shamen,* or wandering Buddhist monk.

Today the term has joined a band of anthropological jargon that includes mana, potlatch, and taboo, among others. These words have been separated from their original cultural contexts and are pressed into usage in alien places, often rather unhappily adapting to their new environment with some culture shock. To come full circle, contemporary

▼

Chinese usage now employs the term *saman*, borrowed from European anthropological applications. The Chinese version incorporates both of the above theories of the linguistic origins of the word: the two Chinese characters *Sa* and *Man* refer, respectively, to the Indo-Buddhist and Manchurian aspects of the scholarly discussion without giving precedence to either. At the same time, the newly coined Chinese term avoids the confusion the more specifically Buddhist technical term *shamen* would introduce.

Interestingly for my present purposes, the term *shaman* seems to have been attractive to Altaic-speaking peoples of Central Asia as the result of the prestige of popular Buddhism, various forms of which were patronized, encouraged, and adopted by generations of Eurasian borderland aristocrats or would-be aristocrats. Some scholars view this fusion of shamanistic practice and high religion as particularly characteristic of the nomadic states founded by peoples such as the Huns, Mongols, and Manchus (Dienes 1981; Pallisten 1956).

Shirokogoroff's allusion to the Chinese connection encourages me to use the word here, although I make no claims about any specific historical connections between the phenomenon I describe as "Chinese shamanism" and the institutions of shamanism among the Tungus or elsewhere in Central Asia. In most discussions of shamanism in Northeast Asia, the most distinctive feature of the Tungus *saman* was his or her entry into ecstatic trance states to perform feats of curing, intercession with otherworldly spirits, and other feats. It is this character of the shaman as spirit medium in a state of ecstasy or trance that has been generalized to other cultural contexts (Basilov 1984). As a working definition of what the term *shaman* means as a classificatory term, I quote a prominent scholar in the field, I. M. Lewis, for guidance: "A Shaman is an inspired prophet and healer, a charismatic religious figure, with the power to control the spirits, usually by incarnating them. If spirits speak through him, he is also likely to have the capacity to engage in mystical flight and other 'out-of-body experiences'" (1984:9).

Recent students of shamanism and spirit possession have emphasized the broader social context in which these ecstatic phenomena are likely to occur. Lewis (1971) in particular believes spirit possession is most frequently observed among marginal and outcast groups (cf. also Walker 1973). This same perception has been largely shared by historians of Chinese society, and the official neo-Confucian position in particular has been to relegate anything that seems to belong to the occult or the

▼

supernatural to the dustbins of history (Ropp 1981:152). Chinese official histories have therefore suppressed evidence of shamanistic activities, especially at the imperial court. Yet, the Chinese historical material is very rich, and enough evidence exists to show that until fairly recently, the Chinese imperial court was the locus of shamanistic activities. The exceptional historical depth afforded by the Chinese historical sources allows us to greatly improve our depth of understanding of shamanistic practices in Chinese culture.

SHAMANISM IN CHINA

The earliest records of Chinese civilization contain evidence that the Chinese have long perceived a close relationship between the living and the spirits of parallel worlds (Erkes 1950; Keightley 1978; Chang 1983). For example, about thirteen centuries before the birth of Christ, the following inscription was carved on the "oracle bones" of the Shang dynasty: "The king is sick. Is this possibly because the deceased Grandmother Chi has cursed him? Or perhaps the Grandmother Keng? Will his condition worsen?" (Chang 1970).

One Chinese character that is often used for a spirit medium, *Wu*, is attested in these same oracle bone inscriptions. The character is still used in modern Chinese to refer to spirit mediums and seems to be related to the homophone Wu, which means to dance, jump, or posture (Needham 1956:134). One of the earliest references to shamanistic activities in Shang times is to a certain Wu Hsien, who is mentioned in the Book of Documents (*Shu Ching*): "In Ta-mo's time [17th century B.C.] there was Wu-hsien who regulated the royal household, and in Tsu-i's time [16th century B.C.] there was a man like Wu-hsien" (*Shu Ching*, Chun Shu, Chun Shih, in de Groot 1969:1,204).

This same personage (or perhaps official title) is mentioned again in the Bamboo Annals, where Ta-mo directs him to make sacrifices to the mountains and streams (de Groot 1969:1,204, note 4). Other texts of the Shang period have numerous references to the personages called Wu, and the archaic society accorded them a central role in religious ritual in the society of the time (Keightley 1978; Chang 1983; and Eichhorn 1976).

By feudal times, during the Chou dynasty (1122–1255 B.C.), the concern with the intervention of otherworldly spirits in human affairs had resulted in the evolution of official titles filled by spirit mediums at the feudal courts. As in the earlier Shang period, these mediums were known as

Wu (or also as *Hsi*, perhaps differentiated from one another by sex, although the evidence is conflicting; Ch'u 1930:1,329). The *Chou Li* (Ritual of the Chou Dynasty) describes these official spirit mediums as being

> of both sexes in indefinite number; their masters (Shih) are four ordinary officers of the middle rank; with two storekeepers, four writers, four adjutants, and forty serfs (Ch. 17, section 1, p. 28). . . . The male *Wu* are bound to turn their faces to the sacrifices and the invited spirits, and to supply the exclamations wherewith to call (the latter) from all sides while waving long grass. In winter, they eject (evil) from the halls, and perform the same task all around, without calculation (of direction or distances). In spring they call (gods or felicity), and avert (demons, or evil), thus warding off diseases. And when the Sovereign pays a visit of condolence, they walk before him with the Invokers or Conjurers. (Ch. 25, section 11, pp. 38ff., trans. by de Groot 1969:1,189)

Although this text is probably from very late in the feudal period, and the state government it purports to describe was likely only an idealized model, it does demonstrate that people of the time felt Wu mediums were acceptable, even desirable, components of official religion. These shamanistic personages were assigned official functions of invocation, placement, and exorcism of spirits.

A Chinese statesman who lived during the late feudal period, from 515 to 488 B.C., discussed the functional role of the Wu as spirit mediums, contrasting them explicitly with secular officials:

> Anciently the functions with respect to the people and with regard to the gods were not exercised by the same persons. Those among the people whose vital spirits (Ching) were in a bright and flourishing condition, and not distracted into different directions; who moreover had the capacity of concentrating all their feelings of reverence, and possessed inward rectitude— their knowledge was able to rise to higher spheres and descend into the lower, and distinguish there the things which it would be proper to do; their perfect intelligence then could clearly observe things in the distant future and explain them; by their sharpsightedness they could see them shine in their brightest light, and by the acuteness of their ears they could hear and

scrutinize them. Being in this condition intelligent Shen descended into them. . . . As functionaries, they regulated the places for the seats of the gods (at sacrifices), the order of their tablets, as also their sacrificial victims and implements, and the ceremonial attires to be worn in connections with the season. (Kuo Yu, Ch. 18, Ch'u Yu, section 11, from de Groot 1969 :1,191)

During the feudal period, most references to and descriptions of these shamanistic Wu are in terms of their functions or involvement in the courtly activities that are the main focus of the sources of the time. We are fortunate that a text has been preserved that is ascribed to Ch'u Yuan (329–299 B.C.); it is called the Nine Songs (Chiu Ko) in the *Ch'u Tz'u* and provides valuable insight into the idiom in which these activities were carried out. The first nine of these songs are apparently transcriptions of invocational chants of mediums to invite the spirits to possess them. These texts are particularly interesting because at this time the struggle between Confucianism and various other religious and philosophical schools was beginning to intensify toward the philosophical ferments of Ch'in (221–207 B.C.) and Han (202 B.C. to A.D. 220) times. One of the most common accusations Confucianists made against their enemies was to charge them with improperly consorting with women—a charge that received prima facie proof when women performed important functionary roles, as was the case with female shamans: "That the female Wu were still numerous in the 2nd century we know from . . . Wang Fu, who bitterly complained of the large number of women in his time who took up the profession" (Needham 1956:127).

If the content of the Nine Songs is any indication of the practices of female Wu of the time, the Confucianists were perhaps not exaggerating their claims. Much of the idiom of the songs is expressed through verbal enticement of an explicitly sexual nature, which is not surprising considering comparative studies of spirit possession (cf. Crapanzano 1977; Deren 1953). The Nine Songs

are descriptive incantations perhaps intended to attract the god by a species of word magic. Their sexual character is obscured by the commentators, who insist on treating them as personal and allegorical appeals by Ch'u Yuan to his ruler. . . . All of [them] . . . are written in irregular five- or six-word lines with a caesura indicated by the particle Hsi, thus differing from the line typical of the

Li Sao and its imitations, where the Hsi normally occurs at the
end of lines which do not rhyme. (Hightower 1965:23)

During the early imperial period, especially during the Han dynasty,
Confucianism began to be established as the orthodox worldview of the
emperor, his court, and his officials; thus the role of Wu shamans became
declassé. Historians of the time began to record the fraternization of
shamans and priests with emperors as a destabilizing and unorthodox
influence, much like the poisonous effects of unbridled sexuality. It was
only over the protests of the Confucians, during the course of the Ch'in
and Han dynasties, that a number of emperors supported the "experi-
ments" of unorthodox magicians and mediums with alchemy, drugs, and
the phenomenon of magnetism. One result of their activities was probably the discovery of virulent poisons, such as the famous *Wu Ku*, or
"shaman's poison," which led to the revolt of the crown prince against
his father, the Wu emperor of Han, in 130 B.C. In the course of this event,
Wu shamans participated both as producers of black magical poisons and
life-threatening curses and as detectors of such malefactors (de Groot
1969:828–843). The official histories that describe these events and place
blame for them on the shamans were composed by representatives of the
Confucian scholar class, which had gradually won control of the state
institutions, "and the more influential Confucianism became during the
Han as the cult of the imperial bureaucracy, the worse it was for the
shamanistic and experimental side of Taoism" (Needham 1956:137).

In fact, it was during and immediately after the Han that elements
associated with Wu shamanism were banished from official participation
in the state religion and, probably in consequence, began to merge with
the philosophical opposition represented by what eventually came to be
known as Taoism. It was shortly after the end of the Han dynasty that the
first legal sanctions against shamanistic practices were recorded. For
example, in the year A.D. 472 the emperor Wen of the To-pa dynasty forbade Wu mediums to participate in the sacrifices of the state religion (de
Groot 1969:1,235). A short time later, the emperor even prohibited the
shamans from carrying out some of their customary functions: "Thus in
A.D. 485 . . . Kao Tsu of the Wei dynasty . . . decreed that the Wu and Hsi
were strictly forbidden to foretell good or bad fortune and under pretext
of doing so by means of Shen or Kwei" (Wei Shu, Ch. 7, section I, p.
1.21, in de Groot 1969:1,217).

At about the same time, the old religious traditions of China were also challenged by the newly introduced Buddhist beliefs. Under attack as "depraved cults" (*Yin-ssu*), the Wu practitioners found some degree of protection in the ideologies developed by the newly emerging Taoist philosophers and divines: "from the fourth to the sixth centuries followers of popular religion became adepts of a Taoist church because they found elements there to which they were accustomed, but which were sublimated and enclosed in a firmer and better-organized framework" (Stein 1979:59).

However, by absorbing the techniques of spirit mediumship, the Taoist ritual repertory adapted a method of religious revelation capable of generating a corpus of spiritual literature that could compete with the sacred texts of the Buddhist tripitaka and the Confucian classics. During the period succeeding the Han, Taoist sects began to become established in isolated places in conscious imitation of the Buddhist practices of building monastic institutions. In places such as Mao Shan, the texts known as the *Chen Kao* recorded the organization and character of the spirit realms of the immortals as revealed to a medium who

> during the years 364–370 . . . underwent a succession of visionary experiences, in the course of which he was visited by some dozen perfected-immortals [Chen, Chen-ren] from the heaven of Shang-ch'ing. They presented him, over those seven-odd years, with certain of the sacred texts current in their own dominions. (Strickman 1979:126)

A similar process, repeated in many locales, created a synthesis of local liturgical and thaumaturgical practices and ideology with the politically respectable Taoism of Chang Tao-ling. During the T'ang (618–906), the Sung (960–1279), and subsequent medieval dynasties, the revelations to Taoist spirit mediums continued to exert a formative influence on Chinese elite culture and to maintain a Taoist presence at court (cf. Strickman 1981:42–45). Many of the texts produced by spirit mediums were eventually incorporated into the *Tao Tsang*, the so-called Taoist canon. But most emperors gave legal sanction to the powerful spirituality of the Taoist sanctuaries, such as Wu Tang Shan, allowing them not only tax exemptions and special privileges for their clergy but also according them imperial patronage and direct financial support (Strickmann 1981:49).

The practices of shamanism and spirit mediumship in the medieval period thus became firmly linked with the institutions and canonical literature of the Taoist religious establishment. To the popular mind, the knowledge and techniques necessary to summon and control the spirits of both gods and ghosts were most effectively achieved by the adepts of the Taoist institutions located in China's mountain monasteries, who sought direct communion with the powerful, pure spirits of the heavens. This supernatural power was then employed on behalf of common mortals by the Taoist practitioners, who functioned as did the old Wu shamanism: invoking, locating, and exorcising spirits.

These practices contrasted with the religious doctrines of Confucianist and Buddhist institutions, which generally discouraged the altered states of consciousness necessary to effective spirit mediumship. Popular cults in medieval China, whatever their philosophical or social origins, thus came to be associated with Taoism, because the Taoists' "own practices were basically, at least in large part, the same as those of the popular specialists, the mediums or sorcerers" (*Wu, Shih*) (Stein 1979:80).

Popular cults in medieval China therefore acquired a patina of Taoist imagery and ideology, whatever their origin. They also frequently claimed a direct tie of "descent" from some Taoist sect established in its own mountain sanctuary, and frequently the gods of these cults were "enfeoffed" in their domains by imperial decrees. Local religious cults in medieval China therefore took on the character of networks focused on Taoist sectarian centers. The ties binding these networks together may often have been weak, but at the least they involved acceptance of a common idiom of expression—whether a common founder of the sect, shared sacred texts, or shared ritual symbolism.

During the Ming dynasty (1368–1644), one of these Taoist centers— the Taoist sect based on Wu Tang Shan in Hupei province—achieved especially high esteem in the eyes of the imperial house. Because the Ming founder and his son both believed they had been greatly aided in their struggles to secure the throne by the god who had made his revelations to the world through Wu Tang Shan, they gave considerable support and protection to adherents of this sect. This god is especially closely associated with one imperial personality—the third, or Yongle, emperor of the Ming dynasty of China—who himself was probably a spirit medium or shaman, because he was possessed upon occasion by a military deity called True Warrior (Zhenwu), a god also known by his more formal title, Emperor of the Dark Heavens (Xuantian Shangdi). This god's cult center is located at Wudangshan.

One consequence of this imperial favor was likely that popular cults devoted to this god became extremely widespread in China (cf. Grootaers 1952). At the founding of the Ming dynasty, power was held by a class of military aristocrats that had been created in the military campaigns against the Mongols and competing hegemons. Because the Wu Tang Shan Taoist sect strongly emphasized the disciplines of the military arts (T'ai-chi-ch'uan is popularly believed to have been revealed to an adept of Wu Tang Shan who later became immortal), the sect naturally appealed to the ruling class of early Ming China. As one might expect from the character of its founders and its patrons, the symbolism of its ritual practices was strongly military in character.

In the popular Daoist pantheon, the Emperor of the Dark Heavens is therefore conceived of as a military figure who commands the northern quadrant of the heavens and the forces that emanate from there. Although the emblematic symbol of the god—the intertwined turtle and snake called the Dark Warrior—is well-known from at least Han times (200 B.C.), the Emperor of the Dark Heavens as an anthropomorphized god is well documented only since the Song dynasty (tenth century) through his sacred scriptures collected in the Daoist canon (Boltz 1987: 86–91). The god is always represented with the seven-star sword and black flag of military command and is closely associated with taijiquan and other military arts in China (Tang 1983).

In present-day Taiwan, the god and his mediums are associated most closely with exorcism, which in ancient and feudal times was performed by the Wu of Shang. Exorcism can be briefly defined as the driving out of and defense against spirits whose presence is unwanted or destructive. In a cognate sense, the Emperor of the Dark Heavens was the "patron deity" of the coup d'etat in medieval China. Further, through the origin myth of the god, the symbolism of a Chinese coup d'état sometimes, surprisingly, implied a Central Asian line of descent for the successful rebel.

The process whereby power is transmitted from one ruler to the next has been troublesome in every political culture. We are fortunate in the Chinese case to have a long historical perspective from which to observe many different succession events. The cycles of dynastic rise and fall are most intriguing to the historian at their high and low points: when the "bad last" emperor is replaced by the "virtuous founder" emperor. With the rise of a true imperium under the Qin dynasty in 221 B.C., the principles invoked to legitimize such centralized and absolute power became very topical when the Han dynasty replaced the Qin within a generation.

In a familistic society, the best claim to legitimate succession is most likely to be determined on the basis of kinship. By Han times a principle of unilineal descent and differential ranking of descent groups (clans) produced dynastic succession from father to son within a surname line, with a pronounced tendency to favor the eldest son. Court ministers as a group, having a vested interest in an orderly succession, basically tended to throw the weight of Confucian public opinion behind this system of succession.

In spite of this well-ordered ideology of patrilineal succession, the evolution of political society and the growth of its external networks produced many perturbations that were impossible to accommodate: internal rebellions destroyed dynasties, and invasions from beyond the Great Wall imposed new ones. How do we account for events that seemingly were beyond control? Many philosophers have answered this question, but one of the more interesting theories for our present purposes is that of Liu Xin, who tried to justify Wang Mang's overthrow of the Han dynasty in A.D. 209. Liu Xin used the so-called Five Evolutive Phases to explain why one dynasty replaced another. According to this theory, each dynasty's appointed length of rule corresponds to one of the five phases (Fire, Earth, Wood, Metal, Water) that produce and destroy one another. In order to account for short dynasties that were quickly overthrown, Liu Xin had an ingenious idea. He likened long dynastic periods to "regular" calendrical phenomena like the phases of the solar or lunar calendars. But he likened short dynasties marked by violent change to intercalary events such as the irregular necessity to insert an extra month into the lunar calendar. After the intercalary month, things could return to a regular, long-term cycle (Chan 1984:30–31).

Shi Huangdi, founder of the Qin dynasty, believed the Water phase corresponded to his dynasty, so he had selected the color black for ritual vestments, north as the controlling direction, and *xuanwu*—the turtle and the snake—as the dynastic emblem. Probably because of the historical associations of the Qin dynasty, violent interludes were most often associated with the Water phase, whereas longer dynastic rules were thought to correspond to one of the other phases. A typical example of this association is found in a popular novel, the *he yi shi*.

> There is an episode under the fifth year of Xuanhe (1123) dramatizing the Jin [dynasty] founder's possession of Water Power. It relates that one night late in this year Huizong [the Xuanhe emperor, last of the Northern Song] took a bizarre journey to the

Great Chilly Palace (Guanghan Gong) in the galaxy on a miraculous blue bird with his Daoist adviser Ling Lingsu. Upon arrival, the emperor found two men sitting north and south under a shadowy tree playing a game of chess; one was wearing black and the other red. They claimed that they were making a match on order of the Celestial Ruler, and whoever won should win the empire. The dark-robed man won the game. Upon inquiry, the Daoist remarked that the loser was the "Fire Lord" Zhao, the Grand Progenitor (i.e., Song Taizu), and the winner was the "Water Lord," the Grand Progenitor of Great Chin (A-ku-ta). This episode, apparently inspired by the Da Jin guo zhi, therefore implies that Jin triumphed over Song because of possession of Water Power, which extinguished Fire according to the cyclical conquest formula of the Five Agents theory. This assertion, however, has no historical basis, and it seems to have been contrived by the anonymous author as a face-saving apology for the loss of North China to the Jurchen invaders. (Chan 1984:79–80)

This passage illustrates that non-Han people, the agents of dynastic change through conquest, are being assimilated in the evolutive phase theory of dynastic succession, as well as in the lineal descent theory. Because these "conquest dynasties" were both located to the north of China proper and typically were of Turkic or Tungusic stock, associating the two perhaps represents a natural evolutionary path. Given the tendency to link the north, the Water Phase, and non-Han barbarians with violent dynastic successions, it is interesting to note that the "Daoist" Emperor of the Dark Heaven's "true origins" are in Central Asia. The popular version of the god's origins is found in the folk novel *The Journey to the North,* which describes his previous incarnations as king of Qocho (Gege Guowang) (probably located in the Xinjiang area) and as crown prince of Xixia (probably a reference to a non-Han state located in the Ningxia-Gansu region) before settling on Mount Wudangshan as the Emperor of the Dark Heavens (Seaman 1989).

In other popular literature relating to the Emperor of the Dark Heavens, the wind from the northeast that secures military victory for those who worship the god takes the form of a black cloud through which the god manifests his aid. In the *Yingliezhuan* example, the founder of the Ming dynasty gains final victory at the battle of the Boyang Lake through the opportune northeast wind that destroys the enemy fleet. In popular iconography, the black cloud becomes transmuted into a black flag, symbolizing the god's control over the powers of nature that come from the north and that can intervene to change the course of battle. The northeast gate of a city—indeed, the northeast direction in general—has traditionally been regarded in Chinese geomancy as the point of greatest danger. Temples at both Nanjing and Peking were dedicated to the Emperor of the Dark Heavens to guard this direction. In popular legend northeast is often connected with fratricide and other events marking irregular succession struggles: the assassination of the crown prince of the T'ang dynasty by his brother, who then became the second emperor, is popularly supposed to have taken place at the northeastern gate of the capital. The associations of the Emperor of the Dark Heavens with this quarter are therefore not completely positive, because they imply a refusal to admit to paternal authority in the matter of the imperial inheritance. If filial piety and submission to one's parents' wishes in succession to the estate are primary values in Chinese culture, as a wide range of literature states, then the Emperor of the Dark Heavens is often the implied agent in overthrowing this value.

REFERENCES

Basilov, Vladimir.
1984.   The Study of Shamanism in Soviet Ethnography. In Hoppal, Mihaly (ed.), *Shamanism in Eurasia*, pp. 46–66. Goettingen: Herodot.

Chan, Hok-lam.
1984.   *Legitimation in Imperial China: Discussions Under the Jurchen-Chin Dynasty (1115–1234)*. Seattle: University of Washington Press.

Chang, K. C.
1983.   *Art, Myth, and Ritual: The Path to Political Authority in Ancient China*. Cambridge: Harvard University Press.

Chang, Tsung-tung.
1970.   *Der Kult der Shang-dynastie im Spiegel der Orakelinschriften*. Wiesbaden: Harrassowitz.

Ch'u Tui-chih.
1930.   Hsieh Wu. *Yen-ching Hsueh-pao* 7:1,327–1,345.

Crapanzano, V. (ed.).
   1977.   *Case Studies in Spirit Possession.* New York: John Wiley.

Deren, Maya.
   1953.   *Divine Horsemen: The Living Gods of Haiti.* London: Viking Press.

Dienes, I.
   1981.   Shamanenaristokratie in den Nomadenstaaten. In O. Ikola (ed.), *Intus Internationalis Fenno-Ugristarum.* Turkey, UNK, August 20–27, 1980, Part 8, pp. 326–338.

Eichhorn, W.
   1976.   *Die alte chinesische Religon und das Staatskultwesen.* Leiden: Brill.

Erkes, Eduard.
   1950.   Der schamanistische Ursprung des chinesischen Ahnenkultes. *Sinologica* 2, No. 4:253–262.

Groot, Jan J.M. de.
   1892–1910 (reprint 1969).
         The Religious System of China. Leyden: Brill.

Grootaers, Willem A.
   1952.   The Hagiography of the Chinese God Chen-wu. *Folklore Studies* 11, No. 2:139–181.

Hightower, James R.
   1965.   *Topics in Chinese Literature.* Cambridge: Harvard University Press.

Keightley, David N.
   1978.   *Sources of Shang History.* Berkeley: University of California Press.

Laufer, Berthold.
   1917.   Origin of the Word Shaman. *American Anthropologist* 19:361–371.

Lewis, I. M.
   1971.   *Ecstatic Religion.* London: Penguin Books.

———.
   1984.   What Is a Shaman? In Hoppal, Mihaly (ed.), *Shamanism in Eurasia,* pp. 3–12. Goettingen: Herodot.

Mironov, N. D., and S. M. Shirokogoroff.
  1924.   Sramana-Shaman: Etymology of the Word 'Shaman.' *Journal of the Royal Asiatic Society, North China Branch*, Shanghai 55:105–130.

Needham, Joseph.
  1956.   *Science and Civilization in China,* Vol. 2. Cambridge: Cambridge University Press.

Nemeth, Julius.
  1913–1914.
          Ueber den Ursprung des Wortes Saman und einige Bemerkungen zur tuerkisch-mongolischen Lautgeschichte. *Keleti Szemle* 14:240-249.

Pallisten, N.
  1956.   Die alte Religion der Mongolen und der Kultus Tschingis-Chans. *Numen* 3:78–229.

Ropp, Paul S.
  1981.   *Early Modern China.* Ann Arbor: University of Michigan Press.

Seaman, Gary W.
  1989.   The Emperor of the Dark Heavens and the Han River Gateway into China. In Seaman, Gary (ed.), *Ecology and Empire.* Los Angeles: Ethnographics Press, pp. 165–177.

Serruys, Henry.
  1955.   *Sino-Jurced Relations During the Yung-lo Period.* Wiesbaden: Harrassowitz.

Shirokogoroff, S. M.
  1935.   *The Psychomental Complex of the Tungus.* London: Allen and Unwin.

Stein, Rolf A.
  1979.   Religious Taoism and Popular Religion from the Second to Seventh Centuries. In Welch, Holmes, and Anna Seidel (eds.), *Facets of Taoism,* pp. 53–82. New Haven: Yale University Press.

Strickmann, Michel.
  1979.   On the Alchemy of T'ao Hung-ching. In Welch, Holmes, and Anna Seidel (eds.), *Facets of Taoism,* pp. 123–192. New Haven: Yale University Press.

———.
  1981.   *Le taoïsme du mao chan. Chronique d'une révélation.* Paris: Fayard.

Tang, Fansheng.
    1983.   *Shaolin Wudang kao*. Taipei: Xuansheng tushu gongsi.

OTHER WORKS

Boltz, Judith M.
    1987.   *A Survey of Taoist Literature, Tenth to Seventeenth Centuries*. Berkeley:
            Center for Chinese Studies.

Chan, Hok-lam.
    1975.   The Rise of Ming T'ai-tsu (1368-1388): Facts and Fiction in Early Ming
            Historiography. *Journal of the American Oriental Society* 95:539–715.

Chang, Chun-shu, and Noan Smyth.
    1981.   *South China in the 12th Century*. Hong Kong: Chinese University Press.

Crespigny, Rafe de.
    1976.   *Portents of Protest in the Late Han Dynasty: The Memorials of Hsiang
            K'ai to Emperor Huan*. Canberra: ANU Oriental Monography Series, No. 19.

Daming Xuantian Shandi ruiyinglu.
    n.d.   Daozang No. 608.

Dreyer, Edward.
    1982.   *Early Ming China: A Political History 1355–1435*. Stanford: Stanford
            University Press.

Eliade, Mircea.
    1972.   *Shamanism: Archaic Techniques of Ecstacy*. Princeton: Princeton
            University Press.

Farmer, Edward K.
    1976.   *Early Ming Government: Evolution of Dual Capitals*. Cambridge:
            Harvard University Press.

Feifel, Eugene, and Hok-lam Chan.
    1976.   Yao Kuang-hsiao [Yao Guangxiao]. In Goodrich, L. C. (ed.), *Dictionary of
            Ming Biography,* pp. 1,561–1,565. New York: Columbia University Press.

Goodrich, L. Carrington (ed.).
    1976.   *Dictionary of Ming Biography*. New York: Columbia University Press.

Hucker, Charles O.
  1978.   *The Ming Dynasty*. Michigan Papers in Chinese Studies, No. 34. Ann Arbor:
          University of Michigan Press.

Hultkranz, A.
  1973.   A Definition of Shamanism. *Temenos* 9:26–37.

Li, An-che.
  1948.   Bon: The Magico-Religious Belief of the Tibetan-Speaking Peoples.
          Southwestern Journal of Anthropology 1:31–41.

Li, Chi.
  1971.   *The Travel Diaries of Hsu Hsia-k'*. Hong Kong: Chinese University of
          Hong Kong Press.

Mano, Senryu.
  1958.   Mincho to Taihosan ni tsuite [The Ming Court and Wudang Mountain].
          Otani Gakuho 38:59–73.

———.
  1963.   Mindai no Budosan to Kangan no Shinshutsu [Development of the
          Eunuch Officials and Wudang Mountain During the Ming Period].
          Toho Shukyo 22:29–44.

———.
  1979.   *Mindai bunkashi* [The Study on the Cultural History in the Ming Period].
          Kyoto: Dohosha.

Michaels, H. N. (ed.).
  1963.   *Studies in Siberian Shamanism*. Toronto: University of Toronto Press.

Nachtigall, H.
  1952.   Die Kulturhistorische Wurzel der Schamanenskelettierung. *Zeitschrift
          füer Ethnologie* 77:188–197.

———.
  1953.   Die erhoehte Bestattung in Nordund Hochasien. *Anthropos* 48:44–70.

Nioradze, Georg.
  1925.   *Der Schamanismus bei den sibirischen Voelkern*. Stuttgart: Stescker
          und Schroder.

Rossabi, Morris.
   1987.   *Kubilai Khan: His Life and Times.* Berkeley: University of California Press.

Seaman, Gary W.
   1987.   *Journey to the North.* Berkeley: University of California Press.

Seidel, Anna.
   1970.   A Taoist Immortal of the Ming Dynasty: Chang San-feng. In T. De Bary (ed.),
           Self and Society in Ming Thought, pp. 483–531. New York: Columbia
           University Press.

Serruys, Henry.
   1955.   *Sino-Jurced Relations During the Yung-lo Period.* Wiesbaden: Harrassowitz.

Voight, V.
   1984.   Shaman—Person or Word? In Hoppal, Mihaly (ed.), *Shamanism in Eurasia,*
           pp. 13–20. Goettingen: Herodot.

Yang, Qiqiao.
   1968.   Mingdai zhudi zhi zongchang fangshu ji qi yingxiang [The effect of the faith of
           Ming emperors in magic]. In Dao, Xisheng (ed.), *Mingdai zongjiao [Religion of
           the Ming Period].* Taipei: Xuesheng shuju.

SHAMANS IN TRADITIONAL
TUVINIAN SOCIETY

Vera P. Diakonova

Shamanism as a social phenomenon played an important role in traditional cultures of Siberian people for many centuries. This phenomenon was a part of the religious ideology of the society and was closely connected to the socioeconomic life of various peoples and ethnic groups.

Tuvinian shamanism is an ancient system of beliefs, although its general formation and existence within the ethnos were not unique. By the time the Tuvinians had formed a single ethnic group with its own economic and cultural society, differentiated by geographical, linguistic, historical, and cultural features, a complex situation existed that was characterized by a syncretism of religious ideas. This situation was complicated greatly by the fact that in the seventeenth century, lamaism, a form of Tibetan Buddhism, had reached Tuva. Its advocates and disseminators among the Tuvinians were Mongolian, or perhaps Tibetan, lamas who had been accepted by the Tuvinian feudal lords. Because of the linguistic barrier, penetration of lamaist dogma and ritual practices, which were quite different from the traditions of Tuvinian shamanism, was difficult.

Active construction of permanent religious centers helped strengthen the new religion. From the middle of the seventeenth century to the middle of the nineteenth century, no *khoshun* or *soumon* (territorial and administrative units) in Tuva lacked their own temple, priest, and adherents. Although lamaism was exported to Tuva from Mongolia, in Tuvinian society it had its own specific features (hierarchical, ritual, and canonical), but from the time of its rise until its decline, its rituals were performed in Mongolian and Tibetan languages, which were alien to Tuva.

By the early twentieth century, twenty-two large lamaist religious centers were functioning in Tuva. These complexes had temple buildings, libraries, and staffs of priests. The lamaist clergy's fight against shamans, with their ancient worldview, rituals, and practices, was never successful. There was, however, an interesting coexistence of the two religious systems among the Tuvinians, as they became mutually complementary rather than mutually exclusive. For example, symbols of the lamaist cult along with important symbols of shamanism decorated Tuvinian felt yurts. But the basic cult symbol system of the traditional dwelling (orientation, accommodation of objects, rituals, and the like) continued to be based on the shamanistic concept of the world, which imagined the universe as consisting of the sky, the underground world, and real earth (Figure 10.1).

By the 1920s and 1930s almost equal numbers of lamaist priests and shamans—573 lamas and 526 shamans—were found in Tuva. Active ministers of the lamaist religion, however, numbered four thousand, many more than were needed for the Tuvinian population.[1]

Tuvinian shamanism has attracted the attention of various scholars, and today a series of publications contains rich data on the subject.[2] In this chapter I attempt to summarize all of the available information, including my own materials collected during ethnographical field work, mostly from the 1960s through the 1980s.

The Tuvinian shamans were most likely to be considered religious professionals, although they also had individual farms, were engaged in cattle breeding, took part in trades, or learned various domestic crafts (wood trimming, tanning, blacksmith's work, and similar skills). Since ancient times, these Tuvinian shamans, as well as the shamans of other Turkic-speaking peoples of South Siberia, had been called *kham* or *kam*. Shamanesses were called *udaban,* which corresponds to the Mongolian *utagan.* The earliest mention of the term *kham* is believed to be in the Chinese chronicle of the T'ang epoch (618–907) for the Kirghiz. The Chinese called the Kirghiz sorcerers and shamans kham and termed them *wu.* The medieval literary monument dating from the twelfth–fourteenth centuries, *Kutadgy bilik* (study of how to become happy) by Yusuph Balasaguni, contains the term *kham.* The well-known scholar Vambery interprets it as sorcerer or magician. According to to Vambery, a kham is different from a doctor in this text because a kham cures people by means of words and invocation.

Not only the Tuvinian but also the Turkic-speaking and Mongolian-speaking peoples of South Siberia and Mongolia had shamans and shamanesses (Figure 10.2). A hypothesis expressed by some scholars gives priority to female shamanism. For instance, shamanesses were already known to the Gao-ghoui peoples, nomads of the Thele confederation

FIGURE 10.1
A homestead in Tuva, with yurt and corral.

FIGURE 10.2
A Tuvinian shamaness.

who inhabited Central Asia in the fourth through the sixth centuries A.D. According to some folk legends, the first shamans in Thele and Tuva were women. To perform religious rites, Yakut and Altayan shamans sometimes wore women's dress, women's decorations, and long hair, which probably invokes an ancient memory of female shamanism. I should note that shamanesses were often considered to be potentially stronger than shamans. But among the Tuvinians, as with other Turkic-speaking peoples, the shamanesses had no right to communicate with the gods and spirits of the celestial sphere.

The path to the shaman's profession was hard; it was regulated by a family-clan tradition that often forced one to take on this kind of activity. As the well-known Soviet ethnographer L. Ya. Shternberg said, "The talent of a shaman is not a gift but a hard burden." In reality, the Tuvinian shamans inherited their gift/burden. When working with a shaman, known in Tuva under the nickname Kok-Bashtyg (Aldyn-Kherel from Ondar-clan), I learned that he remembered well his great-grandfather, Dalai-Ondar, and his uncle Chopchene, who were great shamans in their Ondar-clan. His great-grandfather had performed important shamanistic rites, such as consecrating a horse to the deities (called *ydyk* [holy] after consecration), and his uncle had been buried with a special ceremony in a tomb located in Khanrlyg-Kat, in accordance with the ancient traditions. This example confirms that the Tuvinian shamans inherited their gift or role when they belonged to a family or clan that included shamans among its ancestors.

The chosen one, or shaman, could only be a person who from an early age manifested signs in his or her behavior that were rare among others in the same culture, usually a certain kind of disease. According to some scholars of Tuvinian shamanism, this disease, called *albystaar,* was considered by the Tuvinians to result from a shaman-ancestor's spirit becoming incarnated in a would-be shaman. From the data collected during my field research, I found that if the disease of the chosen one happened at age thirteen or fourteen and continued until age thirty-seven, it was called *dalyp kaar* rather than albystaar. Dalyp kaar was manifested in the frequent faints, dreams, and hallucinations of the novice shaman. An analysis of these manifestations diagnoses no real illness, but it does reveal the conceptual essence of shamanism.

The novices' visions demonstrated the ideas of shamanistic activity. In these visions the traditional worldview is understood, communication with the world of spirits and gods is established, and the chosen ones get to know the structure of the universe and see their future spirit assistants. Later, when the novices perform religious rites, all of the assembly of spirits from the upper and lower worlds that communicated with the novices in their dreams or hallucinations will be reintroduced in their invocations (*algysh*) and will help them to perform their duties.

Shamans explain their role in terms of the traditional worldview and its symbolic imagery. An important part was played by the schooling in which the novices participated with their shaman-teachers. The novices performed their first ecstatic rite in the teacher's yurt using the teacher's ritual costume and drum. Training lasted only seven days, but during this period novice shamans gained an understanding of the world organization, which is the main concept of shamanism. They also learned the roads they needed to travel to reach the land of the dead, the underground world that is the home of the evil spirits (*azalar*) who cause diseases and death. In addition, they became acquainted with the vital substances of man and the interrelation of nature and humans.[3]

The chosen ones also received knowledge of the sacred land *dain deher* (upper world), which was considered very important for their activities. Shamans reached dain deher, the place where nine herbs grew, through the rainbow. Shamans thought this land was between the earth and the thirty-three layers of the sky. Dain deher and *taiga tandy*, which were equal in value, were interconnected; they exerted favorable influence upon the middle world, or earth (*cher ortamchei* or *cher-su*), as well as upon the people and animals inhabiting it. Shamanistic ritual practices were directed to this view of the universe that represented, on one level, a paradise that influenced people's well-being and reproduction and, on another level, the underground world.

The family-clan took care of the shaman's vestments and ritual objects. In the Tuvinian tradition, a shaman had a set of ritual clothes and cult items, which had a special place in his or her dwelling. In addition, after his or her death, the Tuvinians practiced a special form of burial for the shaman.

The shaman's vestments consisted of a cap, footwear, and a robe-caftan that was cut quite differently from secular clothes. The caftan was made of hide (first wild animal and, later, domestic animal skins were used) and cloth. The individual parts of the vestments, as well as the entire set, were taboo while they were being made and could not be tried on. Some Tuvinian shamans had two complete sets of vestments (see Figure 10.3). This was most common for shamans who had a special energy and professionalism and who could perform rites in particularly serious cases, such as addressing the lord of the underground kingdom, Erlic-khan.

The complete set of vestments was a symbolic representation of the shamanistic worldview. Some of the shamans' regalia was considered to be their armor; certain pendants permitted them to change into animals; and other parts gave them the ability to see and communicate with spirits of the other worlds and with the souls of the living and the dead. This belief was also held by most Turkic-speaking peoples of South

FIGURE 10.3
A shaman's vestments.

Siberia. This symbolism of the pendants, robe, and cap allows us to say that the entire costume was considered a "live organism," a mixed image of a beast and a bird.[4] Some plaits on the costume were called snakes (*chylan*) but were also understood as a bird's feathers, and the fringe (*manchak*) on the back part of the coat symbolized a horse's tail. During their rituals shamans drew on the bowstring of an imaginary bow and shot arrows, hitting the enemy (the spirit of a disease or the spirit of a powerful, hostile shaman). The arrow's flight was symbolized by the tinkling of a bell. The pendants depicting arrows were considered to be extremely powerful. A shaman could shoot them for a long distance and even hit targets that were located behind high mountains.

The shamans' costume reflected the ideas about their tutelary and helping spirits. For this purpose most pendants had a direct concern with a disease's nature (bleeding, joint pains, and similar complaints). However, other helping spirits incorporated in the shamans' costume also played a role in searching for and catching thieves, in returning stolen cattle, and in bringing prosperity to people. To a great extent, the costume showed the shamans' status and indicated whether they had the ability to communicate with only one world or all of the worlds. Acting as a mediator between good and evil, a shaman possessed all of the regalia necessary for this function.

In addition to the ritual costume, other necessary items for Tuvinian shamans were, until recently, a drum, a drumstick, and a set of zoomorphic and anthropomorphic representations of their helping spirits (*eheren*; in southern Tuva, *ongout*). These important items were ritually prepared; the manufacturing of a drum and a drumstick was accompanied by elaborate ceremonials. A drum's ring was usually made of larch wood. The larch tree was considered sacred, and every shaman had his or her own tree (*kham-yiash tyt*), near which he or she performed rites and took power from the tutelary spirit. A tree from which a drum was made had a thick, even top and two or three branches inclined to the east. When a tree was cut, it was important that it fall in this easterly direction. Branches were used as resonators; they were knocked down with sticks and caught in the flaps of vestments to prevent them from touching the earth. Before cutting the tree a sacrificial feeding rite had to be performed around it, which included the smoking of sacred herbs for the spirit master of the trees of the forest. Altayan shamans often killed a sheep and sprinkled the tree trunk, especially its roots, with its blood and with an alcoholic beverage called *araka*.

The animal (a mountain goat, deer, or horse) whose skin was used to cover the drum had to be a male without any defects. In Siberian tradition, the drum must undergo the ceremony of enlivening. This rite included sprinkling the wooden parts with tea or araka and performing special invocations. The ceremony of enlivening the animal whose skin was used for the drum was similar, but it also included the ritual of catching, domesticating, and feeding the animal. The most difficult part was the act of seizing the animal's soul, which was caught and swallowed by the shaman during the rite.[5]

Without the ceremony of enlivening, a drum was considered "dirty" (*kara* [black]) and not sacred. A delay in making the vestments, the drum, and other items resulted in disease for the shamans. The spirits who forced them to act left them in peace only after the entire ritual group of objects was ready. Prior to the use of the drum, a drumstick (*orba*) was manufactured for the shamans. In Tuva (except in Todja) it was made of pine or juniper roots. The working surface of the drumstick was covered with the skin of a deer (*maral*) or mountain he-goat; in the past, it was also made of bear skin. Seven metal rings were attached to the opposite side of the instrument, and then it was ornamented with carvings. Some shamans performed rites their entire lives using only the drumstick, although this category of shamans was not connected with the pantheon of the spirits and gods of the upper world. Rites were performed by striking the drumstick on their hands. When the ceremony was finished, the shaman was able to tell the people who were present about their fortunes.

The aspect of the drum's sacred value has been studied in depth by Soviet ethnographers. Among Turkic-speaking people of South Siberia, including Tuvinians, the drum symbolized the animal ridden by shamans in their travels to other worlds. The animal reflected in the drum could be a deer, a horse, or a camel. The current image of the drum as a horse is a rather late tradition that appeared among nomadic cattle breeders. This new meaning was superimposed on the drum of hunters and reindeer breeders, which had originally symbolized deer, elk, and other wild animals.[6] As an animal to be ridden, today the drum is correlated accurately with a horse. Its handle is a spine; the plaits of leather attached to the upper part of the ring symbolize the reins of a horse; the drumstick is a lash, which beats a drum only in certain places. The shaman never strikes the part on which the horse's head is visualized; in fact, Tuvinians and other nomads never strike their real horses on the head.

In addition to symbolizing the image of a riding animal, the drum was a symbol of the cosmological ideas of shamanism. Shamans took precautions regarding their drums. They demonstrated awe and piety before them, thus expressing respect for their forefathers and for the spirit-master of the drum. If the drum fell on the earth during a ceremony, it was considered a sign that the shaman would soon die.

Tuvinian shamans thought that when they beat the drum, major spirits awoke and responded to their call. With the sounds of the drum, shamans appealed to their spirits—they came, entered the drum, and prospered. According to the shamans, the spirits' voices were heard in the drum's sounds, thus giving evidence of their presence. The sounds of the drum could also frighten and drive away evil spirits. When performing a healing seance over a sick person, the shaman drives all evil spirits into the drum. Souls of those who have recently died are also driven into the drum, because they must be removed from the world of the living. After the souls of sick people that are stolen by the evil spirits are returned, they are placed there too.

The most typical items in Tuvinian shamanism are the images of helping spirits (zoomorphic, anthropomorphic, mixed, or uncertain in appearance). The most prestigious category of shamans has more of these than do the other categories. The most common helping spirits in Tuva are called eheren. There are nine of them: *moos eheren, adyg eheren* (a bear), *morzyk eheren* (a badger), *chydyg-khyrza eheren, as eheren, ak eheren, ezir eheren* (an eagle), *kuskun eheren* (a raven), and *khyzungu eheren* (a mirror).[7] At the beginning of their careers shamans do not have all of these. They begin to acquire them, starting with khyzungu. The main function of the shamans' helping spirits is to cure people, but they also help shamans overcome difficult obstacles. For example, moos eheren helps shamans to cross hazardous rivers in the lower world. Some images of these helping spirits were fabricated by a shaman; others were developed by skilled craftspeople.

Shamans must find the magic mirror for themselves in the forest (taiga) or in the mountains. The mirror was considered to have come from the sky. When it fell down, the shaman had to find it. It was difficult to locate and had to be caught by shamans in a sacred piece of cloth. After recovering the mirror, the shamans offered up a horse, or sometimes the life of a man, to the heavenly gods. The mirrors were male and female, and shamans used them in performing ecstatic rites.

They believed the mirrors helped them to see the spirits who caused diseases and to learn whether a sick patient would survive.[8]

The yurt and the utensils of the Tuvinian shaman were like those of the common people but with added items and accessories of his or her practice. They were arranged in strict order. Certain spaces in the dwelling were appointed for certain kinds of images of the helping spirits. In traditional Tuvinian culture, dwellings, including that of the shaman, were considered to be a part of the universe—a model of the real earth that was one of three levels of the universe. The yurt protected those within it and had a vital relationship with the patrons of the universe.

In Tuvinian society the shamans were divided into categories (*ulug kham, kham, tengry boo*). This division was based on the shamans' strength, which was manifested in their communication with the spirits, the gods, and their ancestors. The most prestigious category of shamans received their gift from the sky; they had specific attributes and were known as the "heavenly" ones. A medieval Mongolian monument of literature called the "Concealed Legend" mentions such a Mongolian shaman who approved Chingis Khan as emperor of all of Mongolia. This famous shaman declared that he was able to travel to heaven on the back of his white horse.

Tuvinian shamans played important and diverse roles in the social life of the late nineteenth and early twentieth centuries. Even though the official religion was lamaism, shamans continued to perform calendar prayers (*dagyyr*) for the welfare of the political and economic order of their society. The fertility and prosperity of a Tuvinian family were tied to a dependency upon the entire environment, which could only be understood in terms of the religious-mythological world. Thus, the successes and misfortunes in the individual lives of people were interrelated with the cult of spirits and gods. Shamans had the power to be mediators between personified nature and people and were considered to be able to provide and secure the group's welfare. Within family-clans, shamans performed prayers to spirit-masters of places (*dag dagyyr, art dagyyr, khamyash dagyyr,* and similar prayers) and performed such important rites as praying to fire (*ot dagyyr*) and consecrating animals (*ydyk dagyyr*). They were also continually engaged in doctoring and in conducting funeral rites.

By the beginning of the twentieth century, the social role of shamans had decreased. But as a whole, their status is still high in the traditional Tuvinian society.

NOTES

1. Diakonova, V. P. 1979. Lamaizm i yego vliyanye na mirovozzrenie religioznyye kul'ty tuvinsev [Lamaism and its influence on the religious cults of the Tuvinians]. In Vdovin, I. S. (ed.) *Hristianstvo i lamaism u korennogo naseleniya Sibiri* [Christianity and Lamaism among the indigenous population of Siberia]. Leningrad: Nauka, pp. 150–179.

2. Potapov, L. P. 1969. *Ocherki narodnogo byta tuvinsev* [Essays on everyday life of the Tuvinians]. Moskow: Nauka, pp. 352–369; Diakonova, V.P. 1978. The vestments and paraphernalia of a Tuva shamaness. In Dioszegi, V. and M. Hoppal (eds.) *Shamanism in Siberia.* Budapest: Akademiai Kaido, pp. 325–339.

3. Diakonova, V. P. 1981. Tuvinskiye shamany i ikh sotsial'naya rol' v obschestve [Tuvinian shamans and their role in their society]. In *Problemy istorii obshestvennogo soznaniya aborigenov Sibiri* [Problems of history of social consciousness of the aboriginals of Siberia]. Leningrad: Nauka, pp. 125–137.

4. Prokofyeva, Y. D. 1971. Shamanskii kostjum narodov Siberi [Shaman's costume among the peoples of Siberia]. *Sbornik Muzeia antropologii i etnografii* [Collected Articles of the Museum of Anthropology and Ethnography] 27:5.

5. For similar ceremonies performed by other peoples of Siberia, see, for example, Basilov, V. N. 1986. The Shaman Drum Among the Peoples of Siberia: Evolution of Symbolism. In I. Lehtinen (ed) *Traces of the Central Asian Culture in the North. Memoirs de la Societe Finno-Ougrienne*, No. 194. Helsinki: Suomalais-Ugilainen Seura, pp. 35–51.

6. Potapov, L. P. 1978. The shaman's drum as a source of ethnographical history. In Dioszegi, V. and M. Hoppal (eds.) *Shamanism in Siberia.* Budapest: Akademiai Kaido, pp. 311–323.

7. See also Vainstein, S. I. 1978. The erens in Tuva shamanism, in Dioszegi, V. and M. Hoppal (eds.) *Shamanism in Siberia.* Budapest: Akademiai Kaido, pp. 457–467.

8. Diakonova, V. P. 1981. Tuvinskiye shamany i ikh sotsial'naya rol' v obschestve [Tuvinian shamans and their role in their society]. In *Problemy istorii obshestvennogo soznaniya aborigenov Sibiri* [Problems of history of social consciousness of the aboriginals of Siberia]. Leningrad: Nauka, pp. 148–153.

11

THE SHAMAN COSTUME:
IMAGE AND MYTH

LARISA R. PAVLINSKAYA

The shaman costume of the Siberian peoples has had special interest for many researchers. This can be explained by the fact that shaman attire represents a phenomenon that encompasses a wide strata of ideological imagery. Those who study the spiritual culture of the Siberian region often include the costume in their studies.

In this chapter I analyze the role of the metallic pendants that form the nucleus of the shaman costume among many Siberian peoples. This analysis reveals two distinctive characteristics: (1) phasic dissimilarity of certain images and themes, and (2) a certain regularity in the placement of pendants on the costume.

Both of these peculiarities reflect the history of the development of these ritual vestments, which is bound inseparably to the formation of the system of ideological imagery. Thus, it is important to discover the genesis and meaning of the metallic pendants on the shaman's attire in order to relate the costume to mythological subjects.

Comparative analysis of the metallic pendants on the shaman attire of large groups of Siberian peoples reveals a general unity of images and meaning, artistic devices, and the technology of processing metal. This unity is the principal evidence for a common origin of this cultural phenomenon. Thus, in cases in which the original meaning of some elements of the metallic pendants in the shaman costume of a particular culture have been lost, these can be deduced by using data that is still preserved in the mythological systems of other peoples whose shaman pendants are similar.

E. D. Prokofyeva has presented convincing evidence that, in the archaic stage of its development, the shaman costume aimed to create an animal/bird image. In studying the shaman attire of these archaic types, she found they were made of the entire animal skin, with a headdress of skin that had been separated from the animal's head in one piece. Prokofyeva identified a group of images on which such attire was based: it includes deer, bear, wolf, fox, otter, crane, eagle, and owl.[1] She correctly postulates that having donned such attire, the shaman was incarnated into the animal or the bird, which was thought to be his or her main spirit protector. At an earlier stage, these animals or birds were also the protectors of the clan (kin). This connection between the animal images on the shaman costumes and the clan totems is agreed upon by many researchers.[2]

When compared with earlier costumes made of animal skin, analysis of the metallic pendants of the later shaman costumes—which carry the primary meaning and artistic load—reveals a somewhat different picture. When comparing Siberian shaman costumes, two different animal images in metal can be observed: images of the animal skeleton and images of the realistic figure of the animal. These two types of representation are based upon different worldviews and the different artistic depictions that result from those views, which reflect different stages of ideological development.

The creation of the animal image as a skeleton is more ancient and is closely linked with the ritual costume made of the entire animal skin, which incarnates the shaman into an animal. This can be seen in the arrangement of the metallic skeleton parts on the costume in correspondence with the actual arrangement of animal body parts and with the parts of the body of the shaman. Originally, representation in metal could not have been used, and it must have been preceded by more ancient means of representation such as embroidery or painting.

The roots of this phenomenon go back as far as the Neolithic epoch. Animal images appeared in rock paintings; on their bodies we can see exact representations of a skeleton. In scientific literature, this method of animal representation is called the skeletal, or "x-ray", style.[3] Representations of this kind are widely known in Eurasia. The origin of this phenomenon has not yet been determined. A rather convincing point of view explains the appearance of a skeleton representation as related to the basis of vital power, the idea of resurrection, and a cult of the dying and resurrected animal, which is characteristic of the culture of hunting peoples.[4] The majority of Siberian peoples maintained such beliefs up to the beginning of the nineteenth century.

In more archaic attire, that made of the entire animal skin, various animal images were represented, including the deer, bear, wolf, fox, and otter; on the costume with metallic skeletons, only two creatures are depicted—the deer and the bear. The attire representing the deer served the shaman on trips to the upper world, whereas that of the bear was reserved for lower world trips. Thus, of the diverse animal images in the archaic stage of ritual costume, only two creatures remain in the metallic pendant designs.

The images of the deer and the bear occupied the central place in the mythological systems of the northern Eurasian peoples. The cult of these animals is characteristic of the majority of traditional cultures in Siberia, where the deer and the bear are known to exist in the ideological imagery of almost all peoples.[5]

The deer was a personification of the sun deity and the entire circle of ideas connected with the sun, such as the succession of day and night, the organization of the cosmic order, the possession of the heavens' fire, and so on. The bear was a master spirit of the forest and was also a master of the lower world, which it symbolized. This suggests that at the core of the metallic pendants on the shaman costume was a connection with the main body of cosmological thinking and with the concepts of the "upper" and "lower" worlds that were incarnated in the images of the deer (or elk) and the bear.

Of special interest is the relationship of these images to one of the principal cosmological myths—the myth of the Heavenly Hunt. This myth, known in the majority of northern Eurasian traditional cultures, presents a poetic explanation of the important cosmological phenomena of the succession of day and night, the seasons of the year, and the cycles of nature.[6] The deer (the sun) runs across the heavens from east to west pursued by the hunter, who catches the deer at the end of the heavenly chase. G. N. Potanin and A. D. Okladnikov have made a detailed study of the cosmic hunt theme in the Central Asian and Siberian material and have convincingly proved that the role of the Heavenly Hunter (at the earliest stage of the appearance of the myth) was played by the bear.[7]

It is logical that such an important ideological theme would find its expression in certain ritual acts. The signs of that ritual are seen distinctly in the ceremony of the animation of the shaman's drum. This drum is also the personification of the deer among many Siberian peoples. The ceremony is most vivid among the Selkups, as has been described by G. N. Prokofyev.[8] First, the shaman performs the life cycle, from birth to death, of the deer whose skin was taken to make the drum. Then the shaman faces the most difficult task—to catch the soul of the deer. After great efforts and much time, the soul of the deer is surrounded, and the shaman imitates the hunting of the deer, shooting arrows at it from a small bow. An analogous ritual also exists among other peoples of Siberia.[9]

Two elements are of particular interest in the relationship between the ceremony of drum animation and the ritual reproduction of the Heavenly Hunt. First, the description of the life story of the deer, in either words or dramatic action, is a poetic metaphor that correlates the stages of the life of a living creature with the phases of the movement of the heavenly bodies. As a plot, the life of the deer (the sun) is reduced to escaping from the hunter who is pursuing it. Second, the shaman ritually hunts the soul of the deer and pursues the animal down the pathway of its life. When analyzing such rituals, questions naturally arise. First, why does the shaman reproduce (either orally or in his or her acts) the life of the deer? Second, why, when trying to obtain the soul of the deer, does the shaman hunt it and kill it when, according to the ritual, the soul should be caught alive to be put into the drum? These acts of the shaman can be understood if we view them as the ritual representation of the Heavenly Hunt myth. In this case, the ritual reproduction of the life of the deer (the sun from sunrise to sunset) is logical, as is the deer's being hunted by the shaman, whose acts relate to the theme of the hunt—which has its roots in the cosmological myth.

It is possible to relate the appearance of the deer and bear images, represented by skeleton images in the metallic pendants on the shaman costume, to the ancient complex of ideological imagery in which the images are correlated with cosmological myths. The form of the presentation correlates with the material embodiment of life power in the skeletal bones. In addition, the main element in the shaping of the images of the ritual attire depends upon the complete incarnation of the shaman into the animal represented by his or her attire.

At present, no data give us a clear idea of the ancient ritual that reproduced the Heavenly Hunt or of the ritual attire that existed in early cultures. It is important to note that the entire plot of the ancient cosmological myth takes place in the upper sphere of the universe, but the bear (and later the hunter) ascends to the skies from the earth. Thus, each of those two worlds is part of the ancient plot, and there is no barrier between them; this appeared later. The lower world is not emphasized in this myth; perhaps the shaman personified the two images at once (the deer and the bear) in the developing ritual acts of the plot of the Heavenly Hunt. Furthermore, we may see here the first stage of the "shaman's travel" to the upper world, which could be performed by incarnating both the deer and the bear.

Further development of both shamanistic ideas and ritual attire incorporated a distinct division among all three levels of the universe— the upper, lower, and middle worlds. At the same time, it illuminated the close connections between the image of the bear and the lower world of ancestors and spirits, which is not evident in the original form of the myth. The deer remained the symbol of the sun and heavens— the upper world—whereas the bear, as the image connected with the earth and antagonistic to the deer, descends to the lower world, thus personifying that sphere of the universe. The distinct divisions of the universe and of animal images are reflected by the division of shamans into corresponding categories and the development of the deer and bear attire. This is why, when traveling to these other worlds, the shaman must incarnate the respective animals of those regions, which involves retaining the deer and bear skeleton images and eventually transforming them into metal, a new material of this later time period.

A third basic image of the shaman costume is the bird. Whereas the images of the deer and the bear were applied to distinct types of attire, the image of the bird was combined with the image of the deer on the same costume. The combination of these images on one costume can be explained by the fact that their meaning is alike in many respects. In the traditional ideological systems, the bird as well as the deer was often the personification of the upper world, the sun, and fire.

The correlation between the deer and the bear in the metallic imagery on the shaman attire with one of the main cosmological myths of Eurasia makes us examine the image of the bird from a different point of view. At first glance, the combination of the deer image with that of the bird on the same shaman costume is not quite logical. But it is just this combination, the unity of which represents the incarnation of all three images, that allows us to connect the bird image with an ancient cosmogonic myth spread among many peoples—the myth of the creation of the earth, in which the main personage is a bird. In Siberia, this myth is believed by the majority of peoples.[10] The plot of the myth in all of the cultures is the same. At first only the ocean existed, then a bird dove into the sea and recovered some soil from its bottom; with its continuing efforts, this soil increased to an enormous size.

Further data referring to the bird's function in the shamans' rites allow us to connect the image of the bird into which the shaman is sometimes incarnated with the theme (plot) of another cosmological myth. Common agreement exists among scientists that the bird was the main spirit assistant of the shaman and that it performed both the function of a riding animal and that of a bird that scouts. However, the study of the bird's functions in the shamans' acts (*camlaniya*) shows that the main direction of its flights was not to the upper world, where the shaman most often went on the deer (the horse, in the case of Buriats), but to the lower world, or the world existing underwater.[11]

These mythological plots indicate that the bird (a water bird in the earlier versions of the myth) embodies a basic function as intermediary between two opposite levels or spheres of the universe—the upper world and the lower world. The bird lives in all three levels of the universe—earth, sky, and underworld. Its functional connection with water is embodied in the upper sphere by the heavenly water and in the lower sphere by the earthly water and the underworld water.[12] It is important to emphasize that the significance of the bird in the cosmic system as the intermediary among the three spheres of the universe coincides with the ritual function of the shaman, who also serves in this intermediary role. The constant presence of the bird's image is reflected in the shaman's ritual costume. The three images—the deer, the bear, and the bird—are dominant on the shaman's ritual costume and create a symbolic image of the universe. In accordance with this symbolic structure, all of the later modified images in metallic pendants played a strictly defined role on the ritual costume.

Thus, the analysis of these three images found on shamanistic attire, with its metallic decoration in the form of skeletons, demonstrates that the creation and development of the images were connected with cosmologic and cosmogonic myths and that these myths were embodied in rituals in which the main role was played by the shaman. By leaving the narrow concepts of the clan, shamanism absorbed the most basic worldview categories of cosmology and cosmogony and helped to create more advanced ideological forms, which found their expression in the shaman's ritual costume.

NOTES

1. Prokofyeva, E. D. 1971. Shamanskii kostjum narodov Siberi [Shaman's Costume Among the Peoples of Siberia]. *Sbornik Muzeia antropologii i etnografii* [Collected Articles of the Museum of Anthropology and Ethnography] 27:5.

2. Anisimov, A. F. 1951. Shamanskie dukhi po vozzreniyam evenkov i totemisticheskie istoki ideologii shamanstva [Shamanistic Totemism and Shamanistic Ideology]. *Sbornik Muzeia antropologii i etnografii* [Collected Articles of the Museum of Anthropology and Ethnography] 12:193.

3. Lommel, Andreas. 1980. *Shamanen und Medizinmanner: Magie und Mystic früher Kulturen*. München: Verlag Callweg, p. 189; Nachtigall, H. 1953. Die erhoehte Bestattung in Nord- und Hochasien. *Anthropos* 48: 44–70; Nachtigall, H. 1952. Die Kulturhistorische Wurzel der Schamanenskelettierung. *Zeitschrift fuer Ethnologie* 77: 188–197; Okladnikov, A. P. 1974. *Petrogliphy Bajkala—pamyatniki dzevnej kultury narodov Siberi* [Petroglyphs of Baikal: Cultures of the Peoples of Siberia]. Novosibersk: Nauka; Okladnikov, A. P. 1966. *Petrogliphy Angary* [Petroglyphs of Angara]. Moscow and Leningrad: Nauka.

4. Vasiljev, B. A. 1948. Medvezhii prazdnik [The Bear Celebration]. *Sovetskaia etnografiia* [Soviet Ethnography] 4, pp. 78–87.

5. Zelenin, D. K. 1936. *Kult ongonov v Siberi* [The Cult of Fire in Siberia]. Moscow and Leningrad: Nauka, pp. 10, 12–13; Anisimov, A. F. 1959. *Kosmologicheskie predstavleniay narodov Siberi* [Cosmological Representations of the Peoples of Siberia]. Leningrad, pp. 39, 85; Vasiljev, B. A. 1948. Medvezhii prazdnik [The Bear Celebration]. *Sovetskaia etnografiia* [Soviet Ethnography] 4, pp. 9ff.

6. Yankovich, M. 1980. *Miphicheskoe zhivotnoe na zverzdnom nebie. Skipho-siberskoe Kulturno-istoricheskoe edinstvo* [Mythical Animals in the Wild Sky in the Skythian-Siberian Cultural-Historical Unity]. Kemerovo, pp. 348–357.

7. Potanin, G. N. 1892. *Gromovnik po poverjam i skazaniyam plemen Ujzhnoi Siberi i Mongolii* [The Thunder God in the Popular Belief and Stories of the Tribes of Southern Siberia and Mongolia]. Zhurnal Ministerstva narognogo prosvesh'eniya, feveral, p. 317; Okladnikov, A. D. 1950. Kult medvedya u neoliticheskikh plemen Vostochnoi Siberi [The Cult of the Bear Among the Neolithic Tribes of Eastern Siberia]. *Sovetskaia arkheologiia* [Soviet Archaeology] 12:11.

8. Prokofyev, G. N. 1934. Tseremoniya ozhivleniya bubna u ostyako-samoe-dov [The Ceremony of the Resurrection of the Bubo Among the Ostyako-Samoeds]. *Izvestiya Leningradskogo Gosudarstvennogo Universiteta* [News From Leningrad State University], p. 9.

9. Potanov, L. P. 1935. Sled totemisstiskikh predstavlenii u altaitsev [Totemistic Performance Among the Altai]. *Sovetskaia etnografiia* [Soviet Ethnography] 4–5, pp. 141–142.

10. Prokofjyeva, E. D. 1954. Materialy po religioznym pred-stavleniyam entsev [Material on the Religious Performance of the Nentsi]. *Sbornik Muzeia antropologii i etnografii* [Collected Articles of the Museum of Anthropology and Ethnography] 14:204; Khomich, L. V. 1981. Predstavleniya nentsev o prirode i chelovekie [Performance of the Nentsi About Nature and Man]. In *Prirod i chelovek v predstavleniyakh narodov Siberi* [Nature and Man in the Performances of the Peoples of Siberia]. Leningrad, p. 17; Aleksaenko, E. A. 1981. Predstavleniya ketov o mearie [Representations of Siberian Salmon in Connection With Mear]. In *Prirod i chelovek v predstavleniyakh narodov Siberi* [Nature and Man in the Performances of the Peoples of Siberia]. Leningrad, p. 71; Popov, A. A. 1984. *Nganasany. Sotsialjnoe ustroistvo i verovaniya* [Nganasany: Social Structure and Beliefs]. Leningrad, p. 41; Dyrenkova, N. P. 1919. Ptitsa v kulture turetskikh plemen Siberi [Birds in the Culture of the Turkish Tribes of Siberia]. In C. Dalai, ed., *Kultura i pisjmennostj Vostoka* [Culture and Writings of the East], Vol. 4. Baku, p. 119.

11. Popov, A. A. 1984. *Nganasany. Sotsialjnoe ustroistvo i verovaniya* [Nganasany: Social Structure and Beliefs]. Leningrad, p. 117; Prokofjeva, E. D. 1951. Kostjum selkupskogo shamana [The Costume of the Selkup Shaman]. *Sbornik Muzeia antropologii i etnografii* [Collected Articles of the Museum of Anthropology and Ethnography] 11:533.

12. *Myfy narodov meara* [Myths of the Peoples of Mear], Vol. 2. 1981. Moscow.

12

THE HORSE IN YAKUT SHAMANISM

Vladimir Diachenko

The Yakut live in a vast territory of more than 3 million square kilometers that occupies one seventh of the former Soviet Union. Their territory includes the tundra zone of the Arctic shores in the north and settlements as far south as the tributaries of the Amur River. They are the second-largest native group in Siberia, numbering about 330,000. The Yakut are typical of the seminomadic horse-breeding and cattle-breeding Turkic peoples of Central Asia, even though today they live in the extreme northeast portion of Siberia. The peopling of the Lena River Valley took place in different epochs, as various tribes from the southern areas of the Baikal region and Central Asia moved into the area. Migration occurred in waves, the last of which was in the late twelfth century in the epoch preceding Chingis Khan's empire.

Although isolated from other Turkic peoples, the Yakut bred horses and cattle—the same activities that were basic to the economy of the Turkic peoples of South Siberia. However, they formed their own very expressive and original culture. Historically, the Yakut settled in the taiga and tundra zones, pasturing their horses and cattle everywhere. In some areas, they acquired knowledge of reindeer breeding from the Evenki, Yukaghir, and Chukche peoples. The Yakut groups who farm in the basins of the east Siberian rivers—the Colombia, Indighirka, Yana, and others—often keep both horse herds and domestic reindeer herds. Because they had horses, the Yakut were able to master vast ranges of Siberia, and they brought horse breeding to the Polar circle, including Amerkon, where temperatures as low as −70 degrees Celsius have been registered. Perhaps no other Siberian people maintained a cult of the horse to such a degree as the Yakut. Of major importance in the Yakut economy, the horse's image was also reflected in material culture and religion. The Yakut's historic isolation has promoted this in many respects, and the horse cult has found expression in all spheres of Yakut life: in mythology, heroic epics, and ritual ceremonies.

According to Yakut beliefs, the horse is of divine origin. At first god created a horse from which a half horse–half man descended, and from this creature humankind was born. The Sky-Horse deity, called Uordakh-Djesegei, is one of the main characters in Yakut religion (Popov 1949:268). Yakut legends depict him as a white stallion that appears from the clouds during summer *koumiss* festivals. The peals of thunder are believed to be his passionate neigh. This festival, which is named after him, is celebrated in the spring after the mares have foaled. During this season, the Yakut store the mares' milk and prepare the koumiss for the festival. The family and all of the relatives gather in the house. A carpet of white horsehide is spread flat in the center of the room, and wooden goblets of koumiss are placed upon it. The guests then sit down. The host goes around the inside circuit of the room with a goblet of koumiss lifted in his hands and invites the guests to drink the koumiss.

Yakut mythology depicts many scenes in which deities and guardian spirits descend to the earth as horses. The honorable goddess Ajysyt, the patron of childbearing, appears as a white mare. Another goddess, called Lajahsit, also appearing in the form of a white mare, greets the Yakut with best wishes (Troshanskiy 1903:38). Yakut religion views the horse as the source of childbearing and as a protective force that, in vital situations, may be transferred directly to an individual. At the time of childbirth, a long cord of horsehair is plaited and wrapped around stakes and a cross beam. The woman in labor holds on to this cross beam. It is believed that the horsehair rope makes childbirth easier and more successful.

A particularly expressive cult of the horse can be traced in Yakut shamanism, in which the horse and shaman are inseparable. A Yakut shaman's healing performance is unthinkable without a horse, just as the entire ceremony cannot occur without the shaman's participation. The shaman's main function is to return the patient's soul, which has been stolen by evil spirits. In search of the soul, a shaman journeys to the underground world, which is populated by terrible monsters, or fights in the upper world with other dangerous spirits. If successful, the shaman seizes the lost soul, either by force or by fraud, and returns it to the patient.

A horse, its image, or, at times, an object personifying the animal is always present in the shaman's preparations and performances. Three trees joined by a cord of horsehair are placed near a patient's house before the ceremony begins. These trees are hung with bunches of horsehair and with horses' skulls, the front teeth of which point to the sky. This ritual arrangement, called *bagakh,* is the preliminary sacrifice brought to the spirits. A carpet made of horse's skin, including the head and leg skins, is then spread in the middle of the dwelling opposite the door. Through this symbolism it is thought that the shaman actually sits on the horse. A long birch twig, cleaned of side branches and tied with bunches of horsehair in three, seven, or nine places, is used as an irritant for the evil spirits lurking in the patient. The shaman waves the twig above the patient, rousing the evil spirits and luring them to himself or herself. It is thought that the horsehairs fastened to the birch twig attract the evil spirits.

Before leaving for the upper or lower world, the shaman dresses in a cap of horse skins and a robe decorated with numerous metal pendants. These pendants are in the form of animals and birds and personify the spirit assistants of the shaman. The shaman's robe is sewn of foal's skin or horse's skin. When forging the pendants for the robe, the blacksmith plunges the hot iron into mare's blood (Vasiljev 1910), and the forged pendants are then sprinkled with horse's blood. This ceremony of sprinkling blood is accompanied by invocations and requests to the spirits to recognize the new owner of the costume and to keep him under special protection. Before the shaman's performance, the spirit assistants are also fed horse's blood. When the shaman first dresses in his new costume, he bucks about with great force, like a horse, and sometimes even faints. In this Yakut ceremony, called "breaking in" a new dress, the shaman throws a horse's rein around his neck, signifying that he has become a horse by dressing in this costume. He throws the rein across his collarbone and over his shoulders to his back. Often two rings are sewn on the shaman's suit at either side of his back, and the rein is fastened to them. During the ritual performance, the shaman's assistants never let go of this rein.

The shaman snorts and shakes his head like a horse as he continues the performance. He puts iron objects into his mouth instead of a bit and neighs like a horse as he comes into the yard. He then enters the house on all fours. Four men hold him constantly during the ceremony by the rein of the bridle. Often his motions resemble a trotting horse as he moves his lower body left and right, positioning his feet wide apart and throwing the long fringe of his robe around like a horse's tail. This demonstrates that the shaman has turned into the horse before he departs on his dangerous journey. The shaman's drum also turns into a powerful horse during the performance. The shaman calls the drum a faithful assistant who helps him with his "keen ear" and "sharp-sighted eye" and who protects him from evil spirits. White horsehairs are tied to the crosspiece, or handle, of the drum, and during the performance the drumstick turns into the horse's whip.

During a young man's initiation into the rank of shaman, he is led to the high mountains where he is dressed in a new suit and given a birch twig with a bunch of horsehair. The new shaman pronounces a spell and promises to be the patron of the wretched and poor people and to worship the deities upon which the people's prosperity depends. He pledges to sacrifice horses to these deities (Pripuzov 1884:65). A horse's color determines the deity to which it will be sacrificed: the more powerful the deity, the more rare the color of the sacrificial horse.

The Yakuts make two kinds of sacrifices—bloody and bloodless—depending upon which deities and spirits are needed. Bloody offerings are brought to an evil spirit who has stolen a soul and caused a person's illness. This sacrifice is like an exchange or trade between the spirit who stole the soul and the shaman who is the patient's representative. The shaman offers the evil spirit the animal's soul in exchange for the patient's soul. To perform the sacrifice, the shaman ties the horse's feet. The horse is then brought down on its back, its belly is cut with a knife, and its aorta is removed. The animal's heart and liver are boiled and put on a special table; these parts are considered delicacies for the evil spirits. The horse's skin, head, and hoofs are hung from a tree that grows in an open place. After the ceremony is completed, the shaman and the participants eat the meat of the sacrificial animal.

The second type of sacrifice is bloodless. Here, the Yakut offers horses to the kindly deities in hopes of their protection. In ancient times, rich men—dressed in white fur coats and carrying white wooden poles in one hand—rode saddle horses and drove nine other horses before them far to the east, where they released the animals and abandoned them as sacrifices. Very rich men participated in this ceremony three times during their lifetimes, those who were fairly wealthy took part twice, and the poor participated only once.

Yakut who own big herds of horses give one mare to the shaman for sacrifice. This horse is separated from the others and is kept locked up. The horse's bridle has a rein embroidered with colored cotton and beads, and its mane and tail are not cut. This mare is not bred and therefore is not milked; it is also not ridden or worked. The horse is not killed, but if it dies, it is replaced by another mare of the same color. If, by oversight, it bears a foal, the foal also becomes a sacrifice to the spirits. During summer koumiss festivals, these sacrificial horses are sprinkled with koumiss from a special vessel.

In earlier times, at the beginning of summer, the Yakut organized a national koumiss festival called *Ysyakh*. This was an ancient festival in which major deities, particularly patrons of horses, were honored. Much koumiss was accumulated to be shared with the thousands of people who participated in the ceremony. In the field in which the festival was held, two posts with horizontal crosspieces and images of horses' heads at the ends were set in the ground. Two birches, interwoven at the top, were tied to the posts. Cords of horsehair were hung with ribbons, bunches of white horsehair were stretched between the posts and birches, and a high tethering post was often set nearby. During the festival, a white horse, which was to be sacrificed to the celestial deities, was tied to this post. Large vessels, called *choron,* which could hold about nine pails of liquid, stood near the posts; these huge containers were filled with koumiss and were decorated with bunches of white hair from a horse's mane.

Shamans managed the festival. The Yakut felt that the greater the number of shamans present at the festival, the better it was for the people. These shamans wore caps made from the leg skins of white foals and coats made of white horses' skin. Before the koumiss was drunk, it was scooped up with a wooden ladle tied with white hair from a horse's mane. With this ladle the shamans sprinkled the koumiss upward and to the east, where the Yakuts' deity-patrons lived, and then sprinkled the tied horse with the koumiss. This event included dances and races, which occurred after much group drinking of koumiss.

The main aim of this festival was to propitiate deity-patrons and to offer them sacrifices in exchange for their goodwill. The shaman appeared in the capacity of mediator. A horse, horsehair, or koumiss was brought to be sacrificed. The sacrifice of a horse, or any of its parts, was considered obligatory and was the most desirable form of sacrifice. It emphasized the horse-breeding basis of the Yakut economy and the importance of the horse cult.

I have mentioned that a horse is an embodiment of the life force and of fertility among Yakut people. These forces are given to the shaman during the ritual described earlier and also as part of the performances of other ceremonies.

During the past century, the Yakut held a special ceremony for inducing sexual passion and the forces of reproduction. Shamans were the main participants in the ceremony, and several master shamans presented a special prayer to the spirits of the earth to grant the force of sexual inclination to women. The chosen place for the ceremony was under a big, branching, ceremonial tree. Three posts with carved tops in the form of vessels for koumiss were placed in the ground, and newly blooming birches, joined with a cord made of white and black horsehair, were placed around the posts. Ribbons of cloth and bunches of horsehair were fastened to the cord as a sacrifice to the spirits, and a conical hut covered with birch bark was placed near the posts. Black, or evil, shamans who associated with bloodthirsty evil spirits could not participate in this ceremony; only white shamans could perform the rituals. Nine girls and nine boys assisted the shamans in their ceremonial journey to the spirit of mother earth. Holding birch poles in their hands, these youths danced together with the shamans. The shamans then put on their costumes and picked up the drums.

During the ensuing performance, they addressed the spirit of mother earth, imploring her to give the force of sexual inclination called *dzalin*. When the force of dzalin entered the shamans' spirits, they began to prance, neighing like a horse and uttering screams and invocations. At this moment the women suddenly began to laugh and to neigh like mares. They attacked the shamans with neighing and performed passionate sexual motions. Sometimes the shamans were thrown to the ground, but the men, who stood close by, protected them from the passionate women. The shamans then suddenly got up, whistling and performing circular motions with their drumsticks. At that point the women regained their senses, became tranquil, and sat down.

The shamans' ritual infusion of dzalin was called "the taking of sexual passion from the spirit of earth," or "the inducing of the force of reproduction." According to the tales of old men, the flushed, excited women used to throw themselves at the shamans, at times even stripping off their clothes.

The shamans' performance continued all night, from sunset to sunrise (Ksenofontov 1929:47). Similar erotic ceremonies have been observed recently among some peoples of the north Altai (Satlaev 1971:130–141). This seems to indicate the existence of blood ties between the Yakut and the Altai peoples.

REFERENCES

Ksenofontov, G. V.
   1929.   *Hrestes: Shamanizm i hristianstvo* [Hrestes: Shamanism and Christianity].
            Irkutsk: Nauka, p. 47.

Popov, A. A.
   1949.   Materiali poistorii religii jakutov bivshego Vilujskogo okruga [Material on the
            History of Religion Among the Yakut of the Former Vilujs Region]. *Sbornik
            Muzeia antropologii i etnografii* [Collected Articles of the Museum of
            Anthropology and Ethnography] 7, No. 11:268.

Pripuzov, N. P.
   1884.   Svedeniya dlya izucheniya shamanstva uyakutov yakutskogo okruga
            [Information for the Study of Shamanism Among the Yakut of the
            Yakut Region]. *Izvestiya VSORGO* [News VSORGO]. Irkutsk 15, Nos. 3–4:65.

Satlaev, F. A.
   1971.   Kocha-kan—starinniy obrjad isprashivaniya plodorodiya u kumand intsev
            [Kocha-kan: An Ancient Fertility Rite Among the Kumandirits]. *Sbornik
            Muzeia antropologii i etnografii* [Collected Articles of the Museum of
            Anthropology and Ethnography] 27:130–141.

Troshanskiy, V. F.
   1903.   *Evolutsiya chornoi veri (shamanstva) u yakutov* [Evolution of the
            Black Beliefs (Shamanism) Among the Yakut]. Kazan: Nauka, p. 38.

Vasiljev, V. N.
   1910.   Shamanskiy kostjum i buben u yakutov [Shamanist Costumes and Bubos
            (Drums) Among the Yakut]. *Sbornik Muzeia antropologii i etnografii*
            [Collected Articles of the Museum of Anthropology and Ethnography] 1:6, 8:2.

13

TEXTS OF SHAMANISTIC INVOCATIONS FROM CENTRAL ASIA AND KAZAKHSTAN

Vladimir N. Basilov

A shamanistic rite is a social action. Shamans perform their rites in order to satisfy the requests of the people in their society; therefore, their actions must be understandable to their people. Thus, shamans must explain their actions, and for this reason verbal performance represents an important element of their ceremonies.

Some examples of texts spoken or sung during a seance by the shamans of various peoples of Siberia and the European North were published by scholars in the nineteenth and twentieth centuries, but these early reports do not sufficiently illustrate the significant role of the word in shamanistic rites. This is why contemporary texts of shamanistic invocations collected among the peoples of Central Asia and Kazakhstan have indisputable interest and can help to explain the specificity of these invocations. The texts do not clarify everything. The question of how much the texts are determined by traditions has not yet been analyzed in the ethnographic literature, and we still do not know how independent the shamans were in creating their invocations nor to what degree they were dependent upon established stereotypes. Mircea Eliade feels the ritual songs are "the improvisation of the shaman, and he forgets them after a seance." Eliade expressed this interpretation in connection with a description of a healing seance of a North American Indian shaman.[1] The same view is shared by some Soviet ethnographers studying the peoples of Siberia,[2] but in many publications this issue is not discussed. To understand whether this view is correct, we must compare the texts of invocations sung, first, by various shamans and, second, by the same shamans at different times but in similar situations. We have the data for this comparison from written texts of scholars in Central Asia and Kazakhstan, including my own records made mostly in the 1970s in Uzbekistan.

First, let me give a general description of shamanistic invocations. In Central Asia and Kazakhstan, the shamans usually sing their invocations and address them to their helping spirits, accompanied by a musical instrument. The invocations consist of phrases of a certain meter; in the course of a seance, the rhythm of the invocations may be changed. In an attempt to make their verbal performance expressive and bright, the shamans use the images of their traditional epic poetry and of rhymed neighboring phrases. With a masterly use of epithets, metaphors, colorful comparisons, deliberate repetitions, and allegories, the shamans achieve an artistic effect. The invocations of an effective shaman could attract and hold the attention of the participants and concentrate their imaginations on the content of a ceremony.

Ritual shamanistic invocations in Central Asia and Kazakhstan do not always have a logical connection with a rite itself. Here we see the influence of Islam. In Central Asia and Kazakhstan, as in some other parts of the Muslim world, shamanism exists in a thoroughly Islamized form; this phenomenon has been described in a series of publications.[3] Under the conditions of dominant Muslim ideology, shamanism could survive only if it lost its most obvious ethnic features and absorbed Muslim concepts and ritual elements. The invasion of Islamic ideology destroyed the original logic of shamanistic rites. For example, some Uighur shamans sang lyric songs at the beginning of their healing seances.[4] Turkmenian shamans often performed lyric songs with verses of the fifteenth-century Uzbek poet Alisher Navoi.[5] Songs composed with Navoi's verses were also sung by some Uighur shamans.[6]

The Islamization of shamanism, however, did not entirely destroy the ancient genre of invocations addressed to the spirits and directly connected with the ritual actions of a shaman. The texts of invocations recorded by ethnographers in Central Asia and Kazakhstan contain the extended list of spirits summoned by the shamans for the ceremonies they performed. Many Muslim saints are among these spirits. The invocations, with their many formal differences, have similar contents and identical structures. In the beginning the shamans ask various Muslim saints to help them, then they invite their own helping spirits. The texts of the invocations we know today do not describe the ceremony as a whole but only comment on some of its elements—mostly the beginning, when the shamans address various spirits with a request for help, and the end, when the shamans see their helping spirits off and demand that the malicious spirits leave a sick person and resettle in another place.

I first examine the similarity in the invocations sung by various shamans. Comparison of the available texts shows that they have the same structure, the same images, and the same ideas. Of course, an image or a concept can be represented in a great variety of forms—some cases identical, some cases only distantly related. I illustrate this point with some examples.

For instance, the ritual songs of the Uzbek shamaness Ulpan (Djizak oblast of the Uzbek SSR) began with the words:

> For this my work [I say] *bismillah,*
> For my every work [I say] *bismillah,*
> When I lie down, when I get up [I say] *bismillah,*
> When I set off, [I say] *bismillah.* (Basilov field notes)
> (*Bismillah* is an initial fragment of a sacred Muslim formula in
> Arabic: *Bismillahi-r-rahmani-r-rahim*: In the name of Allah,
> merciful, generous.)

The Uzbek shamaness Aidai began her ritual songs with other words:

> First of all [I say the name of] the God,
> Then [I say the names of] the patron saints (Uzb. *pir*),
> Four friends [i.e., first four Rightful Caliphs—V.B.],
> I appeal to you, help me!

Both versions of these initial phrases are known in a similar form by other Uzbek, Kazakh, and Uighur shamans.[7]

Characteristic of shamanic texts is the mention of suffering experienced by shamans and caused by their spirits. Perhaps the spiritual songs originally described torments felt or imagined by shamans during a period of "shamanistic disease," when they were persecuted by spirits in their hallucinations. The original reason for these torments has not been preserved in the beliefs of the peoples of Central Asia and Kazakhstan, but traditions of the Siberian peoples make it quite clear. They report that the spirits boil shamans, cut them into pieces, and eat them in order to "re-create" them, thus making them beings with supernatural qualities.[8]

Describing the tortures she suffered from her spirits, the Uzbek shamaness Aidai (Djizak oblast of the Uzbek SSR) sang:

[First] I didn't want to take [shaman's role]
Let your name vanish, you infidels [i.e., helping spirits—V.B.]
I didn't want to go your way
[But] you gave the date (Uzb. *jiyda*) into my hand,
(It turned out to be predestined to me).
You gathered [the spirits] and put [them] on me.
You gave an apple into my hand [as a sign of selection—V.B.]
You neglected my reluctance.
Having deceived, you put [the spirits] on me.
My loving father gave me the name.
My loving mother gave me milk.
Milk given me by [my] mother
Because of this "heritage" [i.e., helping spirits—V.B.].
Have flown being yellow water [i.e., brought me suffering—V.B.].
The name, given [me] by [my] father [changed]:
(It turned out to be predestined to me).
I got a name of a shamaness (Uzb. *bakshi*).
Because of these "infidels" [i.e., helping spirits—V.B.].
My end [i.e., end of my life—V.B.] comes, I shall say.
I became like a willow branch [i.e., without fruits and without children—V.B.],
My sins are more numerous than small sweepings [around me],
My sins are more numerous than dried up grass.
Allah, God, what shall I do? (Basilov field notes)

The Uzbek shamaness Karshigul (Djizak oblast of the Uzbek SSR) recited these phrases in another way:

My loving father gave [me] a name.
My loving mother gave [me] milk.
The name given [me] by my father
Has been dedicated to shamanism (Uzb. *bakshilikka ataldy*).
Milk given me by my mother
Has flown having turned to yellow water (Uzb. *Zardab bolyb*).
[To make my] food pure, bread righteous,
Would it not be better if I grazed cattle [instead of shamanizing]?
(Basilov field notes)

The Uzbek shamaness Ulpan (Djizak oblast of the Uzbek SSR) described the same feelings in these words:

My loving father gave [me] a name.
My loving mother gave [me] milk.
[My] dear relatives! [obviously, father and mother—V.B.]
The name left by my father
Having turned to a white drum caught [me] firmly,
Milk given me by [my] mother
Having turned to "heritage" [i.e., helping spirits—V.B.]
entangled [me].
"I shall not take," I said, [but they] made me take,
Delivered me a serpent whip.
You joined [me] when [I was] 25 [years old].
Like a silk thread, [you] twined round [me]
In my childhood a spirit (Uzb. *jinn*) struck me,
In my cradle a patron saint (Uzb. pir) struck [me].
The trace of the patron saint's blow is
His example that I have in my hand [i.e., the shamaness
follows his prescriptions—V.B.]
The trace of the spirit's blow is
His sign that I have on my tongue. (Basilov field notes)

In other expressions, the same subject (motif) is present in the texts of various Uzbek shamanesses. This idea of invocations—a complaint against the spirits who cause sufferings to the shaman whom they chose—can be found in the ritual songs of the Kazakh shamans. For instance, in the text published by W. Radloff, a Kazakh shaman reports that his helping spirits (*peri*) made forty knives cut his body and forty needles prick his flesh; he resisted the call of the spirits, but they made him be humble and obey; they tied him to a dry wood [i.e., to the stringed musical instrument *kobyz,* which was used by the Kazakh shamans instead of a drum—V.B.]. This shaman says: "I didn't honor [my] father, I didn't drink milk of [my] mother";[9] these words resemble the corresponding phrases of Aidai's invocation presented earlier.

Another Kazakh shaman, whose invocation was published by A. Divayev, also complains about his destiny:

I took in my hands a kobyz made of a pine-tree
And wind like a water serpent.
But my kobyz didn't break,
Didn't give peace to my poor soul.
When [I was] 15 years [old] he [i.e., spirit, jinn—V.B.]
stuck to me,
When [I was] 20 years [old] he befriended me.
Having forced me to do this work—against my will.
He bound me to a dry wood [i.e., to a kobyz—A.D.].[10]

Complaint against sufferings caused by the spirits is also heard in the ritual songs of the Altay and Yakut shamans. For instance, an Altayen shaman enumerated his ancestor-shamans who selected him for the shaman's office and caused his "shamanistic disease," thus making him suffer:

Because of shaman Otkon I called [for help].
Because of shaman Yeren' I cried.
Because of shaman Mitka, because of shaman Mitam
Because of shaman Yazi-balyq I cried,
Because of shaman Kobor I ran and turned like a whirlwind
Shaman Ponok lay heavy on me.[11]

A Yakut shaman in his song scolded his spirits: "I was predestined [by you] to be unhappy. . . . My fate was crippled!"[12]

In the texts performed by other shamans, we recognize a similar description of some helping spirits. Several shamans mentioned in their invocations a spirit in the image of an eagle (Uzb. Turkm. *kara kush*). Omar, a Kazakh shaman, for instance, addressed this spirit with the following words:

In the skies flying eagle!
Your wings stretching, come down
[Your] tail pressing [to your body] come down
[Your] legs stretching, come down."[13]

The Uzbek shamaness Karshigul summoned the eagle with different words:

The heavenly eagle,
Defecate on the patient's head!
One of your wings is [made] of silver,
Another of your wings is [made] of bronze.
Sit on my white drum,
Give me a companion [i.e., a helping spirit—V.B.].
Pour down an army [of spirits] at once.[14] (Basilov field notes)

We also possess texts recorded from Uzbek and Kazakh shamans in which other variations of the appeal to the spirit eagle are present.[15] The ancient image of the spirit eagle is also common in the traditions of many Turkic-speaking peoples. The eagle, in particular, was one of the important helping spirits for the Altayen shamans. It was addressed in invocations and depicted on the drum's skin.[16]

The Kazakh shamans also called on a helping spirit shaped like a snake. In my records we find the words:

A red serpent with yellow spots, as high as a yurt's lattice
(*kerege*), [come],
A yellow serpent, as high as a yurt's dome, [come].[17]

Spirit snakes were summoned with very similar phrases by some other Kazakh and Karakalpak shamans.[18]

The most convincing example of the widespread circulation and longevity of stereotypes in shamanistic invocations is a description of a spirit giant who is a helping spirit of the Kazakh shamans. Here is a text recorded by Divayev at the end of the nineteenth century:

Fly [to me] from Qaf mountains, o, Chara-bas!
Ninety sheep skins were not sufficient
To make a winter-coat for you, Chara-bas,
Eighty sheep skins were not sufficient
To make a hat for you, Chara-bas!

And also:

Ninety sheep skins were not sufficient
To make a winter-coat for you, Kokaman,

Eighty sheep skins were not sufficient
To make a hat for you, Kokaman.[19]

Many Kazakh shamans glorified the might of their helping spirit in
their invocations. We find similar phrases in texts recorded from various
Kazakh shamans.[20] Kirghiz shamans also liked this imagery. Shermat, a
Kirghiz shaman, for example, sang to his spirit:

Toktor, you are as great as a mountain.
Ninety sheep skins are not sufficient
To make for you a winter-coat with its end by your knees.
If you don't come, who comes?
Who wins this shaitan [i.e., evil spirit—V.B.]?
Toktor, you are the most mighty person.
Sixty sheep skins are not sufficient
To make trousers for you.
If you don't come, who comes?
Who wins this *shaitan*?[21]

The Altayen shamans depicted the huge size of the spirit with similar words. Among the invocations published by N. P. Dyrenkova are
the following lines:

Sixty bear skins are not sufficient
To cover [your] leg to the end [i.e., to make trousers—V.B.].
Seventy bear skins are not sufficient
To make sleeves [of a coat] for you.[22]

It is interesting that the same type of description was used in the epic
poetry of the Turkmens (*destan* "Yusup-Akhmet"),[23] the Bashkirs (destan
"Alpamysha"),[24] and the Uzbeks (destan "Alpamysh").[25] A Turkish scholar,
A. Inan, was the first to point out similar descriptions in the medieval epic
ballads of the Oghuz Turks—*Kitabi Dedem Korkut* ("My Grandfather
Korkut's Book")[26]—and to suggest that they were borrowed from the
ancient shamans' invocations.[27]

Thus, shamans who lived far away from each other and who belonged
to different peoples used the same or similar images and formulas in their
ritual songs. This similarity is obvious even in translation, and the original
texts in Uzbek, Kazakh, and other languages show the likeness distinctly. It

is important to stress that if we can draw this conclusion by comparing only a few texts, how many more common elements in shamanistic invocations would there be if we possessed a larger corpus of recorded data.

The conclusion that the texts of invocations have been determined by traditional stereotypes coincides perfectly with the characteristics of current shamanistic rites. These rites can be described as an action with a logical structure and plot, performed in accordance with traditional animistic beliefs and with various elements of the rites reproducing the stereotypes. It is natural that the texts of the invocations should have the same specific features as the rites. The texts reflect consistent views of the world of the spirits and of the relations between these spirits and the shaman. Thus, in essence, the different texts represent variations on the same subject.

The next question is, how consistent are the texts of the invocations? Do shamans sing the same ritual songs when they perform the same rite for different people, and do they sing the same invocations when they perform various rites? To answer this question, a scholar must remain with the same shaman for a period of time. I did this when I carried on my field work among the Uzbeks.

In 1974 the Uzbek shamaness Aidai dictated to me the text of her invocation. She said she sang that invocation with the sounds of her drum when performing a seance of ritual healing, regardless of the sex of the patient. In 1979 she gave her blessings to another shamaness, Nobat, when together they performed a rite of renewal in a shamanistic initiation.[28] A tape recording of Aidai's songs was of poor quality; the drum sounded louder than Aidai's voice. She listened to the tape but could not recognize the words. As a result, she began to dictate to me the text she had sung during the renewal of the initiation. Although she had explained to me that the texts for the rites of healing and initiation differ, I found that this was basically the same text I had recorded in 1974. The similarity of the texts can probably be explained by the similarity of the rites—in both cases the spirits are fed and are asked not to harm the people. Also, Aidai is not a "big" shamaness. Women from her area pointed out that her invocations are not rich; the text is short and cannot be compared with the invocations of the other shamans who in the past could carry on a seance during an entire night.

The recorded texts are interesting. First, they are not identical. Some lines that were present in one were absent in another; in some cases the sequence of the phrases was changed; and some sentences

FIGURE 13.1
The Uzbek shamaness Nobat at home with her family. Shamans usually have the same life-style as that of other villagers.

FIGURE 13.2
The beginning of the rite Renewal of Blessing. The shamaness Aidai puts her drum into the flames of the ritual candles. She explains that the drum thus shows reverence for the candles that are dedicated to the helping spirits. Shamaness Nobat is to the left: she is putting on her headdress.

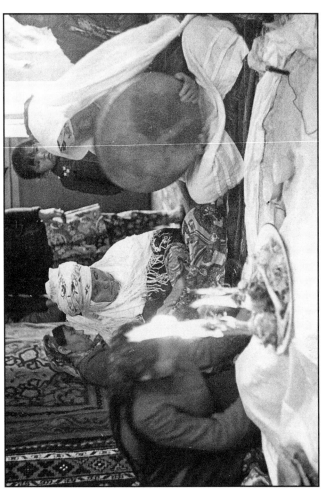

FIGURE 13.3
Aidai is playing the drum and singing as Nobat maintains silence. To the left is Nobat's daughter-in-law, who bows respectfully to the altar.

FIGURE 13.4
Aidai has given her drum to Nobat, who is now playing and singing.

were given in different forms. We can, therefore, conclude that the text of Aidai's invocations was not always performed in the same unchangeable order with a strictly fixed number and sequence of the phrases. Obviously, the text could be lengthened or shortened, and some of its fragments could be sung earlier or later. The general structure of the text must be constant, but the size and details of the text can differ depending upon the circumstances and inspiration.

As a result of my work with the tape recordings in 1979, I also concluded that a text of invocations dictated by a shamaness under nonritual conditions is more accurate and consistent than the same text sung during a rite. Tape recordings showed that some of Aidai's slips of the tongue probably occurred because during a seance, she performs a text learned years ago rather mechanically, without deep attention to the words.

This observation was supported by my impressions when working with Nobat. More than once I asked for her help as I transcribed her invocations from tape to paper. Sometimes it was difficult to hear her voice over the noise of her drum; in such cases Nobat, like Aidai, dictated the text to me. I was surprised that sometimes she could not understand herself and could not reconstruct the phrases or separate words she sang. Some of the phrases she dictated were obviously not the same as those on the tape. Sometimes Nobat successfully explained the fragments I did not understand, but often she spoke a phrase in a different way without concern for what was on the tape. She demonstrated vast resources for devising variations, easily putting together well-known and often-used epithets and colorful combinations of words. Thus, we can see that the tape-recorded texts are examples of her performance, but by no means do they represent an established and constant text, always repeated in the same ways in similar situations. Even when discussing the meaning of a phrase clearly heard on the tape, Nobat often changed it. She could easily substitute another phrase for the original sentence and change the words as well. Nobat was known in the area as an experienced shamaness, and her creative potential was much stronger than that of Aidai. Nobat attributed her capacity for producing good invocations to the influence of her helping spirits.

Freedom or, rather, wide flexibility in performance of the invocation appears to be acceptable in the shamanistic tradition. Shamans who were sensitive to the artistic effect of the words perfected the texts inherited from their predecessors and introduced their own innovations. The shamans' worldview is based on a belief in the existence of the spirits; the spirits inspire the shamans' creativity and enrich the texts of their ritual songs. But does this mean that the texts performed during the rites are improvised? No. The shamans' artistic choices and innovations follow existing stereotypes. Let us again compare texts and rite. Although the same rite was carried on similarly, but not identically, by different shamans, the rite did not lose its importance in the traditional order of ritual. The same can be said about the invocations. Although they often take great latitude with the text, shamans do not distort the traditional world of images and concepts in their variations. Improvisation no doubt has its place, but it does not influence the essence of the text. Although words and phrases may change, the descriptions of the spirits, emotions, and actions remain the same. Improvisation, as a rule, does not manifest itself in a new phrase or a new image created by shamans. Instead, improvisation usually means that shamans, in accordance with their mood and the purpose of a rite, select from a huge stock of stereotypical expressions those epithets and phrases in their memory that seem proper at the moment. We must also keep in mind that the stereotypes in the shamanistic ritual texts have changed over time because of cultural innovations and the re-evaluation of former religious ideas caused by the Islamization of shamanistic ritual practice.

The belief that the words of the ritual texts come to a shaman's mind from the spirits is reflected in the way these invocations are performed. A special "language of the spirits," used by shamans in some cultures, is not typical in Central Asia and Kazakhstan. However, some shamans do change their voices and manner of pronouncing the words. Among the Kazakh shamans, the tradition of singing invocations in a hoarse and constrained voice is known.[29] The Uzbek shamanesses Nobat, Aidai, and some others—after singing a phrase of their invocation during a seance of curing or divination (i.e., in a state of ecstasy)—usually uttered a whistle or a long-drawn high sound while inhaling air.[30] When I asked Nobat why she created this sound, she answered, "The spirits pull me." In addition, some shamanesses slightly torture the language when singing their invocations by lisping or imitating a way of speaking characteristic of children. The Uzbek shamaness Ulpan sang her invocations in this way. A. L. Troitskaya witnessed the same style when she visited an Uzbek shamaness in the vicinity of Samarkand in the 1920s; she reported that the shamaness spoke to a spirit (Uzb. *pari*) with a somewhat squeaky, twittering voice, mixing tortured words with usual speech.[31]

The study of the texts of shamanistic invocations helps us to better understand the nature of ecstasy. A shaman begins to sing his or her stereotypical formulas while in a normal state of mind and continues to perform while in a state of ecstasy. This is borne out by other observers as well as by my own impressions. Let us look at an extremely interesting description of a Kazakh shaman's ritual performance at the end of the nineteenth century, made by an unknown Russian author who obviously spoke the Kazakh language.

> Suddenly [the shaman] Oken deftly and strongly drew his bow upon the strings of his *kobyz* and began to play. . . . As he played he became more and more inspired and moved his bow more strongly; he closed his eyes and twitched his shoulders energetically; perhaps, he already had forgotten us and all that surrounded him. . . . It seemed he already played unconsciously and came into ecstasy. Having played so for about 20 minutes, Oken began to sing with a hoarse bass. . . . When he finished an invocation, he shook in convulsions and wriggled badly, uttering at the same time crazy sounds and hiccuping loudly as if he had eaten a whole ram with bones; it meant that a spirit had come; and the more spirits that appeared [to his call] the stronger he twitched his shoulders, and there was foam on his twisted mouth. Now he was completely mad; he crept along the floor and sometimes cried out incantations in a threatening way; suddenly he pulled his head back and showed the whites of his eyes.

But it was not really an unconscious state with a lack of control over his actions. Oken understood what he did.

> While singing, Oken pictured to us his spirits as images of different people who had been granted immortality; this was why he frequently changed the melodies of his song in accordance with the spirits' age and sex. For example, to summon the girls of "charming beauty," as he described them, he performed a tender and voluptuous melody. It is especially interesting that among his evil spirits there were "five Russians"; to summon them he played, to our surprise, the melody of a popular Russian song.[32]

We can conclude, therefore, that the ecstatic state does not prevent shamans from following traditions and singing the text needed for their rite. Clearly shamans can control themselves while in a state of ecstasy.

NOTES

1. Eliade, Mircea. *Shamanism: Archaic Techniques of Ecstasy.* Princeton: Princeton University Press, 1972, p. 303.

2. See, for instance, Taksami, Ch. M. Shamanstvo u nivkhov (Shamanism Among the Nivkhs). In *Problemy istorii obshchestvennogo soznaniya aborigenov Sibiri* (Problems of History of Social Consciousness of the Aboriginals of Siberia), ed. I. S. Vdovin. Leningrad: Nauka, 1981, p. 177; Gurwich, I. S. Ot redaktora (Editor's Comment). In Alekseyev, N. A. *Shamanism tiurkoyazychryh narodov Sibiri* (Shamanism Among Turkic-Speaking Peoples of Siberia). Novosibirsk: Nauka, Siberian branch, 1984, p. 3.

3. See, for instance, Sukhareva, O. A. *Islam v Uzbekistane* (Islam in Uzbekistan). Tashkent: Izdatel'stvo Akademii Nauk Uzbekskoi SSR, 1960, pp. 41–44, 52; Sukhareva, O. A. Perezhitki demonologii i shamanstva u ravninnykh tadjikov (The Survivals of Demonology and Shamanism Among the Plains Tadjiks). In *Domusul'manskiye verovaniya i obriady v Srednei Azii* (Pre-Muslim Beliefs and Rites in Central Asia), ed. V. N. Basilov and G. P. Snesarev. Moscow: Nauka 1975; Snesarev, G. P. *Relikty domusul'man-skikh verovaniy i obriadov u uzbekov Khorezma* (Relics of Pre-Muslim Beliefs and Rites Among the Uzbeks of Khorezm). Moscow: Nauka, 1969; Basilov, V. N. New Data on Uzbek Shamanism. *Besinci Milletler arasi Türkoloji Kongresi.* Istanbul, 23–28 Eylul 1985. Tebligler. 3. Türk tarihi, cilt 1 (Fifth International Türcological Congress. Istanbul, July 23–28, 1985. Papers. 3. History of Turkic Peoples, Part 1), Istanbul, 1986, pp. 119–128; Basilov, V. N. Popular Islam in Central Asia and Kazakhstan. *Journal Institute of Muslim Minority Affairs* 8, No. 1, January 1987, pp. 7–17.

4. Tenishev, E. R. *Uygurskiye teksty* (The Uighur Texts). Moscow: Nauka, 1984, pp. 19–23.

5. Basilov, V. N. Perezhitki shamanstva u turkmen-göklenov (Vestiges of Shamanism Among the Turkmen-Geoklen). In *Drevniye obriady, verovaniya i kul'ty narodov Sredney Azii* (Ancient Rites, Beliefs and Cults of Central Asian Peoples), ed. V. N. Basilov. Moscow: Nauka, 1986, p. 98.

6. Pantusov, N. Taranchinskiye bakshi. Peri uynatmak (The Shamans of the Taranchi [Uighurs]). *Izvestiya Turkestanskogo otdela*

Imperatorskogo Russkogo Geograficheskogo Obshchestva (Proceedings of the Turkestan Section of the Imperial Russian Geographic Society) 6. Tashkent, 1907, p. 40.

7. See, for instance, Radloff, W. *Proben der Volkslitteratur der Turkischen Stamme Sud-Siberiens.* 3, St. Pbg., 1870, p. 63; Sejpulla ulM (Saken). Qazaq edebijeti 1-inci kitap (Kazakh Literature, First Book). Qzml-Orda, QazaqMstan baspasM, 1932, pp. 88–91; Basilov, V. N. Nekotoryye materialy po kazahskomu shamanstvu (Some Materials on the Kazakh Shamanism). In *Polevyye issledovaniya Instituta etnografii,* 1976 (Field Researches of the Institute of Ethnography, 1976). Moscow, 1978, p. 158; Pantusov, Taranchinskiye bakshi, p. 47.

8. For more details see Ksensfontov, G. V. *Legendy i rasskazy o shamanakh u yakutov, buriat i tungusov* (Legends and Tales on the Shamans Among the Yakuts, Buriats, and Tunguses), 2d edition. Moscow, 1930. See also Friedrich, A., and G. Budruss. *Schamanengeschichten aus Siberien.* Munich and Planegg, 1955.

9. Radloff, *Proben der Volkslitteratur* 3, pp. 63–64.

10. Divayev, A. Iz oblasti Kirgizskih verovanii. Baksy kak lekar' i Koldun (From the Sphere of the Kirghiz [here: Kazakh] Beliefs. Baksy [Shaman] as a Medicine-Man and Sorcerer). In *Izvestiya Obshchestva archeologii, istorii i etnografii pri Imperatorskom Kazanskom Universitete* (Proceedings of the Society of Archaeology, History and Ethnography at the Imperial Kazan University) 15 part 3. Kazan, 1899, pp. 321–322.

11. Dyrenkova, N. P. Materialy po Shamanstvu u Teleutov (Materials on Shamanism Among the Teleut). In *Sbornik Muzeya Antropologii i etnografii* (Collection of Articles of the Museum of Anthropology and Ethnography) 10. Moscow-Leningrad: Izdatl'stvo Akademii Nauk SSSR, 1949, p. 124.

12. Ksenofontov, G. V. *Legendy i rasskazy o shamanah,* 2d edition. Moscow, 1930, p. 35.

13. Basilov, Nekotoryye materialy po kazahskomu shamanstvu, p. 159.

14. In the Uzbek traditional beliefs this was considered to be a good sign. When Uzbeks wished to explain that a certain person was very gifted, they used to say: "A crow defecated on his head (*Boshiga qarga sychkan).*"

15. See, for instance, Divayev, Iz oblasti kirgizskih verovanii, p. 314; Sejpulla ulM (Saken), Qazaq edebijeti 1-inci kitap, p. 89.

16. See, for instance, Dyrenkova, Materialy po Shamanstvu u Teleutov, pp. 119, 124; Sieroshevskii, V. L. Yakuty (Yakuts) 1, St. Petersburg: *Izdaniye Russkogo Geograficheskogo Obshchestva*, 1896, p. 626.

17. Basilov, Nekotoryye materialy po kazahskomu shamanstvu, p. 159.

18. Alektorov, A. Ye. Baksa. Iz mira kirgizskih suyeveriy. (Baksy [Shaman]. From the World of Kirghiz [here: the Kazakh] Superstitions). *Izvestiya Obshchestva archeologii, istorii i etnografii pri Imperatorskom Kazanskom universitete* (Proceedings of the Society of Archaeology, History and Ethnography at the Imperial Kazan University) 16, part 1. Kazan, 1900, p. 34; Sejpulla ulM (Saken), Qazaq edebijeti l-inci kitap, p. 90; Esbergenov, Kh., and T. Atamuratov. *Traditsii i ih preobrazovaniye v gorodskom bytu karakalpakov* (Traditions and Their Transformation in the Urban Life of the Karakalpaks). Nukus, 1975, p. 112.

19. Divayev, Iz oblasti Kirgizskih verovanii, pp. 319–320.

20. Divayev, A. A. *Ethnograficheskiye materialy* (The Ethnographic Materials), part 5. Tashkent, 1896, p. 36; Zhil'tsov A. Baksy. Nechto o kirgizskoy meditsine (Baksy [Shaman]. Some Remarks on the Kirghiz [here: Kazakh] Medicine). *Pravoslavnyy blagovestnik* (Orthodox Good Messenger) 1, No. 5. Moscow, 1895, p. 263; Alektorov, Baksa, p. 33; Erzakovich, B. G. Vrachevatel'naya pesnia baksy (A Curing Song of a Shaman). In *Narodnaya muzyka v Kazahstane* (The Folk Music in Kazakhstan). Alma-Ata, 1967, pp. 105–106.

21. Il'yasov, S. Perezhitki shamanizma u kirgizov (Vestiges of Shamanism Among the Kirghiz). In *Trudy Instituta istorii, yazyka i literatury Kirgizskogo filiala Academii Nauk SSR* (Transactions of the Institute of History, Language, and Literature of the Kirghiz Branch of the Academy of Sciences of the USSR), part 1. Frunze, 1944, p. 145.

22. Dyrenkova, Materialy po Shamanstvu u Teleutov, p. 132; see also p. 145.

23. Magrupy, G. *Yusup-Ahmet.* Ashgabat, 1943 (in Turkmenian), p. 24; see also p. 64.

24. *Materialy i issledovaniya po folkloru Bashkirii i Urala* (Materials and Studies in Folklore of Bashkiria and Ural), part 1. Ufa, 1974, p. 226.

25. Zhalolov, Gh. *Uzbek folklorida zhanrlaro munosabat* (Interaction of Genres of the Uzbek Folklore). Tashkent, 1979 (in Uzbek), p. 53.

26. *Kniga moyego deda Korkuta* (My Grandfather Korkut's Book). Moscow-Leningrad, 1962, p. 30.

27. Inan, A. *Dede Korbut kitabindaki bazi motiflere ve kelimelere ait notlar* (On Some Motifs and Words in "Kitabi Dedem Korkut"). *Ülkü*, 10, no. 55, Ankara, July 1937 (in Turkish), pp. 78–80.

28. The photographs that show some moments of this rite can be seen in *Nomads of Eurasia,* ed. V. Basilov. Seattle and London: Natural History Museum of Los Angeles County in association with University of Washington Press, 1989, p. 166.

29. Novolineyets, A. Chary Shamana v Kirgizskom aule (The Charms of a Shaman in a Kirghiz [here: Kazakh] Village. *Orenburgskiye Gubernskiye vedomosti,* 1848, 25; Daulbayev, B. D. Rasskaz o zhizni kirgiz Nikolayevskogo uyezda Turgayskoy oblasti s. 1830 po 1880 god (A Description of the Kirghiz [here: Kazakh] Life in Nikolayevskiy District of the Turgayskaya Oblast in 1830–1880). *Zapiski Orenburgskogo otgela Imperatorskogo Russkogo Geograficheskogo Obschchestva* (Transaction of the Orenburg Section of the Imperial Russian Geographic Society), part 4. Orenburg, 1881, p. 109.

30. The same whistling sounds were performed by some Kazakh shamans as well. See Alektorov, Baksa, p. 35; Chekaninskii, I. A. Baksylyk (Tracks of the Ancient Beliefs of the Kazakhs). In *Zapiski Semipalatinskogo otdela Obshchestva izucheniya Kazakstana* (Transactions of the Semipalatinsk Section of the Society of the Kazakhstan Studies) 1. Semipalatinsk, 1929, p. 31.

31. Troitskaya, A. L. Lechenie bol'nyh izgnaniyem zlzh duhov (Kuckuruk) sredi osedlogo naseleniya Turkestana (A Medical Treatment of the Patients by Expelling Evil Spirits Among the Sedentary Population of Turkestan). In *Bulleten' sredneasiatskogo Gosudarstvennogo universiteta* (Transactions of the Central-Asian State University), part 10. Tashkent, 1925, p. 152.

32. Nevol'nik. Vo mrake nevezhestva (In the Darkness of Ignorance). *Turgayskaya gaseta* (Turgay Newspaper), 1896, no. 77.

APPENDIX: BIBLIOGRAPHY OF PUBLICATIONS IN CONJUNCTION WITH THE MUSEUM EXHIBITION "NOMADS: MASTERS OF THE EURASIAN STEPPES"

GARY SEAMAN

A condition set by the Soviet organizers of the exhibition was that the United States host an academic symposium at each venue: the Museum of Natural History in Los Angeles, the Smithsonian Institution in Washington, D.C., and the Denver Museum of Natural History. Over one hundred papers were presented at these three symposia, of which sixty-five have been published in four volumes of proceedings, including the present one. The publisher of the first three volumes was Ethnographics Press (Center for Visual Anthropology, University of Southern California, Los Angeles, Calif. 90089–0032, U.S.A. Telephone [213] 740–1900. FAX [213] 747–8571).

VOLUME 1
ECOLOGY AND EMPIRE: NOMADS IN THE
CULTURAL EVOLUTION OF THE OLD WORLD

The first volume of the proceedings was published at the end of 1989. It contains sixteen papers on ethnographic and ethnohistorical topics. They primarily address the geopolitical implications of Eurasian cultural ecology, a concept usually identified with the name Owen Lattimore. This concept provided the organizational theme for the Los Angeles symposium held in February 1989. The papers featured in volume 1 are:

1. Richard Feynman and the Tuva Adventure
   Ralph Leighton
2. Chokan Valikhanov: Explorer of the Nineteenth Century Asian Nomadic Peoples
   Ramazan B. Sulejmenov

3. An Ecological History of Central Asian Nomadism
   Rhoads Murphy
4. The Ecology of the Ancient Nomads of Soviet Central Asia
   and Kazakhstan
   Boris A. Litvinskii
5. One of the Paths of the Origins of Nomadism
   Sevyan I. Vainstein
6. The Decline of the Silk Road Trade
   Morris Rossabi
7. Main Tendencies in the Development of Hunting in Ancient and
   Traditional Nomadic Societies
   Leonid B. Ermolov
8. The System of Nourishment Among the Eurasian Nomads:
   The Kazakh Example
   Nurila Zh. Shakhanova
9. Some Problems of Male Social Organizations Among the Tadjiks
   Rachmad R. Rahimov
10. The Social Functions of Traditional Hunting With Game Birds in
    Central Asia and Kazakhstan
    Georgii N. Simakov
11. Central Asian Concepts of Rule on the Steppe and Sown
    Richard Frye
12. Dunhuang as a Funnel for Central Asian Nomads Into China
    Victor H. Mair
13. The Emperor of the Dark Heavens and Wudang Mountain:
    The Han River Gateway Into China
    Gary Seaman
14. The Nomadic Peoples of China Along the Great Wall
    Kui Bai and Rui Gao
15. Folk Cultures of Inner Mongolia and Their Preservation
    Hao Wen
16. Contemporary Khanates: Compromises Adopted by Kazakh and
    Kirghiz Leaders
    Andre Singer

A P P E N D I X

VOLUME 2
RULERS FROM THE STEPPE: STATE FORMATION
ON THE EURASIAN PERIPHERY

The second volume of the proceedings was based mainly on papers delivered at the symposium held at the Smithsonian Institution in Washington, D.C., in November 1989. Published in 1991, that volume focused on aspects of the interaction among political cultures with widely differing ecologies. It contains fifteen papers, most of which are directly or indirectly concerned with the impact of the Mongol empire on the Eurasian world system:

M

10. Changing Forms of Legitimation in Mongol Iran
    Thomas T. Allsen
11. Buddhism in the History of Mongols and Buryats: Political and
    Cultural Aspects
    Natalia L. Zhukovskaya
12. The Culture of the Golden Horde and the Problem of the
    "Mongol Legacy"
    Mark G. Kramarovsky
13. The Volga Tatars: Modern Identities of the Golden Horde
    Azade-Ayse Rorlich
14. Evolution of Nomadic Culture Under Modern Conditions: Traditions
    and Innovations in Kazakh Culture
    Olga B. Naumova
15. Sedenterization, Socioecology, and State Definition: The Ethnogenesis
    of the Uighur
    Dru C. Gladney

VOLUME 3
FOUNDATIONS OF EMPIRE: ARCHAEOLOGY AND
ART HISTORY OF THE EURASIAN STEPPE

Archaeological and art historical work in Central Asia is the focus for this volume of the symposia proceedings. The richness of archaeological finds within Soviet Central Asia is matched by the extensive literature on the excavations and museum collections. The third volume of the proceedings focuses on the material evidence for the formation of early steppe societies, mainly in the early historical periods from the first millennium B.C. through the Mongol imperial era. Because this volume was already in press at the time the Union of Soviet Socialist Republics ceased to exist, nomenclature in this volume reflects usage prior to December 1991. The papers featured in volume 3 are:

1. Theoretical Considerations on the Origin of Pastoral Nomadism
   Maurizio Tosi
2. Symbolic Structures as Indicators of the Cultural Ecology of the
   Early Nomads
   Esther Jacobson

▼

▼

CATALOG OF THE AMERICAN EXHIBITION
"NOMADS OF EURASIA"

In addition to these symposia proceedings, there is also an excellent catalog of the U.S. exhibition. The text was edited by Vladimir Basilov and Robin Simpson from translations by Mary Zirin. It was published in 1988 by the Natural History Museum of Los Angeles County and the University of Washington Press.

1. The Culture of Eurasian Peoples, Prehistoric Times Through the Middle Ages
   Larisa R. Pavlinskaya
2. The Scythians and Sakians, Eighth to Third Centuries B.C.
   Evgenii I. Lubo-Lesnichenko
3. The Turkic Peoples, Sixth to Twelfth Centuries
   Sev'yan I. Vainshtein
4. The Mongol-Tatar States of the Thirteenth and Fourteenth Centuries
   Mikhail V. Gorelik and Mark G. Kramarovskii
5. Yurts, Rugs and Felts
   Vladimir N. Basilov and Ol'ga B. Naumova
6. Clothing and Personal Adornment
   Nina P. Lobacheva
7. Household Furnishings and Utensils
   Vladimir N. Basilov, Vera P. D'yakonova, Vladimir I. D'yachenko, and Vadim P. Kurylev
8. Harness and Weaponry
   Vadim P. Kurylev, Larisa R. Pavlinskaya, and Georgii N. Simakov
9. Bowed Musical Instruments
   Vladimir N. Basilov
10. Religious Beliefs
    Vladimir N. Basilov and Natal'ya L. Zhukhovskaya

CATALOG OF THE DANISH EXHIBITION
LANGS SILKEVEJEN: NOMADER OG BYFOLK
I SIBIRIEN OG CENTRALASIEN

When the exhibition traveled to the Moesgard Museum near Aarhus, Denmark, it was reorganized by the director of the museum, Peder Mortensen, with Rachmad R. Rahimov of the Institute of Ethnography in

▼

Leningrad as curator. Under the editorship of Annette Damm of the Moesgard Museum, a new catalog was prepared by a team of Soviet and Danish authors: O. M. Bronnikova, J. Damm, T. Emiljanova, L. B. Ermolov, V. R. Janborisov, V. P. Kurylev, T. A. Popova, R. R. Rahimov, N. Z. Shakhanova, G. N. Simakov, and N. L. Zhukhovskaya. The catalog was published by the Moesgard Museum in 1990 under the title *Langs Silkevejen: Nomader og byfolk i Sibirien og Centralasien* [Along the Silk Road: Nomads and Townspeople in Siberia and Central Asia].

INDEX

Pepper, tobacco and, 56, 57, 58

Petuniodes, 48

Peyote (*Lophophora williamsii*), 21, 22, 23, 130, 139, 167; Aztec use of, 17; importance of, 180; obtaining, 181, 186; prohibition on, 183, 184; sacred, 147, 179, 182. *See also Datura* (spp.)

Peyote Cult, The (La Barre): on hallucinogens, 19

Peyote Hunt: The Sacred Journey of the Huichol Indians (Myerhoff), 132

Peyote pilgrimages, Medina Silva's, 115, 122, 132, 135, 136, 142, 145, 146, 162–63, 165, 166

Peyote religion, 18, 186; spread of, 179, 180–81, 182–83, 184–85

Peyotists, 157, 166, 181; harassing, 183–84, 185; religious freedom for, 186

Pharmaceutical industry, 16; shamans and, 13–14

Pipes, 61; predominance of, 62; types of, 52, 54, 62–63

Pitchkosan (clan bundles), 189, 195

Plotkin, Mark J., 13, 15

Plowman, T.: on coca chewing, 53

Popcorn, symbolism of, 159, 160

Popol Vuh, shamanistic rituals and, 102

Popular cults, spread of, 234, 235

Potanin, G. N., 259

Potawatomi, 189, 190, 193, 199; Dream Dance and, 200, 201; ethos of, 188, 192; Wananikwe and, 200

Power contests, 213

Power symbols, 218

Prayer-makers, 101

Prechtel, Martin, 83

Preuss, Konrad Theodor: curing ceremonies and, 158; on Kauyumari, 119

Primitive Man as Philosopher (Radin), 137

Primitivism, vocabulary of, 203–4

Primordial condition, 11, 30, 36

Prohibition Law (1897), 183

Prokofyev, G. N., 259

Prokofyeva, E. D.: on shaman attire, 257–58

Psychic equilibrium, 113, 130

Psychoactive plants, 146; shamanism and, 167–69. *See also* Hallucinogens

Psychopomps, 12, 35

Psychotropic drugs, 51, 167; shaminism and, 16–25; snuffing, 59–60. *See also* Hallucinogens

Q'isom, 79, 103–4

Quiché, 102–3; dream interpretation and, 97

Quieju, Maxuan, 94

Radloff, W., 277

Rain, origin of, 137–38

Raincloud, Dan, 197

Rain forests, conserving, 15–16

Rajawal, 93, 94

Rapé, 64, 65; snuffing, 55, 59–60

Ray, Verne, 211, 215, 220

Reason in Religion (Santayana), quote from, 77

Reciprocity, principle of, 2

Reichel-Dolmatoff, Gerardo, 17

Renewal of Blessing, photo of, 283

Rite of renewal, 281

Ritual clowns, 159–60

Ritual texts, stereotypes in, 281, 287

R'kan Sak R'kan Q'ij (Footpath of the Dawn, Footpath of the Sun), 84, 85–86, 88, 90

R'muxux Ruchliew (Umbilicus of the World), 93, 97

Roadmen, 186; missionary life of, 182–83, 185

Roads, 97–98

Rock paintings, animal images on, 258

Roosevelt, Franklin D., 185

Ruchiliew (Face of the World), 83, 91, 92, 93, 99

Ruíz de Alarcon, H., 20, 21

Ruki kik 'om, 103

Rxin ch'oj (lust-insanity) tradition, 81, 96

INDEX

◤◢